PQ
2249
.C75
1986

Critical essays on
Gustave Flaubert

Critical Essays on Gustave Flaubert

Critical Essays on
World Literature

Robert Lecker, General Editor
McGill University

Critical Essays on Gustave Flaubert

Laurence M. Porter

G. K. Hall & Co. • Boston, Massachusetts

Library of Congress Cataloging in Publication Data

Critical essays on Gustave Flaubert.

(Critical essays on world literature)
Bibliography: p. 223
Includes index.
1. Flaubert, Gustave, 1821–1880 — Criticism and interpretation. I.
Porter, Laurence M., 1936–   II. Series.
PQ2249.C75   1986   823'.8   86–12114
ISBN 0-8161-8831-9

This publication is printed on permanent/durable acid-free paper
MANUFACTURED IN THE UNITED STATES OF AMERICA

For Ben

CONTENTS

INTRODUCTION

Flaubert has long been considered the dominant novelist of nine-teenth-century France — a great age for the novel. He has also stimulated an exceptional variety of critical approaches. At first glance his preeminence is surprising because he is less purely entertaining to read than are his great contemporaries. He lacks Balzac's melodramatic intensity and range of character types; Stendhal's wit, verve, and political sophistication; Zola's violence, raw sex, and visionary fervor. In Flaubert's "exotic" novels *Salammbô* and *La Tentation de saint Antoine*, the historical background seems remote and labored; in his "realistic" novels *Madame Bovary*, *L'Éducation sentimentale*, and *Bouvard et Pécuchet*, the protagonists are obscure middle-class figures: their conversations are uninteresting; their ideas, clichés; their lives produce only the ripple of a passing scandal in society; and at best they are only dimly aware of the historical process around them. So what accounts for Flaubert's durable prestige? His realism and his psychological acuity.

Flaubert was the most thorough-going, consistent realist of his century: his characters seem in perfect balance with his settings. Neither dominates the other. The emotional life and its material frame have become so interwoven that they are inseparable. In contrast, Stendhal imagined psychological relationships between characters, and then sketched in tenuous, overtly symbolic backgrounds. Balzac and Zola accumulated descriptions and documentation concerning physical settings, and then devised characters to inhabit them. Stendhal, Balzac, and Zola *affirm* connections between their characters and the environment. Flaubert *shows* these connections in a style that is nearly always appropriate to his characters' limited awareness. Flaubert's narrator does not intervene to comment on the action: he prevents the reader-narrator relationship from becoming a distracting ghost flitting between the reader and the subject.

In addition to avoiding authorial intervention and thus destroying the realistic illusion, Flaubert also deploys a major stylistic instrument for psychological analysis: the systematic use of "represented discourse" (called *style indirect libre* in French, *erlebte Rede* in German). This means

1

that he reports a character's thoughts or words without using the first person; without a pronoun in the same sentence to show who is doing the thinking or saying; and without a verb identifying the mode of that thinking or saying. For example, direct discourse would read "I said: 'I'm tired.' " And represented discourse: [He said or thought that] "He was tired." In isolation you can't tell this last sentence from a thought or statement by another character, or from a comment by the narrator. Context must provide clues. Critics may disagree as to whether a particular sentence is written in represented discourse or not. Sometimes only the author knows for sure.

That's just why the device is so useful. It works like the gearshift in a car. It allows the author to slip inobtrusively in and out of the character's point of view; to report inarticulate feelings without seeming to psychologize; to glide back and forth among spoken words, musings, narrative comments, and summary. For example, at the end of chapter 1, part 1, of *Madame Bovary*, the words "she . . . began to talk to him of her troubles: *he was neglecting her, he loved another*" [emphasis added for the segment in represented discourse] function to report Madame Dubuc's direct statement: "You are neglecting me; you love someone else." But they also serve the narrator by summarizing her lengthy complaints in seven words; by adding a dramatic highlight to the paragraph; and by reporting a frequent occurrence as if it were a one-time event. The needs of economy and of liveliness are satisfied simultaneously.

Represented discourse appeared in the ninth-century *Cantilène de sainte Eulalie*, the oldest known literary work in French. Many authors, notably La Fontaine and Marivaux, have used it since. But Flaubert's contribution to literature was to use represented discourse far more often and more systematically than before, as did Jane Austen and the Goethe of *Wilhelm Meisters Lehrjahre*. The device builds a bridge between narrator and character. The former no longer needs to pronounce against or in favor of the latter. The secret of Flaubert's celebrated impersonality is not that he suppresses his personality, but that he finds a way to blur the boundary between his selfhood and his characters'. Thus he anticipates the modern novel.

A few kindred spirits, great authors in their own right, appreciated Flaubert from the beginning—Baudelaire; Banville; Sand; Zola; Proust. Aside from their reactions, there are three main overlapping stages in the evolution of Flaubert criticism. First, normative criticism, which called Flaubert a realist; then, thematic criticism, which considered him an idealist; and finally, structuralist and post-structuralist criticism, which consider him an indeterminist, a writer who resists conclusions.

Normative criticism predominated from the appearance of *Madame Bovary* in 1857 until the centenary of Flaubert's birth in 1921. The normative critic chooses an aesthetic or moral standard, or both, and then judges literary works according to how closely they conform to that standard. Usually they fall short. The earlier normative criticism directed at Flaubert is represented in this volume by the reviews and essays of Duranty and Barbey D'Aurevilly on *Madame Bovary*, and elsewhere by Henry James, Sainte-Beuve, and others. Its underlying presupposition was summed up by l'abbé Batteux in the early eighteenth century, in what became an axiom of neoclassical aesthetics: literature should devote itself to "l'imitation de la belle nature."[1] Literally, this expression means "the imitation of beautiful nature," but Batteux was not actually recommending a literature of landscape descriptions. By "nature" he meant mainly "human nature," and by "beautiful," "what is beautiful in human nature." In other words, literature should select from human behavior what is most noble and inspiring, so as to set a good example for its readers. The major corollary to this view was that the reader needed guidance: an author should therefore explicitly intervene to praise virtue and condemn vice, like George Eliot or Dickens, tugging the reader by the sleeve and telling him or her what to feel.

Since most critics of Flaubert's time adhered to such views, they were too moralistic fully to appreciate realistic literature as we can today. After reading *Madame Bovary* in 1857, they granted that Flaubert observed keenly and described with power; but they condemned him for selecting only what was trivial and base in human nature, and neglecting what could have inspired us. Worse yet, they complained, Flaubert did not denounce his characters' baseness. He reported it calmly, impersonally, without telling us how we should react. His dispassionateness seemed to condone the immorality he depicted. And he failed to defend the good: when his narrator observes that in adultery Emma Bovary "rediscovered all the platitudes of marriage," marriage and adultery seem equally bad. Critics found Flaubert's detached attitude cynical and depressing.

So Edmond Duranty, himself the moving spirit of a journal called *Réalisme*, nevertheless assailed *Madame Bovary* as a novel where "there is no emotion, no feeling, no life." Sainte-Beuve, the leading critic of the century, saw only "meanness, misery, pretentiousness, stupidity" in Flaubert's characters. "Why not provide the good in one figure at least, in one charming or venerable face. . . . That provides relief and consolation, and the view of humanity is only the more complete."[2] In a more peremptory manner, Barbey D'Aurevilly exclaimed: "human nature is loath to have a subject in hand without feeling some passion for or against. But Flaubert escapes from this custom which seems a law of the human spirit." And Henry James condemned *La Tentation de saint Antoine* as consisting entirely in "a strangely artificial and cold-blooded picturesque — abounding in the grotesque and the repulsive . . . When the author has a really beautiful point to treat — as the assembly of the Greek deities fading and paling away in the light of Christianity [a morally edifying spectacle of the Triumph of the Good] — he becomes singularly commonplace and ineffective."

During the remainder of Flaubert's career, critics gradually came round to a grudging, backhanded appreciation of *Madame Bovary*, contrasting it with his later novels and claiming that he had outlived his genius. They universally damned *Salammbô* in 1862, finding it contrived, frenetic, and artificial, an orgy of sadism and horror with flat, unbelievable characters. Critics welcomed Flaubert's return to the contemporary world in *L' Éducation sentimentale* (1869), but found once again that his skill in observation, his keen treatment of detail, and his carefully-wrought style were offset by his concentration on the trivial and degrading, while he preserved an inappropriate detachment. They did appreciate his impersonality, however, insofar as it represented a departure from the confessional effusions of the romantics. *La Tentation de saint Antoine*, published in 1874, was the last full-length work to appear during Flaubert's lifetime. In it he seemed to have slid back into incoherent, excessively bookish exoticism, depicting a limp-wristed saint passively watching a parade of visions. Most readers of the time — like Valéry, Butor, and Culler after them — failed to realize that the generative principle of the work was psychic projection (frequently signalled by Flaubert), a defense mechanism that attributes one's own shameful feelings to people outside oneself. The devils and monsters that beset Anthony in his hallucinations and dreams are extensions of his own personality, embodiments of his memories. Like the fantastic tales of Nodier and Nerval before him, Flaubert's visionary work, on which he labored intermittently for twenty-five years, anticipates depth psychology by exploring the operations of the unconscious and the fantasies to which they give rise.

In 1881, the year after Flaubert died, Maxime Du Camp's *Mémoires* revealed that he had composed a first version of the *Tentation* early in his career, and suppressed it after harsh criticism from his friends. And the posthumous publication of the unfinished *Bouvard et Pécuchet* showed Flaubert had returned to a drably realistic mode as he portrayed two retired copy clerks who try to master all practical applications of human knowledge. These two publishing events revealed the complete trajectory of Flaubert's literary endeavors, and created a durable image of a Flaubert torn between two opposite extremes, yielding first to one and then to the other:

ROMANTIC EXCESS	REALISTIC EXCESS
1. *Tentation* (1849)	2. *Madame Bovary* (1857)
3. *Salammbô* (1862)	4. *L'Éducation sentimentale* (1869)
5. *Tentation* (1874)	6. *Bouvard et Pécuchet* (1881)

According to this view, Flaubert over-indulged his imagination, becoming grotesque and incoherent. While composing his romantic historical novels, he tried to rein in his fancies through the discipline of exhaustive documentation. The result was that he wrote in a manner that was bookish and uncontrolled at the same time. Then he reacted with an excess of self-restraint, choosing for his next subject a trivial contemporary topic, at the cost of becoming dry. Only from the late 1970s on has literary criticism begun consistently to challenge this scheme, by emphasizing the psychological realism of the *Tentation* (see Porter in the present volume), and the relevance of the history in *Salammbô* to Flaubert's own era (see Donato and Green). Ever since Baudelaire, critics have tellingly analyzed the elements of personal fantasizing in *Madame Bovary* (e.g., Flaubert's androgyny), but more remains to be done to bring out the personal fantasies of *L' Éducation sentimentale* and *Bouvard et Pécuchet*.

All Flaubert's novels center on temptations afflicting the central character. For example, just as *La Tentation de saint Antoine* dramatizes the temptation of metaphysical knowledge, *Bouvard et Pécuchet* dramatizes the temptation of material knowledge. The difference is that the historical characters, Anthony and Salammbô, are fanatics who preserve a clear vision of their guiding ideal most of the time: the contemporary characters, Emma Bovary, Frédéric Moreau, Bouvard and Pécuchet, confuse their ideals with debased, desacralized, material forms of them, and stumble from one object to another through their lack of conviction. For Flaubert to create such a contrast reflects his view of the decadence and corruption of contemporary society. The human condition never lent itself to triumphs, Flaubert believes, but on top of that, the modern age has no more heroes and its failures lack grandeur.

Normative criticism, which dominated the Victorian Age and the French "Belle Époque" (1880–1914), reappeared in new guises after World War I. Revulsion at the horrors of the war, added to a groundswell of reaction against late nineteenth-century positivism and scientism ("vice and virtue are products like sulphuric acid and sugar"), produced strong religious revivals in France and England. As a result, critics like J. Middleton Murry appeared, condemning Flaubert for not having been Christian. More complex and influential was the position of Marxist criticism. From this viewpoint, the French Revolution had been led by, and worked primarily for the benefit of, the middle class. They replaced the feudal system of the formerly dominant aristocracy with capitalism. Middle-class capitalists developed more efficient means of production and accumulated wealth at the expense of a growing urban proletariat. The latter was exploited without mercy. Around the middle of the nineteenth century, writers, also middle-class, recognized themselves as members of a social group that had become morally bankrupt. Seeing no positive values to uphold, they reacted with disillusionment, despair, and nihilism, becoming—in Sartre's words—"knights of nothingness."[3]

The most influential representatives of this school of criticism are Roland Barthes and Jean-Paul Sartre. In *Writing Degree Zero*, Barthes argues that *Madame Bovary* exemplifies a crisis of the loss of values in the novel around 1850: Flaubert tries to revalidate the novel in capitalist terms, on the basis of how much work has gone into producing it. The third volume of Sartre's monumental study of Flaubert, *The Family Idiot* (1972 — too intricate and long-winded to excerpt for this volume), criticizes Flaubert for sharing the middle class' "bad faith," the self-deception which masks an initial deliberate choice to claim special privileges for oneself at the expense of justice and logic. Sartre argues that Flaubert tried to escape from his class into a pseudo-nobility during the last nine years of the Second Empire (1861–70). He accepted the cross of the Legion of Honor in 1866 (having ridiculed his character Homais for prostituting himself to gain that same cross, nine years earlier), and became a regular guest of Princess Mathilde, whom he referred to as "*our* princess." After the disaster of the Franco-Prussian War in 1870, Flaubert was forced to realize the sham of the bourgeois values by which he lived, but could only reaffirm them without conviction. He refrained from writing a satiric novel on the Second Empire, although he had thought about one, because the loss of his special status as an honored guest of the Imperial Family depressed him.[4]

Normative criticism, which we have been describing up till now, attempts to situate the ultimate meaning of the literary work outside the work, in a parallel but more extensive frame of reference — moral values, the historical process. Thematic criticism (using the term in its broadest extension) seeks the work's meaning within itself or within the corpus of the author's works. The assumption is that an author does not explain everything, and that the task of criticism is to bring out what the author has implied or hidden. Normative criticism serves social values: it tries to make them more vivid. Thematic criticism serves the artist, to disclose his or her richness, complexity, and interest. Normative criticism usually states its presuppositions: thematic criticism takes them for granted. Normative criticism claims to represent values which the work of art is always vehemently suspected of having flouted: thematic criticism sees the work of art either as existing in harmony with its tradition, or as inaugurating a new and equally valid one. With the exceptions just noted, thematic approaches dominated Flaubert criticism from about 1920 to 1970.

Georges Poulet summed up the attitudes of this style of criticism by insisting on the organic unity of the work of art. "The main purpose of [*Madame Bovary*] is to create relation and order."[5] "What man attains in the Flaubertian experience is . . . the intuition of life in its cosmic expansion," he adds in the present volume. His general essay here is an outstanding example of phenomenological criticism, which assumes that only our subjective representations of the world — of time and space, self and other, thought and object — are knowable, whereas that world in and of itself is not. Poulet argues that "Flaubert arrived at an integral phenomenalism. The mind being what it represents, and the object existing only in its representation in the mind, what remains is simply a unique being that can be called indifferently mind or nature." Poulet tries to demonstrate how Flaubert enters this state of awareness and then re-emerges from it to reconstitute a novel. He considers as part of a single, uniform whole everything that Flaubert wrote, at every period of his life. He takes no account of development, of chronological order, assuming that Flaubert's thought was always already fully formed; and he does not give special consideration to Flaubert's literary masterpieces. Forty per cent of his citations here refer to the Correspondence, and forty-five per cent more to the youthful works. Nevertheless, Poulet's method works well with nineteenth-century French authors in general, and with Flaubert in particular, because most of them share the organic world-view of romanticism, in which every part reflects the whole as the chromosomes in a single cell reflect the organism from which it comes.

As Poulet has dominated the thematic criticism of nineteenth-century French literature in general, Victor Brombert has dominated the thematic criticism of the nineteenth-century French novel. Here he discusses "the metaphorical unity [the inevitable word] of L'Éducation sentimentale" in terms of prostitution—literal and figurative, male and female, individual and social. "Society itself, as represented by various groups, corporations or institutions, is the great whore who always embraces the winner." Anne Green places a similar motif into a broader context by treating the historical novel Salammbô as a reflection of the corruption Flaubert deplored in his own day. She explains that Flaubert selected a historical period with features similar to his own. Vitality (the liberal revolution of 1848 / the mercenary barbarian armies) confronts decadence (the authoritarian reaction leading to the Second Empire / the city-state of Carthage), only to be defeated; yet triumphant decadence is itself doomed (Carthage will be overwhelmed by Rome, and Flaubert anticipates a similar fate for the Empire—it was realized eight years later by the Prussian invasion).

Flaubert's fantastic and visionary literature—La Tentation de saint Antoine, and from the Trois contes, Hérodias and La Légende de saint Julien l'hospitalier—have lent themselves particularly well to a psychologically oriented thematic criticism. Theodor Reik's classic essay here illustrates the traditional psychoanalytic study of the repressed contents of the unconscious. These, unbeknownst to the author, manifest themselves in the symbolic disguises of the literary work. Reik examines the "link between [unresolved] incestuous infantile fantasies and the masochistic ascetic idea" in La Tentation de saint Antoine. More recent approaches usually are influenced by ego-psychology, which without denying the reality of repression, nevertheless stresses the self-healing function of literary creation. In this view, writing is held to constitute "regression in the service of the ego":[6] it provides a means of getting in touch with primordial fantasies in order to bring them to consciousness. In this vein, Benjamin F. Bart studies the evolution of Flaubert's lifelong struggle to come to terms with his sexuality. He focuses on the core fantasy of a youthful dream, and traces its refinement down to the Saint Julien legend written in Flaubert's mid-50s. Laurence M. Porter studies *La Tentation de saint Antoine* in detail, examining how the devil figure is a projection of Anthony's inner, religious doubts, and stressing how carefully Flaubert revised the work over the years to imply that the sources of Anthony's visions could be situated in his own lived experiences. Such studies make it clear that Flaubert was an innovative, sophisticated psychologist. More could be done to study him as such in the realistic works.

Dr. A. W. Raitt does just that, contributing substantially toward understanding the originality of character depiction in *L' Éducation sentimentale*. There Flaubert "is no longer using the techniques of character construction that had served him in *Madame Bovary* . . . and that his contemporaries in general were using. Name, place of residence, occupation, social class, origins, moment in time, determinism of behavior — all of these are systematically blurred or substantially reduced in a way which would have profound effects upon Proust, Gide, and the New Novelists of the 1960s. And Jean Rousset, in the most frequently reprinted essay in Flaubert criticism, insists upon Flaubert's desire to compose *Madame Bovary* as "a book about nothing, a book without reference outside itself," an enterprise which makes Flaubert "the first in date of the non-figurative novelists" such as Joyce and Woolf.

Rousset's essay, pointing to Flaubert's nihilism, had been anticipated by Paul Bourget in 1884. His great influence in 1962, however, announced a major shift in thematic criticism. Earlier thematic critics like Harry Levin had depicted Flaubert as a saint of art, a martyr to style, sequestering himself in an eremitic retreat in order to dedicate himself to his novels. Once Flaubert's Correspondence became widely known in the 1930s, critics could find abundant evidence of Flaubert's idealism. He called himself a "Platonist" more than once. He suggested that any subject properly treated would allow one to approach the ideal. He reported ecstatic visions of perfection. As Charles Du Bos explained in his pioneering essay, "Sur le milieu intérieur dans Flaubert," "Art had to make demands upon him as strict as those of the strictest religion, as stern even as the most ardent form of mysticism. Only then will art be a complete religion for him, intimate, mystical in an almost Platonic sense, since the exhilaration he derives from the masterpieces fulfills his desire for the absolute."[7] This view of Flaubert was echoed in major articles by critics like Frank Laurence Lucas (1933),[8] Paul Valéry (1942)[9] and Benjamin F. Bart (1965; 1967).[10] As recently as September 1984, Jacques Derrida opposed the notion of Flaubert's "Platonic idealism."[11]

But once thematic critics like Rousset had joined the Marxists in proclaiming that Flaubert's novels of disillusionment pointed to no meanings valid outside themselves, it was only a short step to the structuralists who studied the works as self-contained linguistic systems. The structuralists were ultimately inspired by the International Phonetic Alphabet, a system that successfully described and categorized the sounds of all known human languages. This great achievement led the Russian Formalists of the 1920s and 1930s to try to emulate it by devising a universal grammar for literary works, analogous to the grammar and syntax of sentences. The structuralists, further inspired by anthropological classifications of human behavior in the 1950s and 1960s (Marcel Mauss, Claude Lévi-Strauss) tried to continue the work of the Formalists. Their efforts are reflected in titles such as Tzvétan Todorov's *The Grammar of 'The Decameron'*. Raymonde Debray-Genette states the structuralists' presuppositions unequivocally in her article on *Un coeur simple*. She explains that a literary work is organized like a sentence. It is organized "horizontally" (across its successive narrative segments) by a kind of syntax (a set of rules for putting things together) analogous to the syntax of a sentence; it is organized "vertically" (across multiple levels of meaning) by rhetorical devices analogous to "the great figures of speech which nourish classical discourse" (asyndeton, repetition, metonymy, metabole, synecdoche, and metaphor). At the conclusion, she finds that these figures of speech "are figures of nothing if not of themselves. They refer to one another, they circulate meaning, they do not halt it." She thus refuses to "interpret" the literary work; that is, to try to connect it to some ultimate meaning inside ("organic unity") or outside (social or moral values) of itself. In the eyes of such post-thematic criticism, meaning is a system of transactions, of exchanges, of shifting axes rather than fixed points.

The intertextual approach, whose leading exponent is Michael Riffaterre, stands halfway between the old and the new. Inspired in part, like structuralism, by classical rhetoric, it studies how a complete work can be generated by the elaboration of one of its parts, by saying the same thing over and over again in different ways. But it also studies the relationships between parts of one text and parts of another, like old-fashioned source criticism. It differs from source criticism, from "influence" studies, in three ways. It does not limit itself to the impact of one great author on another. It recognizes the existence of "paratexts," of popularized and vulgarized second-hand sources, as frequent and influential vehicles for ideas. And rather than seeing an earlier text as the "cause" of a later text, it sees both texts as parts of an overall system of socially shared meanings. And it goes beyond paraphrases and verbal parallelisms to recognize how kernels of ideas can be enormously expanded. In this volume, Riffaterre examines *Madame Bovary* as the development of commonplaces in the "sociolect," the fund of "common knowledge" which we share without examination. Flaubert built his novel on the cliché that adultery inevitably leads to degradation. When Riffaterre uses words "interpret" and "interpretation," he refers to translating the idiosyncratic sign system of the author into the communal system of social discourse. He does not judge that discourse as being uplifting or disappointing, wise or foolish, propitious or disadvantageous for the creation of a work of art.

Shoshana Felman studies Flaubert's early works, *Mémoires d'un fou* and *Novembre*, from a semiotic-deconstructionist viewpoint. Semiotics aspires to explain every instance of meaningfulness and of communication as part of a system of signs — the length of your hair or lawn, the make and year of your car, the conventions of professional wrestling and so forth as well as language. When focused on a literary text, semiotics goes beyond the dictionary definitions to explore how concepts are socially and culturally "loaded," analogous to the psychoanalytic criticism which explores how concepts are individually and emotionally "loaded." Semiotics tends to find systems of binary oppositions (e.g., "good and evil"). Deconstruction challenges these oppositions as delusions based upon their users' vested interests, upon selfish hypocrisy, or self-deception. (Compare Nietzsche's title, "Beyond Good and Evil," or William Blake's, "The Marriage of Heaven and Hell".) Felman examines the connotations of the concept of "madness" to show Flaubert's rapid maturation as a writer. In the *Mémoires d'un fou*, he still is trying to exploit the notion of madness like a romantic, to prove that he is different from other people, to assert his independence, originality, and creativity. Sanity refers to otherness, madness to the unique self. But in *Novembre*, completed when Flaubert was only 21, "the narrator discovers that the difference once so diligently searched for in 'madness' is in fact found not in the subject, but in the language: insofar as it is the place of the other." In other words, "sanity" and "madness" both belong to the shared system of conventions which is language. You can't use "madness" to make yourself different, because as a part of language, "madness" is a [linguistic] "commonplace," and also a social "common place," always already occupied by others. Madness, and the narrator's death itself, become in *Novembre* clichés that undermine "the very status of the narrative, of the event in general . . . Neither a romantic nor a realist, Flaubert puts signs to rout, sends them drifting away from their playing field."

Eugenio Donato's two articles in this collection illustrate deconstructive criticism at its most lucid and persuasive. His essay on *Salammbô* dismantles the traditional dichotomy between "realist" and "romantic." "The opposition between a Flaubert centered upon a contemporary reality and a Flaubert in quest of an exotic bygone Orient is untenable." (We recall that Anne Green reached the same conclusion in her fine conventional study.) Flaubert, avers Donato, writes from the perspective of the end of time, the death of society: there the foreignness of ancient Carthage, Alexandria, or Jerusalem is merely a literary illusion with no real referent. All differences will be leveled as they and we fall into oblivion. Finally, Donato depicts the Flaubert of *Bouvard et Pécuchet* as a deconstructionist replacing the metaphors of Newtonian physics (based upon separate locations in space, and on the mass, motion, and interaction of individual objects) with those of the new science of thermodynamics (based on the physical properties common to all objects). Metaphorically speaking, the title characters try to constitute a museum, a tableau of nature and of history immobilized "as an eternally present spectacle with transparent origins and anthropocentric ends." They are defeated again and again by crossbreeding, decay, and fire, by forces that abolish difference. Their naive optimism, illustrative of the positivistic age, is refuted by Flaubert's "epistemological nihilism."

Felman, Rousset, Donato, Raitt—many of the best recent Flaubert critics, thematic and deconstructionist alike, believe that his fiction depicts nothingness or functions to abolish difference. They stress the texts' fragmentation, self-contradictions, resistance to interpretation—in short, their drift toward entropy. The opposition, whose most eloquent recent spokesperson has been Victor Brombert,[12] emphasizes the texts' ultimate coherence, unity, and decodability. What both camps share—and Flaubert criticism has been particularly blessed in this—is a broad familiarity with what Flaubert wrote and an informed respect for the historical context in which he operated.

Since the first publication of *Madame Bovary* one hundred thirty years ago, criticism has moved beyond an almost exclusive focus on that novel to Flaubert's other works, and from peremptory moral judgments to a due respect for his genius. The *Trois Contes* have been studied particularly often of late because they are short enough to permit detailed analyses, and because their grouping by the author invites speculation on how they are related—both approaches being particularly appealing to structuralists. Still neglected are *L' Éducation sentimentale*—studies of which are often pedestrian and superficial—and the Correspondence. Some consider Flaubert's letters his masterpiece, and surely they are livelier than most in literary history. We also need a book-length study of Flaubert's style. Among promising recent developments is feminist criticism, illustrated by the outstanding contributions of Carla Peterson and Naomi Schor.[13] Another is comparative literature. Although efforts to situate Flaubert in world literature had till lately just scratched the surface, new studies by Lilian Furst, Mark Conroy, and Patricia Merivale go far toward remedying this deficit.[14] And finally, Charles Bernheimer's ingenious attempt to update psychoanalytic criticism so that it can swallow up deconstruction reminds us that literary criticism will eventually move on to new and as yet unforeseeable modes.[15]

In selecting the essays for this volume, I have tried to balance the conflicting needs of general readers and of specialists. The general reader requires clarity, straight-forwardness, and exposure to the classical essays (such as those by Poulet and Rousset), as well as an introduction to the criticism of earlier periods and of Flaubert's less well-known works. The specialist should have a few surprises, and encounter some alien critical methods. For all readers, there are obvious gaps, such as essays by Baudelaire, Proust, and Sartre.[16] The annotated bibliography at the end tries to fill some of them. I have chosen to omit studies of Flaubert the man—his mother-fixation, his ambiguous sexuality, his courage as a social critic, his acceptance of patronage under the Second Empire – in order to concentrate on his works. Those who wish to study his life should start with Benjamin Bart's biography and with Hazel Barnes's study of *Sartre and Flaubert*.[17] At the other extreme, essays were omitted if they used Flaubert mainly as a pretext for general theoretical statements.

The publishers who kindly permitted republication are thanked at the end of the first page of each selection. Five essays are found in English here for the first time. I am particularly indebted to their translators: Debora V. Traas (Felman), Robert Steele (Barbey D'Aurevilly), and Tina M. Gikas (Reik) of Michigan State University; Mark W. Andrews (Debray-Genette) of Vassar College; and Robert Magnan (Raitt) of the University of Wisconsin. He and I were most graciously corrected by Dr. A. W. Raitt himself. Michigan State University has provided years of generous support through All-University Research Grants, and the Michigan State University Library, as usual, granted me a quiet place to work and gave unstinting, exceptional professional support. Laurel Porter helped substantially to clarify the introduction. I should particularly like to remember here the late René Jasinski, who first introduced me to Flaubert in a seminar in 1958, and who offered much encouragement since. This volume, however, is dedicated to Benjamin F. Bart, mentor and friend, who first enabled me to write on Flaubert, and who has greatly enriched my professional life.

LAURENCE M. PORTER

Michigan State University

Notes

1. See Charles Batteux, *Les Beaux Arts réduits à un même principe* (Geneva: Slatkine, 1969 [1746]), pp. 20–22, 159–378.

2. Charles Augustin Sainte-Beuve, "*Madame Bovary* par M. Gustave Flaubert," in his *Causeries de Lundi* (Paris: Garnier Frères, 1850–60), 16 vols, XIII, 346–63, reprinted in George Becker, ed., *Documents of Modern Literary Realism* (Princeton, N.J.: Princeton University Press, 1963), pp. 99–104 (p. 103).

3. See Jean-Paul Sartre, *L' Idiot de la famille: Gustave Flaubert de 1821–1857* (Paris: Gallimard, 1971–72), 3 vols. III, 160–206, esp. 193–202.

4. See Hazel E. Barnes, *Sartre & Flaubert* (Chicago: University of Chicago Press, 1981), pp. 278–309.

5. Georges Poulet, "The Circle and the Center: Reality and *Madame Bovary*," pp. 392–407 in Gustave Flaubert, *"Madame Bovary": Backgrounds and Sources; Essays in Criticism*, edited and translated by Paul de Man (New York: W. W. Norton, 1965), p. 407.

6. See Ernst Kris, *Psychoanalytical Explorations in Art* (New York: Schocken Books, 1964 [1952]), pp. 60–63, 197–99, 220–22 et passim.

7. Charles Du Bos, "On the 'Inner Environment' in the Work of Flaubert," pp. 360–71 in Flaubert, *Madame Bovary*, edited by Paul de Man (see note 5), p. 363.

8. Frank Laurence Lucas, "The Martyr of Letters: Gustave Flaubert," pp. 227–47 in his *Studies French and English* (London: Cassell, 1950 [1933]).

9. Paul Valéry, "La Tentation de (saint) Flaubert," in his *Oeuvres complétes* (Paris: Gallimard, 1957), 2 vols., I, 613–19, reprinted from his *Variété V* (1944).

10. Benjamin F. Bart, "Flaubert's Concept of the Novel," *PMLA*, 80, no. 1 (March 1965): 84–89; and Bart, *Flaubert* (Syracuse, N.Y.: Syracuse University Press, 1967).

11. Jacques Derrida, "An Idea of Flaubert's 'Plato's Letter,' " *MLN*, 99, no. 4 (September 1984): 748–68.

12. Victor Brombert, "Flaubert and the Status of the Subject," pp. 100–15 in *Flaubert and Postmodernism*, edited by Naomi Schor and Henry F. Majewski (Lincoln, Nebraska: University of Nebraska Press, 1984). A variant statement by Brombert appears in the Spring 1984 issue of *Nineteenth-Century French Studies*, pp. 280–96.

13. See Carla L. Peterson, "The Heroine as Reader in the Nineteenth Century Novel: Emma Bovary and Maggie Tulliver," *Comparative Literature Studies*, 17 (1980): 168–83; Naomi Schor, "Salammbô enchaînée; ou, Femme et ville dans *Salammbô*," pp. 89–104 in *Flaubert: La Femme, la ville*, edited by Marie-Claire Bancquart (Paris: Presses Universitaires de France, 1983).

14. See Lilian R. Furst, *Fictions of Romantic Irony* (Cambridge, Massachusetts: Harvard University Press, forthcoming); Mark Conroy, *Modernism and Authority: Strategies of Legitimation in Flaubert and Conrad* (Baltimore, Maryland: Johns Hopkins University Press, forthcoming); Patricia Merivale, "Learning the Hard Way: Gothic Pedagogy in the Modern Romantic Quest," *Comparative Literature*, 36, no. 2 (Spring 1984): 146–61.

15. See Charles Bernheimer, *Flaubert and Kafka: Studies in Psychopoetic Structure* (New Haven, Connecticut: Yale University Press, 1982).

16. See Charles Baudelaire, "*Madame Bovary*, par Gustave Flaubert" (1857), pp. 336–43 in Flaubert, *Madame Bovary*, edited and translated by Paul de Man (see note 5); Marcel Proust, "A propos du style de Flaubert" (1920), pp. 193–206 in his *Chroniques* (Paris: Gallimard, 1928): and Jean-Paul Sartre, *L'Idiot de la famille* (see note 3).

17. Cited in notes 4 and 10 above.

Flaubert

Georges Poulet*

I

> Sometimes (during my grand days in the sun) when I was lit up by an illumination that made my skin tingle from my toes to the roots of my hair, I had an inkling of a state of mind so superior to life that compared to it glory would be nothing, and happiness vain.[1]

Those grand days in the sun, those "happy days when the mind is as open to the sun as the countryside,"[2] form in the life of Flaubert a series of radiant peaks about which works, thought, existence, all cluster. He is, primordially, a romantic: a romantic not so much for his love of the picturesque, as for the consciousness of an exceptional interior experience. But unlike that of the Romantics, the consciousness of this interior experience does not turn Flaubert in upon himself; it opens his mind to the sun; it turns him outward. Like Diderot, like Gautier, from the moment he makes use of his faculties for literary ends, those faculties which he exercises the most and which dominate all the others are precisely those which direct the mind not toward a knowledge of the self but toward a grasp of the non-self and a representation of the world:

> I have an extraordinary faculty of *perception*. . . .[3]

> I have almost voluptuous sensations simply from seeing things, so long as I see them well.[4]

> Only rapports are true, that is to say, the manner in which we *perceive* objects.[5]

The starting point with Flaubert is thus not Flaubert himself; it is the rapport between the perceiving self and the object perceived:

*From Elliott Coleman, trans., *Studies in Human Time* (Baltimore: Johns Hopkins University Press, 1956), 248–62. Reprinted by permission of Johns Hopkins University Press.

Often, a propos of no matter what, a drop of water, a shell, a hair, you stopped and stayed motionless, eyes fixed, heart open.

The object you contemplated seemed to encroach upon you, by as much as you inclined yourself toward it, and bonds were established. . . .[6]

Sometimes by dint of gazing at a pebble, an animal, a picture, I felt myself enter into them. Communications between human beings are not more intense.[7]

Certainly these are capital passages; they reveal to us the fundamental orientation of Flaubert's mind. Self-awareness is fully experienced by him in the moment when he emerges from himself to become identified — by the simplest but most intense of the acts of the mental life, perception — with the object, whatever it may be, of this perception. Thus objectivity, far from being an acquired discipline with Flaubert, is a natural state, the only truly natural state of his thought. If it is realized fully only in exceptional instances, that is because ". . . man is so made that each day he can savor only a little of nourishment, colors, sounds, feelings, ideas",[8] but this nourishment, made up in the first place of colors and sounds and secondarily of feelings and ideas, is the sole possible food. It is to it that one must turn for support and subsistence. Life exists, but only where there are colors, sounds, the outdoors, the sun. One must incline toward it, penetrate into it or be penetrated by it, and become what one feels by the very act of feeling.

An act of identification by which there are abolished not only the interval between subject and object, but their existence as distinct beings: "Then, by dint of looking, you no longer saw; listening, you heard nothing, and your mind itself ended by losing the notion of that *particularity* which kept it on the alert."[9]

The particularity of the object exists only for him who maintains in his consciousness a gap between the thing perceived and the perceiving mind; it no longer exists for him who, effacing within him any idea of a representing self and a thing represented, limits his present consciousness to the representation itself. In his moments of "contemplative effusion,"[10] in his "grand days in the sun," Flaubert arrived at an integral phenomenalism. The mind being what it represents, and the object existing only in its representation in the mind, what remains is simply a unique being that can be called indifferently mind or nature: "The interval between yourself and the object, like an abyss whose two sides come closer and closer together, was getting increasingly narrower, so much so that this difference disappeared. . . . One degree more and you became nature, or nature became you." [11]

This "one degree more" by which one becomes nature is reached elsewhere: "By dint of being penetrated by it, of entering into it, we also *became nature*, feeling that it was overpowering us, and taking a measureless joy in that process,"[12] It is a joy that becomes measureless from the moment one is identified with the whole extent of nature and of the activity which animates it: "Everything in you palpitates with joy and beats its wings with the elements, you are bound to them, breathe with them, the essence of animate nature seems to have passed into you. . . ."[13]

At this degree of pantheistic ecstasy, the conception of a mere spatial and logical order proves to be transcended. It would be inexact, therefore, to see in Flaubert only a poetic transcription of Spinozism. What man attains in the Flaubertian experience is less the sense of an *ordo et connexio idearum* than the intuition of life in its cosmic expansion. Life is diffusion, a tireless projection of forms in a space that is the divine immensity: "There is no nothingness! There is no emptiness! Everywhere there are bodies that move in the immutable depths of Vastness."[14]

To be identified with cosmic life is to be diffused over a divine vastness which can be considered indifferently as holding the variety of things and that of the representations which one makes of them. Thought and the world are an identical extent: "I was, in the variety of my being, like an immense forest of India, where life palpitates in each atom. . . ."[15]

But precisely because it is sheer variety, life cannot be apprehended except through the motion by which it varies. It is not enough to reach some point from which the sentient mind can spread its thoughts over the whole representative field. It is also necessary that, from this point, and without leaving this point — which is the durationless point of the present — the mind should "live within all that life in order to array all its forms, *to endure together with them*, and forever varying, to extend forth its metamorphoses under the sun of eternity."[16] Since life is duration, the moment that absolutely expresses it must be a moment in which the very working of duration is visible. Sometimes this presence of duration in the moment is found by Flaubert in a direct intuition of the genesis of things: "O happy am I! I have seen life born, I have seen motion begin";[17] but more often it seems occasioned in his work by a sensory event. There are the moments when sensation is so perfectly yoked with the general life of things that one becomes, so to speak, the metaphorical expression of the other. Then to feel oneself live is to feel oneself live life, to feel the pulse of duration beat. For instance, we have the scene of carnal love in *Madame Bovary*: "The silence was everywhere; a sweetness seemed to emanate from the trees; she felt her heart begin beating again, and the blood circulate in her body like a stream of milk. Then she heard afar off, beyond the woods, over the hills, a faint and prolonged cry, a protracted voice, and she listened silently to its mingling, like a strain of music, with the last vibrations of her stirred nerves."[18]

In this passage Flaubert succeeds in giving the moment a spatial and temporal density so particular that one could say (and it is undoubtedly the effect Flaubert wished to produce) that this moment belongs to a different duration from that of ordinary days, a duration whose *tempo* of things is made sweeter, slower, and therefore more perceptible; a duration that spreads out. It is as if time, like a passing breeze, could be felt in the renewed beatings of the heart, in the blood that flows like a stream of milk. It is no longer the bitter consciousness of an interval, there is no more interval; there is only a gliding motion which carries away simultaneously the things and the sentient mind with the sense of an absolute homogeneity between the different elements that compose the moment. The mind, the body, nature, and life, all participate in the same moment of the same becoming.

II

The state of mind glimpsed by Flaubert in his grand days in the sun is thus not different from that experienced by all the great pantheist mystics: a moment of ecstasy when, in the union of the sentient mind and pure sensation, the self is identified with the universe and has for a moment the experience of eternity.

But with Flaubert, even in his grand days in the sun, that state is only *glimpsed*. Thought can neither be established nor isolated within it. The point at which it happens is not a state but a boundary point; a point that is the extremity of a temporal line, a boundary that is that of a movement of thought. Without an antecedent line and movement, it is as inconceivable as a beach without a tide to flow toward it and mark its delimitation.

It is the same with Flaubert when the substance of the lived present is this time constituted not by sense experiences but by memories. There are, for Flaubert, other grand days in the sun when the mind is not open to the present sun, but to the "golden haze" still emanating from suns which have set long ago. There is for him a present that is the terminal place of recollected images as well as a present that is the terminal place of sensorial images.

For the predilection that Flaubert always had for memory, even at the expense of actual sensation, is not due to a particular preference of his for what belongs to the past as such. What does he look for in sensation except a total intimacy with the object of sensation? Now this feeling of total intimacy is rare by reason of the inflexibility of a self that "will not let itself go," the mind naturally here and the object there. But when the sensation is reborn under the form of memory, it reappears not as a thing outside but as something inside. It is regained within. All distance is now abolished, as in the rarest and most perfect sensuous union. The reviviscence is, like pantheistic ecstasy, a pure viviscence. It has the same intensity, the same richness, it ends in the same synthesis of the object and the self.

And to begin with, it has the same starting point. Just as with Flaubert, sensory activity takes its origin from an object encountered ("Often, a propos of no matter what, a drop of water, a sea-shell . . ."), so it is also through the fortuitous encounter with an object that the retrospective imagination takes birth: "anything, the slightest circumstance, a rainy day, a hot sun, a flower, an old piece of furniture, recalls to me a series of memories. . . ."[19] Sometimes it happens at the sight of a garment worn in days gone by, of an engraving hand-colored a long time ago, at the smell of an odor long ago familiar; it recurs oftenest upon revisits to past places. The object, whatever it may be, lets loose a series of memories. A *series*: the most striking characteristic indeed of the phenomenon of memory in Flaubert is seriality. One memory calls up another, then still another, and so on; and each rises into view under the form of an image which is covered and replaced by the following slide, as in the projections of a magic lantern: ". . . He saw again, like ghosts conjured up, the different days of his past, some gay, others sad; *and first* those when he played, a child laughing at life, without dream or desire; *and the one* on which he entered high school, *and that other* on which he left, *the one* when he arrived at M. Renaud's, *the one* on which she came into his room. . . ."[20] These images are all distinct. Each of them presents a definite picture but brings also with it other images, trains of feelings, the very emotions of the past surging up from the depths. Now all this awakening of the affective memory takes place, as it were, in the environs and in the gaps in the series of perceptible images; it connects them, suffuses them, and ends by mingling them: "My travels, my memories of childhood, all are colored by one another, fall into line, dance with wonderful gleamings and mount in a spiral."[21] A spiral, enveloping a thousand diverse images and traversing different zones of the past — such is the recreative synthesis which crowns the operation of memory in Flaubert. It does not consist in drawing upon a repository, in combining elements of different periods, but rather in allowing layers of images to rise in tiers in the mind, each of which keeps the particular form it occupied in time, but, on the other hand, takes color from the reflection of the others. Thus, the consciousness that evokes them appears to itself like a painting in perspective, in the depths of which there appear at unequal intervals with their particular hues — but in a unique ambience (which is the true self) — the phantoms of the past: "I passed along the Rue des Orties which opens on the court of the college . . . . I saw the chestnut trees under which we played. . . . I saw myself there once more, on the first day, entering, unknown, amongst all of you, and you who first came and spoke to me; *and then all the rest slowly unrolled in my memory*, the cries when we were at play, and the racket of our balls against the wire lattices of the windows, and the hot, humid and stifling air of the classrooms. . . ."[22]

In the same manner, Emma, noticing on a letter from her father a little of the ashes with which he had the habit of drying wet ink, sees her father once more, "bending over the hearth to pick up the tongs"; then, this first image leading to others, she recalls "summer afternoons full of sunlight"; and step by step, from memory to memory, she follows the course of her life down to the present moment: "What happiness then . . . what abundance of illusions . . . Nothing remained of them now. She had used them up in the surprising experiences of her mind, through all its successive conditions . . . losing them continually in this way *her whole life long*, like a traveler who leaves something of his wealth at every inn along the way. . . ."[23]

One feels that the whole force of this passage (leaving aside the feeling of the attrition of experience, of which more later) relates to the *depth of duration* which it suggests — a depth that is glimpsed through a descending perspective, in which the images are spaced out like milestones, along *the whole length of life*. The first memory is like the top of a slope; from that point there is nothing to do but descend again; and to redescend the slope is to retraverse the whole life, to render visible the very pathway of lived time: "Then, swept along on her memories as if upon a foaming torrent, she soon came to recall yesterday. . . ."[24]

More rarely (for Flaubert's prospective imagination is poor), the same phenomenon is discovered with regard to time to come: "And immediately pictures unrolled endlessly. He saw himself with her, at night in a postchaise, then on the bank of a stream on a summer evening, and then under the reflection of a lamp at home together."[25]

But the moment when the "contemplative effusion" is most completely realized is the one when the *pictures without end* instead of seeming to approach or withdraw from the present appear to unroll within its span: "Then all of his past life appeared to Smarh, swiftly, in one stroke, like a flash of lightning."[26]

It is as if suddenly the whole field of existence, without losing anything of its intrinsic multiplicity, were contemplated by the interior gaze in the interior of the moment. For example, when Félicité sees the lights of Honfleur: "A feeling of faintness seized her; and the misery of her childhood, the deception of first love, the departure of her nephew, the death of Virginie, like the waves of a rising tide, returned all at once, and rising in her throat, suffocated her."[27]

In this simultaneity on which all existence is brought to bear, the retrospective movement attains its perfection and its terminal point: a revelation of a temporal expanse filled up by the mind just as in the sensuous ecstasy the mind fills up exterior space.

III

What is there beyond this *eternal moment*? All the internal activity is engaged. The mind perceives with an hallucinatory clearness a series of images whose motion is accelerated. They multiply, they surround it, they besiege it. Exaltation is followed by disquietude, then by anguish. The images that the mind watched appearing within itself it now sees disappearing outside itself. It is like "a kind of hemorrhage of innervation,"[28] as if existence drained away through a bleeding wound: "My thoughts, which I would like to clasp together . . . slide away one after another and *escape me*, like a sheaf of arrows from the hand of a child who cannot hang on to them, they fall to the ground hurting his knees. . . ."[29]

The same thing goes for the moment of union with the past as for the moment of union with the present and with nature. In each case, without any transition, fissure succeeds fusion. The abolished distance is suddenly rediscovered, gaping in the mind: "One says to oneself: 'Ten years ago I was there,' and one is there and one thinks the same things and the whole interval is forgotten. *Then it appears to you, that interval*, like an immense precipice in which nothingness whirls round."[30]

It is exactly the inverse motion of that by which the subject had been absorbed in the object of its sensation or of its memory. Then it was a question of an "interval like an abyss whose sides come closer and closer together . . . so much so that the difference disappeared." Now it is a question of the same interval reappearing and affirming the same difference.

A difference which reveals a double change in the nature of space and time. Space is no longer the field of expansion, from the center of which the mind diffuses itself and radiates outward; time is no longer that extent of the past which the mind — starting out from some given memory — fills and overflows with the flux of its reminiscences; on the contrary, extension has become an empty void separating the self from the object, and time another kind of empty extension which no less irremediably separates the present self from its past: "How far away all that is! Did I not live then? Was that indeed I? Is it myself now? Every minute of my life seems cut off at a stroke from every other by an abyss; between yesterday and today there is an eternity that appals me."[31] This eternity is properly called an abyss; it is abysmal because it is the negation of the eternity of plentitude to which it succeeds. It is the infinite absence of things of which one experienced the presence, a sort of atrociously neuter time, since nothing fills or traverses it, whose extent, indifferently comparable to both eternity and a minute, expresses simply an absolute gap. Sometimes this gap is depicted under the aspect of a general petrification of things: "It seems, at certain moments, that the universe is immobilized, that everything has become a statue and that we alone are alive."[32] At other times it takes the form of a perpetual repetition of the same action: "From then on he continually climbed that stairway. . . . He continued to ascend with the strange facility one experiences in dreams."[33] But repetition and immobilization are the unconscious metaphors by which the human mind both expresses and conceals the nakedness of a void, the horror of which he is the only one to perceive. There is no possibility here of that intermediary time which we place mechanically between ourselves and a period of the past which we recall: a consciousness of a duration that is more or less continuous, which joins this moment and that one together. The abysmal time is the time that creates and asserts the abyss, which sees to it that moments do not rejoin each other. The human being is no longer supported from behind by his past. He leans back against nothingness: "Despite the hubbub in his head, he perceives an enormous silence that separates him from the world. He tries to speak; impossible! It is as if the general bond of his existence were dissolved. . . ."[34] "Something undefined separates you from your own person and rivets you to nonbeing."[35]

In a flash our past self is carried to the other side of an abyss, to a side that is directly opposite to us. We see it from afar, and it appears to us as a stranger: "Startled by the fidelity of his memories, rendered still vivid by the presence of those places where they occurred in the form of events and feelings, he asked himself if all of them belonged to the same man, if a single life could have sufficed for them, and he tried to connect them with some other lost existence, so far away was his past from him!"[36]

Existence is divided in two. Actual life now seems only a feeble reflection of another life already lived, one which must have been the only true life: "There are days when one has lived two existences, the second is already a mere memory of the first. . . ."[37]

Then one turns toward that past with an ambiguous nostalgia. One half-fancies having already lived in some far-off epoch of history. One experiences what Flaubert calls "the thrill of history."[38] It is an inordinate sadness over the idea that those ages have passed with no possibility of returning. "What would I not give to see a triumph, what would I not sell to enter Suburre one evening at the time when the torches were burning at the doors of the brothels. . . ?"[39] One sets oneself to the endless pursuit of retrospective myths; one ruminates upon past existences lived or dreamed. But the more one's thought is absorbed in them, the more the present appears as an illusion. The past "devours it" and "devours us": "I roam in memories and am lost in them."[40]

It is then that the actual moment reveals all its narrowness and dearth: "I do not experience, as you do, that feeling of a life that is beginning, the wonder of a newly-hatched existence."[41] "The world is not big enough for the mind: it suffocates in the present hour."[42]

To the "interminable series of the passions that have faded away,"[43] to the lassitude and to the distaste for the ephemeral, it is vain to try to oppose an activity directed toward the future. The imagination, so intense under its retrospective form, sees nothing ahead of it. Since it is entirely representative and cannot picture perceptible objects in the future, it sees nothing at all there: "And from the past, I go dreaming of the future, and there I see nothing, absolutely nothing. I am without plan, without idea, without project, and what is worse, without ambition.[44]

Deprived of a future, devoured by the past, crushed by the weight of the present, the mind cannot any more experience time except as a motion that slows down, as a *tempo* that is slackening. One feels oneself old from having lived through so many of the "minutes that are as years."[45] The sense of existence becomes that of a continuous addition to this length of duration. Life is reduced to being a repetition: "Must you not awake every morning, eat, drink, go, come, repeat that series of acts which are always the same?"[46]

At this point one would say that the course of duration stops. It is no longer a stream, but still water, "a sleeping fen, so quiet that the slightest event that falls into it makes innumerable circles. . . ."[47] An agitation on the surface, and a general feeling of illusion and of wearing away: with Flaubert it is in these things that the feeling of human time is in grave danger of getting lost.

IV

There is in the *Première Éducation sentimentale* a passage that is particularly important because it seems to give us the profound reason for the difference, so visible in Flaubert, between the works of his youth and those of his maturity. This passage begins with a long, morose meditation that one of the characters pursues on the formlessness and dejection of his existence. Then gradually, the thought is transformed into images, and once again the past is put to unrolling a series of memory-pictures. But this time the dominating factor in this succession of images is neither the kind of spontaneous homogeneity which is given to the most disparate things by the current of emotions that carries them along nor, on the reverse side, the feeling of radical heterogeneity which reveals itself in them and between them when the current fails to link them together. This time, on the contrary, it is possible to find there a certain coherence. For the first time one can distinguish not only sensory and imaginative events but also events penetrable by the mind: "Nevertheless from all that there resulted his present state, and this state was the sum of all those antecedents, one which permitted him to review them; each event had of itself produced a second, every feeling had been fused into an idea. . . . Thus there was a sequence and a continuity to this series of diverse perceptions."[48]

It would be hard to imagine a reflection more ordinary or more commonplace. Nevertheless, it is around this reflection that Flaubert tried to reform a life and a work abandoned of themselves to the power of images. The solution he accepts is the middle solution, it is an option in favor of order — an order, moreover, which is perceived and which perhaps exists only when it is discovered as the order of accomplished facts. For it is discovered only in things that are completed and in the postulate that they are completed by reason of other things which have determined their completion: "The thought that comes to you now has been brought to you . . . by successions, gradations, transformations and rebirths."[49] Thus, the order does not depend on the assumption of any transcendence. It is an adequate relationship between what exists in this moment and what existed in all preceding moments. It is an *a posteriori* construction that the mind imposes upon the universe to make it hold together. Thanks to this formula, there are no more *gaps*, no more intervals between things, nor an abyss between the present and the past. We are in the kingdom of immanence, and of so integral an immanence that everything is representable and implied there. Beyond the chain of causes and effects as they are represented in the mind, there is the supposition that the same chain and the same interactivity of causes and effects persist indefinitely; there is nothing else; no mystery; nothing veiled or inexpressible. What the imagination cannot revive the mind can represent to itself.

Representative thought, therefore, chooses a particular moment of life. It perceives this moment and all the sense-data it contains as a relationship between the human being and its immediate environment. Then it proceeds to discern how those sensations are modified by the action of other images coming from the past. From this stage backward, reconstructive thought will begin an ascending movement. It will see how in their turn those images of the past were linked to objects of the past. Behind the environment in which the present self lives, it will discover the milieu in which it has lived and felt; and behind this double past, which is that of being and milieu, it will discover another, and then still another, always making sure of its discoveries and in this way creating a proportionate density of duration in which there is neither hiatus or rupture; a movement which, by its direction as well as by its very nature, is the exact reverse of the "flight of memories," that is to say, the sudden jump by which the mind discovered itself, in the works of Flaubert's youth, thrown away, so to speak, into any moment of the past.

For it is no longer now a question of a sudden plunge into the depths of a former time, from whence one is allowed to descend haphazardly the course of existence. The design of Flaubert is no longer a lyrical but a methodical design. He sketched it in a passage in the *Première Tentation*; there he makes Science speak in the following terms: "If I could penetrate matter, grasp idea, follow life through its metamorphoses, understand being in its modes, and thus from one to the other, reascending the ladder of causes like a series of steps, reunite in myself those scattered phenomena and put them back into motion in the synthesis from which my scalpel detached them."[50]

Thus, the first movement of the Flaubertian reconstruction is the ascending movement by which thought climbs, in a series of inferences, the stairway of causes, and so progressively withdraws from the domain of sensation or of actual images, in order to pass into that of the order of things, into the domain of law. It is a method strictly opposed to that of Balzac, who, starting with an *a priori* creature, posits at the outset the existence of a law-force, of which there remains simply to express next, in terms more and more concrete, the descending curve into real life. Balzac, novelist of the *determining*; Flaubert, novelist of the *determined*.

But precisely by reason of the fact that in Flaubert that which is first given is this *determined* actual, indubitable, and resisting object upon which the representative faculty can rest all its weight, the Flaubertian construction, as high as it may rise, never risks becoming abstract. The law is not a non-temporal thing. It does not exist in itself but in the action by which it is exercised. In proportion as one ascends to it, one gathers up, at each step, the perceptible matter with which the human being has remodified itself in each of the antecedent moments of its duration. Thus the human being is somehow found to exist in two ways: by its sensations, whether immediate or remembered, which form its variable, contingent reality, though in intimate contact with the reality of things; and on the other hand, by the synthetic order that the concatenating series of causes imposes upon its existence.

A double synthesis, or rather a recapture, in the framework of an objective synthesis, of what had always — but in a subjective, fragmentary, and fugitive fashion — been synthetically expressed in the works of Flaubert's youth.

This is what he himself seems to indicate in a note written in 1859: "The artist not only carries humanity within him, but he reproduces its history in the creation of his work: first confusion, a general view, aspirations, bedazzlement, everything is mixed up [the barbarous epoch]; then analysis, doubt, method, the disposition of parts [the scientific era]; finally, he comes back to the first synthesis, made wider in the execution."[51]

Having arrived at this peak of synthesis, thought turns itself about to begin its downward movement. If it raised itself up into the regions of causes and antecedents, that was in order to prepare itself to understand and show how, starting out from this region and from the past, the actual is organized. So then the descending movement of Flaubert's thought takes on the aspect of a prospective representation of life which, through a series of states, is brought out of the past up to the present and ends there by giving it the significance of being an effect that is the consequence of all the vast perceptible genetic travail in space and duration — a perspective similar to that which one has when, on the shore, one lifts his eyes slowly to the open sea in order to follow from out there the course of a wave that draws nearer and nearer, and finally perishes at one's feet — an experience that one also has when in writing, say, a periodic sentence (the periodic sentence of Flaubert) one finds that from the protasis to the apodosis the different elements are composed in a rising and falling synthesis which, in coming to its completion, affords the discovery in the written sentence of an indissoluble unity in which everything becomes present. From that point on, the problem of time is simply a problem of style.

Notes

[All of the following references are to the *Oeuvres complètes de Gustave Flaubert* (Paris: Conard, 1923–54), 21 vol., except those preceded by the abbreviation *OJ*, which refer to the *Oeuvres de jeunesse*, vols. 10–12 of the *Oeuvres complètes* (Paris: Conard, 1910–54), 28 vol. Emphasis added by Poulet in all quotations. Letters I–IX correspond to volumes II–X.]

1. II, 395. Letter to Louise Colet, April 24, 1852.

2. XIII, 424–25. "Corse," in *Par les champs et par les grèves; Pyrénées; Corse* (travel journals).

3. III, 270. Letter to Louise Colet, July 7–8, 1853.

4. I, 178. Letter to Alfred Le Poittevin, May 26, 1845.

5. VIII, 135. Letter to Guy de Maupassant, August 15, 1878.

6. XV, 417. *La Tentation de saint Antoine*, 1849 version.

7. III, 210. Letter to Louise Colet.

8. XIII, 131. "Par les champs et par les grèves."

9. XV, 417. *La Tentation de saint Antoine*, 1849 version.

10. XIII, 131. "Par les champs et par les grèves."

11. XV, 417. *La Tentation de saint Antoine*, 1849 version.

12. XIII, 130. "Par les champs et par les grèves."

13. XIII, 425. "Corse."

14. XV, 173. *La Tentation de saint Antoine*, 1874 version.

15. *OJ* II, 180. "Novembre."

16. XIII, 131. "Par les champs et par les grèves."

17. XV, 200. *La Tentation de saint Antoine*, 1874 version.

18. XII, 223–24. *Madame Bovary: Moeurs de Province.*

19. *OJ* I, 500. "Mémoires d'un fou."

20. *OJ* III, 84. "L'Éducation sentimentale," version de 1845.

21. III, 371. Letter to Louise Colet.

22. *OJ*, III, 36. "L'Éducation sentimentale," version de 1845.

23. XII, 239. *Madame Bovary.*

24. XII, 424. *Madame Bovary.*

25. XI, 453. *L'Éducation sentimentale: Histoire d'un jeune homme.*

26. *OJ* I, 106. "Smarh."

27. XVII, 51. *Trois Contes.*

28. III, 270. Letter to Louise Colet, July 7–8, 1853.

29. XV, 236. *La Tentation de saint Antoine*, 1849 version.

30. III, 331–32. Letter to Louise Colet, September 2, 1853.

31. *OJ* II, 178. "Novembre."

32. III, 317. Letter to Louis Bouilhet, August 23, 1853.

33. XIV, 102. *Salammbô.*

34. XV, 15. *La Tentation de saint Antoine*, 1874 version.

35. III, 332. Letter to Louise Colet, September 2, 1853.

36. *OJ* III, 242. "L'Éducation sentimentale," version de 1845.

37. *OJ* II, 192. "Novembre."

38. III, 19. Letter to Louise Colet, September 4, 1852.

39. II, 6. Letter to Louise Colet, early 1847.

40. VI, 377. Letter to Madame Roger des Genettes, May 15, 1872.

41. V, 240. Letter to George Sand, September 29, 1866.

42. I, 253. Letter to Louise Colet, August 15, 1846.

43. III, 308. Letter to Louise Colet, August 21–22, 1853.

44. II, 201. Letter to Louis Bouilhet, June 4, 1850.

45. I, 368. Letter to Louise Colet, October 10, 1846.

46. XV, 434. *La Tentation de saint Antoine*, 1849 version.

47. III, 289. Letter to Louise Colet, August 14, 1853.

48. *OJ* III, 244. "L'Éducation sentimentale," version de 1845.

49. XV, 418. *La Tentation de saint Antoine*, 1849 version.

50. XV, 349. *La Tentation de saint Antoine*, 1849 version.

51. The reference, not provided by the author, is too vague to trace. [Editor]

Mémoires d'un fou; Novembre

Modernity of the Commonplace   Shoshana Felman*

WRITING, SILENCE

> It is too easy to say what a cliché appears to be. But what it is in reality,
> who can say?
>   —Léon Bloy, *Exegesis of Commonplaces*

It might seem paradoxical to speak of a modernity of the commonplace.[1] What is more opposed to the idea of modernity than the mechanical repetition of a ready-read formula, of a language of stereotypes? Does
modernity not consist of novelty, that is, of an attempt to break with the
clichés of the past and to escape, to the extent possible, from cultural
memory? Is not the commonplace indeed the closure of this memory,
within its worst automatisms, the rut in the interior of the language, of an
already-read, already-seen, already-said? How then may modernity be
associated with the reproduction of this *already*?

It could seem even more paradoxical to attribute the modernity of the
commonplace to Flaubert. Was not writing for Flaubert, more than for
any other, a declaration of rupture with the commonplace? Did not
Flaubert compile the *Dictionary of Accepted Ideas*—"Apology of Human
Vulgarity in all its Forms"—specifically in order that, "once one has read
it, one would no longer dare to speak for fear of saying naturally one of the
sentences to be found there"?[2] It is with a similar ambition, with the same
aim of a utopic *silence*, that Léon Bloy will establish, several decades after
Flaubert, around the turn of the century, his *Exegesis of Commonplaces*:
"Of what is it a question, really, if not of wrenching away the language
from the imbeciles, from the redoubtable and definitive idiots of this

---

*From *La Folie et la chose littéraire* (Paris: Editions du Seuil, 1978), 191–213. Translated
for this volume by Debora V. Traas, Michigan State University. Reprinted by permission
of Editions du Seuil.

century. . . ? To at last obtain the silence of the Bourgeois, what a dream!"[3] To write — in order that "one would no longer dare to speak": to establish the repertory of the banalities themselves so that *one* should keep silence: by the very repugnance inspired in him by the cliché, Flaubert designated it as the privileged spot from which a decisive question is posed: that of the relationship of writing and silence.

But this question was to entail, from Flaubert forward and into modern consciousness a reversal of perspective with regard to the cliché itself. For, if Flaubert wanted above all to coerce his reader, and himself, to the silencing of the cliché, *to silence the commonplace*, the question was raised of knowing to what extent and at what cost such a silence was possible. It is to measure himself against this question that Flaubert *wrote*: he *spoke* only to learn if not speaking was possible. A similar preoccupation, in Beckett, governs and causes to speak the narrator of the *Unnamable*: "In conclusion: shall I be able to speak of myself, of this place. . . ? shall I ever be able to keep quiet? is there a relationship between these two questions? People love wagers. Here are several, perhaps only one."[4] It is from the starting point of such a question and such an exigency that Flaubert had to understand that to keep silence *was necessary* precisely *because* keeping silent was not possible; but also that silence, far from being the negation of the *word*, was interwoven all through it, and that the commonplace word, more than any other, was deeply possessed by it. From there, to rejoin the cliché in its modernity, was to discover that which, from the cliché, was nonetheless unforeseeable: to understand that the déjà-vu was not yet *seen*, that the already-read, *as such*, was not yet read; to understand that the task of the writer was therefore to seek to *read*, to meet and rejoin — within language — this *place*, singularly common, with his own anonymity.

MADNESS, ORIGINALITY, MODERNITY

Such a discovery, part of a veritable revolution, is outlined, it seems to me, throughout the text of *November*: a decisive text marking a turning point not only for Flaubertian writing but for the impact which Flaubert left on literary consciousness and criticism. It goes without saying that such a discovery can be neither fully conscious nor fully clairvoyant: it is not a phenomenon of thought but an event of writing. It is only therefore after the fact that Flaubert will be able to gage the importance of *November* which he refused, however, to publish during his lifetime. On December 2, 1846, four years after its completion, he will write to Louise Colet: "If you have listened well to *November*, you must have sensed a thousand *unsayable* things which perhaps explain what I am. But that age is past, that work was the closure of my youth. What is left of it is little enough, but still holds true."[5]

To comprehend *November* (1842), it is thus necessary to begin by situating it at this point of juncture, in Flaubert's text, which was to mark, according to the author's own word, the opening of maturity: the registering of a change of direction, by which writing, after the fact, found itself to be transformed, reoriented. *November* would be better understood in relation to what comes before it, notably the *Memoirs of a Madman* (1838), which he takes up again, after a four-year hiatus. The fable, *grosso modo*, is the same, that of an initiation to love which opens into the frustration of a life whose sole axis is that of memory, the bitterness of a memory without a tomorrow. From a thematic point of view, the *Memoirs of a Madman* prefigure the entire work of Flaubert: the first text said everything. Why then take it up again? Why rewrite the same story?[6] It will be necessary to try to see in what respect the reprise *modifies* the text, and how the repetition interprets — and transforms — that which it copies: how the copy deconstructs the model: for *November* is, above all, a rereading of the *Memoirs of a Madman*.

However, let us remember this: a metaphor of originality, "madness" in the *Memoirs of a Madman* presents itself as the reverse of the cliché, the transgression of society's commonplaces. It constitutes, curiously, a sort of guarantee, at once of poeticity and of modernity. "Madness" is thus literally "original" in both senses of the term, as defined in the *Robert*: 1) "which appears to derive from nothing anterior, which resembles nothing else, is unique": 2) "By extension — Marked by new and singular characteristics to the point of appearing bizarre, abnormal". "For the wind of the century is toward madness," Baudelaire will say, "the barometer of modern rationality indicates a storm."[7] The task of "madness" in the *Memoirs of a Madman* is to cause the wind of the century to blow on through the pages of the book. "All these unknown echoes of the sumptuous dignity of classical literatures had for me a *flavor of novelty*, an attraction which drew me incessantly toward this giant poetry, which makes you dizzy and causes you to fall into the bottomless pit of the infinite."[8]

But this "flavor of novelty", unknown to the classical texts is conveyed precisely by reading:

> I would go off, with a book of verse, a novel, some poetry. . . . I remember with what sensuous pleasure I then devoured the pages of Byron and of *Werther*; with what transports I read *Hamlet, Romeo*, and the most burning works of our age, all those works, finally, which melt the soul in delight and burn it with enthusiasm. I thus nourished myself on this rough Northern poetry, which reverberates so like the waves of the sea, in the works of Byron. Often I retained from them, on the first reading, whole sections, and I would repeat them to myself, like a song which has charmed you and whose melody follows you still (V, p. 233).

Illness of modernity, axiom of originality, "madness" functions, thus, at the same time as a mark of genre (intimate journal, "memoirs," or "confessions," lyric or subjectivist poetry), that is as reference to a certain reading space, as a *signal of literarity*: however, this function has only become possible because "madness" has, in its turn, *instituted* itself as a commonplace, a banality, a *cliché* of romanticism; a mark of originality, but *mark* above all, that is, a conventional sign, calling for recognition by means of its repetitive character and its capacity for iteration. The ambition of romantic "madness," which subverts all codes, in order to say precisely that which will never allow itself to be encoded, thus comes into conflict with romanticism's paradoxical attempt to encode even the refusal to be encoded, to thereby institute "madness" itself as an intentional or supposedly secret, indeed individual code.

After the manner of so many romantic texts[9] which reflect the vogue of wertherism and byronism by a naive and mystified reading, the *Memoirs of a Madman* thus inscribes a contradiction of which it is not aware: the subject employs the code — of "madness" — to signify the subversion of all codes; the narrator places himself, rhetorically, within the cliché, to affirm, thematically, his refusal of all clichés. The intent to signify difference is in itself a cliché, a mark of resemblance. Thus, the *Memoirs of a Madman*, and the whole tradition — in this literature of the period — of the commonplace of "madness," functions exactly like, in Poe's story, the diverted, purloined letter: the commonplace of the madman, of the "I" who would be the proprietor or occupant of madness, could be the literary equivalent of the theft of the aforementioned letter, but at the same time, this cliché also conceals the *unperceived piece of evidence*: it is the evidence of its banality itself which remains hidden, which is of no consequence, permitting the functioning of romanticism as myth of unicity and illusion of originality. A "purloined letter," the commonplace of madness incarnates in this fashion the paradox of that which is *unconsidered by romanticism*: of a rhetoric which suffers less from the ineffable than from a lack of critical reflection on language, and from a fundamental *misreading of the cliché as such*.

MADNESS AND COMMONPLACE

Thus, and typically, the stake of madness in the *Memoirs of a Madman* is double, and contradictory: by its signified, the metaphor of the "madman" designates a place of unicity, of otherness; but by its signifier, it designates to the contrary a place of iteration and of conformity. "Madness" thereby marks the gaping hole, in the very heart of the language of the text, at which the signifier divorces the signified, and expression divides itself from that which is expressed.

This inversion of the text by itself, this contradiction which governs it, is the blind spot of the *Memoirs of a Madman*, from which point the text functions. But *November*, while copying the rhetoric of "madness," vaguely perceives the blindness underlying it, and *presents to the reader* its own shifts, its own paradoxes. The demand for originality juxtaposes itself, by metonymic and narrative contiguity, with the descriptions of the joys of reading, with the result that the desire for exclusivity of expression arises almost literally from the completely mechanical repetition of the recitation:

> . . . pages by which others were left cold transported me . . . , I wantonly ravaged my mind with them, *I recited them to myself* along the seashore. . . .

> Woe . . . to whoever does not *know by heart* amorous *stanzas to repeat to himself* by the light of the moon! It is a fine thing . . . to possess the passions in their highest form of expression, to love the loves rendered immortal by genius.

> From that time onwards, . . . *I sought to discover words that other men did not in the least understand*, and I opened my ears to listen to the revelation of their harmony; I composed enormous images with clouds and sun, *which no language could have expressed*, and, in human actions as well, I suddenly perceived the relationships and antitheses whose luminous precision dazzled even myself (p. 251, emphasis added).

The original, however, avers itself hackneyed: spontaneity, rereading itself, is discovered to be stereotyped:

> Yes, it seemed to me at one time that I was possessed of genius, . . . style flowed from my pen like the blood in my veins; at the slightest brush with beauty, a pure melody welled up in me, . . . I had complete dramas in my mind . . . humanity reverberated in me with all its echoes. . . . I was shaken by it, dazzled; but when I discovered in others the thoughts, even to the very forms that I had conceived, I fell, without transition, into a bottomless discouragement; *I had believed myself their equal and I was but their copyist!* I passed then from the intoxication of genius to the disheartening feeling of mediocrity, with all the rage of *dethroned kings* and all the torments of shame (pp. 254–55; emphasis added).

In its relationship to the purloined letter, the place of the king could be none other than that of the gaze that sees nothing, that of blindness: that is why, cured of his blindness, perceiving the purloined letter, the king finds himself necessarily dethroned. As early as *November*, Flaubert himself foresaw that his vocation as a writer, that *the* vocation of the writer, is condemned to be that of Bouvard and Pécuchet: the vocation of a copyist.

If then *November* truly takes up again the rhetoric of "madness," it is in order, this time, to overturn it, to challenge it: rather than give voice to the cliché of "madness," *November* gives a voice to *the very madness of the cliché*. Flaubert's *"realism"* takes shape, from this time forward, less as a simple attention to what is *banal*, than as a revealing of the *unconsidered*, *of that which goes without saying:* of the constitutive theft of the letters. Flaubert's, from then on, is a gaze which scrutinizes the blindness of what is evident, which simultaneously plumbs the obscurity — and the efficacy — of commonplaces.

It is thus that in *November*, the rhetoric of "madness" dispossesses itself of its title, as an authority of meaning, a word of signification *par excellence. November*, in effect, has as a *subtitle* the irony appropriate to the apprehension of the misapprehension which entitles the *Memoirs of a Madman*: specifically, *Fragments of some sort of style*. The commonplace at last recognizes itself, names it absence of name, subtitles its absence of titles. "Some sort of style" — is this not precisely the reverse side of "madness"? — and which says that indeed "madness" is not, within language, a place native to subjectivity, a place exclusive of others, but, to the contrary, that language is always, already the place of the other: commonplace. Thereby the rhetoric of singularity weakens and its frequency decreases. The 26 occurrences of "madness" in 18 pages, in the *Memoirs of a Madman*, are reduced to only 10 occurrences in 29 pages in *November* (same edition); that means that instead of 4 to 5 occurrences every 3 pages (on average) one no longer finds more than one single occurrence every three pages. But, what is of even greater importance that this diminution of the frequency of "madness" within the change of tone manifest in *November*, is the explanation of the arbitrariness of the sign, of its rhetorical and linguistic conventionality: "What is this restless pain then, of which one is as proud as of genius, and which one hides like a love? . . . Poetic rhapsodies, memories of bad readings, rhetorical hyperboles, such are all these great nameless pains" (p. 252). "Madness" no longer presents itself as the outside of all language, but, to the contrary, as the inside of the very artifice of rhetoric. And if the cliché of madness once again reproduces itself in the "fragments of some sort of style," the "madman" as quality and qualification of the "I," the "madman" as substantivation of the qualificative adjective, has disappeared. It is no longer a "madman" who "has written these pages," but, says *November*, measuring all the critical distance which separates it from its language, "a man who . . . greatly abused his epithets" (p. 275).

That language cannot go outside of itself to tell of its origin; that the arbitrariness of the sign does not allow itself to be preceded by an essence of meaning; that conventional rhetorical form is fundamentally inaugural — this is what Flaubert learns and teaches us in writing *November*. But at the same time that the concepts of originality, spontaneity and authenticity inherited from romanticism are dislocated, there arises, in the "fragments of some sort of style," a new attitude with regard to conventional language and the constraints of the commonplace and of rhetoric. For if, in the cliché, the content is preconceived and stereotyped, the content, as a result, is of lesser import than the formal action and the structure of the signifier; that which is expressed is of lesser importance than its *functioning*, the *effect* of the act of expression. The structural order takes precedence over, from then on, and overrides the semantic order, which it modifies, displaces, predetermines. Working within the cliché and using it as a point of departure, writing determines itself, and apprehends itself, no longer as a blind haste toward meaning, a naive and precritical rapport with the signified, but as a complex critical relationship to the signifier.

ITALICIZING

The signifier functions, from then on, no longer as a reference to the signified, but as a *reference to the code*. This reference, in any case, has the effect of short-circuiting the code: for the code is effective only when it passes — as such — unnoticed, when it seems merely to transmit natural information, to be nothing more than a direct and unmediated passage from the signifier to the signified. To make explicit the code is, precisely and paradoxically, to subvert its authority, to shatter its illusion of naturalness. From that point on the commonplace will no longer be taken up by writing as a meaning, but as a signal: a signal of the code.

Firstly a typographic signal, as the cliché cites itself, puts itself in quotes, or rather in italics.

> Certain words overwhelmed me, that of *woman*, of *mistress* especially. . . . As for a *mistress*, that was for me a satanic being, the magic of whose name alone would throw me into long ecstasies: it was for their mistresses that kings ruined and won provinces; for them, Indian rugs were woven, gold was spun, the world was moved; a mistress has slaves . . . (p. 249, Flaubert's italics).

> When it became necessary to choose a station in life, he hesitated among a thousand repugnances. . . . And then, are those even "stations"? *It is necessary to establish oneself in life, to have a position in the world, one becomes bored by remaining idle, one must be useful, man is born to work:* difficult maxims to understand and which people took pains to repeat frequently to him (pp. 273–74, Flaubert's italics).

The placing between quotes, the putting in italics: this typographic and metalinguistic signposting, written by *November*, this marking of the commonplace with signal beacons within the language of the text will be, as we know, a typical and recurrent trait in the work of Flaubert.

But the essence of Flaubert's revolution is not in this technical discovery. For the cliché transcends, in fact, in the *Fragments of some kind of style*, not only the typographical boundaries of italic, but the very limits of discourse, in order to penetrate the order of the narrative and of the story. While the *Memoirs of a Madman* made up, in a clichéed discourse, a narrative of originality, *November*, paradoxically, inversely, is a discourse which has no other originality than that of narrating the very apprenticeship of the cliché. That which is expressed, in other words, recounts the apprenticeship of expression: the narrative tells how the "some sort of style" *is learned*, and learns itself for what it is; how the "some sort of style" — subject of writing — informs the process of writing and, at the same time, the narrator — thus the process of narration, of its loss of titles, over and within the language.

The story, the very plot of *November* is set in motion, in fact, by the intoxication with stereotypes. At the origin of the events, the narration discerns the repetition of four words: "mistress", "woman", "adultery", "love."[10] "For me, human life revolved around two or three ideas, around two or three words" (p. 251). Two or three words to which the narrator would attribute the weight and the value of events; two or three words, discursive, repetitive paradigms, which he seeks to transform into unique expressions, indeed, into narrative and consequential syntagmas. Thus, the story of the initiation into passion is itself initiated — by the clichés. The events arise by means of the word: their causal unfolding originates in the words and in the iterative use of commonplaces.

That presupposes that clichés are able to decipher, to *interpret* the deepest desires of the narrator; and that, through that interpretation, the story may be made, dictated by clichés. The story here, in this narrative; but indeed perhaps also, structurally, the story in general, which would not be so much a causal and temporal series of *facts*, as a totally discursive chain, a string of *interpretations* and interpretations of interpretations. "It is a greater affair," said Montaigne, "to interpret the interpretations than to interpret the things themselves." What the cliché cuts through in *November*, then, is the very status of the narrative, of the event in general, of consequentiality as the originating singularity of the fact.

PROSTITUTION AND COMMONPLACE

Thus is also explained the role of the *prostitute* as lover-initiator, while the *Memoirs of a Madman* marked the loved woman, the woman who "inaugurates" love, more as: forbidden, inaccessible, and, naturally, irreplaceable. The body of the prostitute marks by contrast the place of access to replacements and to substitutions: "How many I have seen arrive here . . . some, after leaving a ball, in order to concentrate in a single woman all those they have just left; others, after a wedding, exalted by the idea of innocence; and then young men, so as to caress at their leisure the mistresses to whom they dare not speak, closing their eyes and thus seeing her in their hearts; husbands to make themselves young once more and savor the common pleasures of their good times; priests pressed by the demon and desiring not a woman, but a courtesan, sin incarnate . . ." (p. 268). The common place, literally and physically, of illusion and desire, the prostitute's body, welcomes the imaginary vows of her lovers, in the same way that the cliché — body of the language, matter of the words —

welcomes and interprets the narrator's desire for meaning. Stretched out on "the common pallet where the crowd passes by" (p. 267), the "call-girl"[11] (p. 263) fulfills exactly the function that Baudelaire will assign to the cliché: "meeting-place for the crowd, eloquence's public trysting-place."[12]

> Soon I became known, it was a question of who would have me, my lovers would commit a thousand follies to please me, every night I would read love notes delivered during the day, to find there the novel expression of some heart of a different cast from the others and made for me. But they were all alike, I knew in advance the ends of their sentences and the way in which they were going to fall to their knees (pp. 266–67).

Meeting-place of the crowd, eloquence's trysting-place, the courtesan — medium of illusions — is a witness at once to the very body of the language as a vehicle of the carnal drive, and of desire as the flesh of words, the very matter and body of rhetoric. The experience, the testimony of the prostitute is that of desire itself, as the common-place of the devalued word.

The initiatory trial becomes, for the narrator, an initiation into the repetition of clichés, and into the erosion of the matter of the sign. But this erosion itself consists of the illusion of an inaugural act, of a *first* event and, as such, without equal:

> When I had plainly told her that I had never had a mistress, that I had searched everywhere for one, that I had long dreamed of it and finally that she was the *first* to accept my caresses, she moved closer to me with astonishment as if I were an illusion that she wished to seize: ". . . Ah! how I would love you if you wanted! . . ."
>
> These were the *first words of love* that I would hear in my life. *From wherever they come*, our hearts receive them with a shudder of true happiness (p. 262, emphasis added).

At the trysting-place of eloquence, caught in the snare of devalued language, desire, although sprung from cliché, "from wherever it comes," marks itself nonetheless as virginal, *first*, without precedent. The courtesan thus resells, as she says herself, an illusory virginity: "I came running here, as if I still had a virginity to sell." But if the courtesan — by the very power of illusion which the language conveys — is still a virgin, the narrator — by that very same power — is one no longer:

> At that age I was still a virgin and had not loved at all (p. 257).

> During that period when I was a virgin, I took pleasure in contemplating prostitutes, I went down the streets where they lived, I haunted the spots where they walked (p. 252).

> It seems to me sometimes that I have endured for centuries, and that my being encloses the debris of a thousand past existences (p. 248).

> . . . I felt old and full of experience of a thousand things not yet felt (p.
> 252).

In language, one does not remain intact. The paradox of this story of
initiation, of this narrative of the narrator's loss of virginity, is that it
teaches him that he is losing precisely what he has never had: virginity. In
language, *one cannot be a virgin*, has never been one, because one lives
within the common-place.

But, on the other hand, *one is always a virgin*: the young man is
dedicated and condemned to virginity, if the alternative to virginity, its
loss, is the setting up of a "possession" or of a "property" of some sort. One
has never been a virgin, because one is penetrated — from birth — by
language, because one has always already sustained a long concubinage
with an anterior language; but one remains always a virgin because one
can never *possess* his language in his own right; in language, one is always
dispossessed. Thus it is that the virginity of the narrator is not lost but on
the contrary, returns, proves itself to be repetitive and recurrent: "It was
especially at the approach of spring . . . that I felt my heart filled with the
need to love. . . . Still each year, for several hours, I rediscover in myself a
virginity which pushes me forth with the buds; but joys do not reblossom
with the roses" (p. 257). That which never took place does not cease at the
same time to repeat itself. "It is in vain that they have worn down, the
courtesan will likewise say, each part of my body, by every pleasurable
sensation with which men regale themselves. I have remained as I was at
the age of ten, a virgin, if a virgin is she who . . . has not known pleasure
and who dreams incessantly of it, who creates charming phantoms for
herself and who sees them in her dreams . . . I am a virgin! That makes
you laugh? but do I not have the vague presentiments, the ardent languors
of that state? I have all of it, save virginity itself" (p. 268).[13] It is therefore
no simple accident that the prostitute is named Marie, thus doubling the
Virgin, who is elsewhere evoked in the erotic fantasies of the narrator.[14]
Marie: she who possesses all the qualities of virginity, save virginity itself;
she whose essence is therefore the lack of essence and who can have neither
identity nor name of her own: for Marie is not the true name of the
prostitute.

> ". . . Tell me your name, eh! your name."
> In my turn I wanted to learn hers.
> "Marie, she replied, but I had another, that's not what I was called at
> home" (p. 260).

Prostitution becomes, thus, the symbol for the impropriety of the common-place, which engulfs all possession and all property, which therefore
has neither its own meaning nor its own name, and which can have, for its
name, only the face of virginity itself insofar as it is constitutively
substitutive and figurative. Centered on the non-particular, the initiation
into the *common-place* can only open onto a *non-place*, and transform the

initial act of replacement into an illusion of the irreplaceable, and the illusion of the irreplaceable into a chain of replacements and of commutations of *place*: ". . . it was she whom I pursued everywhere; in the bed of others, I dreamed of her caresses" (p. 270).

Places of the narrative: returns to the place.

The commutation of places, however, can only reveal that the journey is impossible: with the common-place as point of departure, one finds oneself necessarily, on arrival, still within the commonplace; to arrive is perhaps no more than to arrive there from whence one originally left. "But, *returning always to the point from which I had left*, I was turning in an inescapable circle, in vain I butted my head against it, desiring to have more room" (p. 257). The very logic of the narrative proves itself to be rigorously *topical*. The commonplace becomes a topological knot which one explores like a labyrinthine space. *November*, in effect, traces the plan of the labyrinth, as Michel Serres has defined it: "I lose myself in a labyrinth only for the simple reason that I find myself indefinitely in the same spot. I am lost because I continually return here . . . , all the other paths are identical there."[15]

The narrator thus journeys from common-place to common-place: all the spots by which the narrative passes are in effect, literally, common places, places of erosion, marked by the other.

— The bed of the prostitute: "Look on the headboard of my bed at all these intercrossed lines on the mahogany, these are the fingernail-marks of all those who have thrashed about there, of all those whose heads have rubbed there" (p. 268).

— The law-student's bedroom, in Paris: "He went to lodge in a furnished room, where the furniture has been bought by others, used by others than himself: it seemed to him that he was living among ruins" (p. 274).

But if the narrator must journey in the labyrinth of the common-place, displace himself, lose himself only to find himself again in the same point, stray from his path to reach once more the same places, it is in order to learn that, without exception, *every* place is common-place; that the most private places, the most secret, the most intimate — for oneself, within oneself — are in reality the domain of the other.

It is precisely there, that which the narrator discovers at the time of his journey, to X . . . , a journey which echoes, toward the closing of the book, a first journey to X . . . of which the narrative stressed the importance at the very beginning. At the two extremities of the text, at the beginning and at the end, the story is thus marked by this repetitive and symmetrical structure, *two* trips *to the same place* — a place without a name, the reference to which is of little moment: X . . . In the last pages of the book, the narrator leaves Paris once again, as he had formerly left the village of his birth, to see X . . . again, to rediscover there a memory of his youth, a bit of dream for himself, his private corner:

A memory of youth kept running through his head, he thought of
X . . . , this village where he had gone one day on foot . . . : he wanted
to see it again. . . . Around ten o'clock in the morning, he got off at Y
. . . and from there made the trip on foot as far as X . . . ; . . . He
noticed that the signposts which indicated the way had been overturned
. . . He pushed forward, he was eager to arrive. . . .
    . . . There was a little spot in the cleft of a rock, where he had often
gone to sit . . . , he would settle himself in all alone, on his back on the
ground, to look up at the blue of the sky between the white walls of the
sheer crags; it was there that he would see the sails of vessels plunge
beneath the horizon, and that the sun, for him, had shone warmer than
anywhere else on the face of the earth.
    He returned there, he found it once again: but others had taken
possession of it, for, digging in the soil mechanically with his foot, he
discovered the end of a bottle and a knife. People had doubtless gone
there for an outing, they had come there with ladies, had picnicked
there, had laughed there, joked there. "Oh my God," he said to himself,
"are there nowhere on earth places which we have loved enough, where
we have lived enough, so that they belong to us until death, and that
others than ourselves should never lay eyes on them!" (pp. 275–76).

If the narrator wanders the same byways, travels the same paths,
journeys and displaces himself to arrive in the same places, it is in order to
learn not only that all places are common-places, but equally that the
same places, the common-places, are not the *same*, but *other*: the
commonplace is incommensurable with itself. Thus the return does not
appropriate for itself a space of identity with itself, but, to the contrary,
produces a difference: the commonplace does not resemble itself. The
narrator discovers that the difference once so diligently searched for in
"madness" is in fact found not in the subject, but in the language: insofar
as it is the place of the other. Difference, ironically and paradoxically,
resides at the heart of the commonplace: in the repetition of the signifier.
By its very repetition, the space of the common-place loses its *directional-
ity*, its meaning, overflows or perhaps overturns its *road signs* ("he noticed
that the signposts which indicated the way had been overturned"), its
unique and directing consistency: it decenters itself.
    Let us recall that at the beginning the commonplace presented itself,
in the imagination of the narrator, precisely as the center, and as a passion
for the writing of the center: "These passions that I would have desired to
possess, I used to study them in books. Human life revolved, for me,
around two or three ideas, . . . *around which all the rest turned* like
satellites around their star (p. 251). What the narrative — the apprenticeship of the commonplace — brings about then in the space of the commonplace is a decentering of the writing of the center. The *event*, from then
on, is the *return from the place* or the *return to the place* as difference,
separation, *distance produced at the heart of the place*: the displacement

of the place itself to the same place as that which abolishes the particular identity of the place. Such was, already, the status of the first displacement to X . . . , which involved a double journey, a going and a returning:[16]

> I went out and I went away to X . . . .
> Then everything on earth seemed beautiful to me . . . ; I returned home at night, I wandered the same paths, I saw again the trace of my feet on the sand and the place where I had lain down in the grass; it seemed to me as though I had dreamed. There are days when one has lived two existences: the second is already nothing but the memory of the first, and I would often stop along my route before a bush, before a tree, at the corner of a road, *as if there*, that morning, *there had taken place some event* of my life (pp. 256–57).

Between the coming and going, the high point, "the event," is merely the appearance of the place as otherness from itself. The very instance of the narrative rejoins, from then on, by its mode of functioning, that of the discourse in its iteration of clichés. For the status of the event is not the unique singularity of the fact, but, to the contrary, its iterative recurrence. The event is that which, having happened, happens (at least) twice but which, occurring twice, does not take place, or only takes place in the mode of "as if." The status of the event, like the status of the cliché itself, is that of the distance from the self of a double reading: at once *seen* and *already-seen*, the event is but the disjunction of the one from the other, the cleavage between the seen and the already-seen. "He entered a bar, where he had occasionally gone to drink some beer, he asked for a cigar, he could not stop himself from saying to the good woman who was serving him: 'I have come here before.' She answered him: 'Ah! well, this is not the summer, m'sieu, it's not the summer,' and she gave him his change" (p. 276). "I have come here before": distance, suspense of this *already*, non-place of *here*. Already, here: already come and not yet departed; behind and ahead of time of arrival. Here, in the common-place, in the *same* place, in the place which is *other*; here, it is therefore the point of the undetermined which conditions wandering, the empty center where everything, rediscovering itself, is lost. "I have come here before"; simple phrase of purely phatic function, barely meaningful for the interlocutress, and which nevertheless sums up — in a cliché, as is fitting — all the irony of this story of the apprenticeship of the commonplace. But the rejoinder of the serving-woman, "Ah! . . . this is not the summer, m'sieu," replies, for its part, with a second cliché, to the very title of the text, *November*, invoking it unknowingly, in this autumnal image (season, said the narrator, of memory), beneath the banal face of the cycle of the seasons, the repetitive and circular temporality of the commonplace: a temporality without origin, at once changing and recurrent, never coinciding with itself, always in displacement, in hiatus, always already and not yet come.

DEATH AND CLICHE: THE DEATH OF THE AUTHOR

Caught in this temporality of repetition, the cliché has neither start nor finish. The end, in a *narrative* which is itself a *discourse* of the common-place, can only be an artifice of rhetoric. Thus one reads, in the last pages of the book: "The manuscript ends here, but I knew its author, and if someone, having passed, in order to arrive as far as this page, through all the metaphors, hyperboles and other figures of speech which fill those preceding it, desires to find an ending to it, let him continue; we are going to give it to him" (p. 272). The prefabricated ending can construct itself only arbitrarily, as a response to a desire to read itself conditioned by clichéed structures, as an echo to conventional and stereotyped expectations.

Veering from the "I" to the "he," the text will relate for us from that point on an event which had not taken place in the *Memoirs of a Madman*: the death of the narrator, Death — the sole event which will happen only once — will it be able, in this narrative, to escape repetition? The narrator has said it explicitly however: death itself is commonplace; the common-place *par excellence*.

> One day, in Paris, I stopped a long while on the Pont-Neuf: it was winter, the Seine . . . was greenish; I thought of all those who came there to end it all. How many people had passed by the place where I was then standing, running head high to their loves or to their business matters, and who had returned there one day, walking with gingerly steps, palpitating at the approach of dying! They approached the parapet, they mounted it, they jumped. Oh! what miseries ended there, how many happinesses began there! What a cold and damp tomb! How it expands to hold them all! how many there are within it! They are all there, at the bottom, rolling slowly with their contorted faces and their blue limbs; each icy wave carries them off in their sleep and drags them gently to the sea (pp. 255–56).

To die, then, is definitively to rejoin the commonplace: to rejoin the Other. But in the death of the narrator, such as it is recounted in *November*, the commonplace is doubly rejoined: "Finally, last December, he died, but slowly, little by little, by the sole force of thought, without any organ being ill, *as one dies of sorrow* — which will appear difficult to people who have greatly suffered, but which must be tolerated within a novel, for love of the marvellous" (p. 276).

Of course, it will be said, people do not die of love or of sorrow other than figuratively, in literarily coded, conventional clichés. But therein resides all the irony of the text. For what can be this strange death by thought alone, if not precisely a death by cliché? A death, one might say, between quotes? An utterly novelistic death, totally romantic,[17] but above all, totally *linguistic*, literally following the trace of the cliché itself in the language. Ironically taken literally, clichéed hyperbole does not literalize itself ("he died") except to allegorize ("as") the arbitrariness which obscures the linguistic automatism ("one dies of sorrow"), to make explicit there the logical leap between sign and meaning, between the rhetorical ("as one dies of sorrow") and the semantic ("he died"): he died *as* — one (does not) die of sorrow. "As one dies of sorrow" equivalent to "as one dies in literature,"[18] is the entire novel which, at its end, becoming a figure-cliché of itself, reflects and ironizes itself.

A clichéed figure of itself, the death of the narrator is not, from then on, a simple syntagmatic accident, but a paradigmatic necessity. The death is the totally symbolic one of the sender of the message, as inscribed in the structure itself of the mark (iterative and stereotyped); the inescapable death of the subject to the cliché. It is the disappearance, at the same time, of the author as authority, mastery of meaning, as source or origin of writing. *To die*, then, *of sorrow*, is just this, *to die in the language* in order to be born, precisely, to writing; dying without end and repeating, thus, infinitely and indefinitely, by writing and by the life itself of the cliché, its own death.

"I" TO "HE"

Death, in other words, is the completely linguistic process by which the "I," in the narrative, becomes a "he"; a process by which the "I" itself places itself in italics and assigns to itself — on the level of the other — the status of a purely grammatical event: thereby anticipating the effort of modern texts to relinquish their power of saying "I." Such is, for example, in Beckett, the effort of the hallucinating narrator of the *Unnamable* and his shifts from "I" to "he":

> What I say, what I shall perhaps say, on this subject, on my subject, on the subject of my place of residence, is already said, for, having been here forever, I am still here.[19]

> I have to speak, having nothing to say, nothing but the words of others (p. 39).

> I. Who *is* that? (p. 73).

> He knows that they are words, he does not know if they are his. . . . Yes, I know that those are words, there was a time when I was ignorant of that. . . . I should not say me anymore . . . it's too stupid. I shall put in its place, each time that I hear it, the third person, if I think of it. If that amuses them. That won't change anything. There's only I, I who am not there, there where I am (p. 100).

> Useless to quibble, from here on, over pronouns and other such trivia. No matter the subject, there isn't any (p. 109).

> . . . one finishes by not knowing any more, a voice which never stops, from whence it comes (p. 121).

The "he," dismissing the "I" from its function as the signified, becomes what Maurice Blanchot calls the "neutral," a phantom, spectral voice, incapable of making itself central, which, on the contrary, prevents the text from having a center: "the *he*," writes Blanchot, "does not simply take the place traditionally occupied by a subject, it modifies, a mobile fragmentation, what is understood by place: fixed spot, unique or determined by its placement. . . . The narrative *he* . . . thereby marks the intrusion of the other — understood as neuter — in its irreducible strangeness, its devious perversity. The other speaks. But when the other speaks, no one speaks, for the other . . . is no more one nor the other. . . . The narrative voice derives from thence its loss of voice."[20]

It is indeed toward the loss of voice of Flaubert's subsequent work[21] that *November* moves, by its passage from the "I" to "he": the "he," pronoun of the other, of the non-person, is explicitly introduced here as the very figure of silence: silence of emotion and of meaning.

> It is imperative that feelings have few words at their service, without that this book would have been completed in the first person. Doubtless our man will have found nothing more to say: there is a point at which one ceases to write and thinks all the more; it is at this point that he stopped, worse luck for the reader! . . .
> . . . He saw fit to complain no more, perhaps proof that he began truly to suffer. Neither in his conversation, nor in his letters, nor in the papers that I searched through after his death, and where I found this [manuscript], I seized on nothing which unveiled the state of his soul, from the time when he ceased to write his confessions (pp. 272–73).

At the antipodes of the "I," bearer of the cry, the "he," a sort of blank at the heart of the text, is no longer anything but the possibility of a stop, of a short-circuit.

From then on, an esthetics of reserve, of understatement will muffle the early pomposity and the hyperbole of affectivity. But euphemism will always be, in Flaubert's work, itself a hyperbole of silence, and silence the underside of the cry.

Short-circuited by the silence of the "he," the voice of the text loses its authority: the narrative itself becomes aleatory, hypothetical, offering to the reader, in anticipation — yet again — of so many modern texts, the alternative of two versions, one affirmative, the other negative: ". . . The barrel-organs which he used to hear playing beneath his window would tear at his soul, . . . he used to say that those boxes were full of tears. *Or rather* he would say nothing . . ." (p. 274). He used to say, or rather, he would say nothing: one thinks, there again, of Beckett: "How to do it, . . . how to proceed? By pure aporia or else by affirmation and negations invalidated as we go along, sooner or later. . . . The yes and no, that's something else, they will come back to me as I progress."[22]

It is the loss of authority of the text; the uncertainty for which the silence of the "he" is responsible, is the opening to a multiple reading, the opening to interpretation: "He wept—was it from cold or sorrow?" (p. 276). The uncertainty, the choice offered here to the reading, is significant: it marks the location of the "he" as the place of confusion, precisely between the object and the subject; cold and sorrow.

STORY / DISCOURSE: THE GENERALIZED ITALIC

Purposeful confusion, insistence upon non-alternativity, *deconstruction*, precisely, of *the very structure of the opposition* between object and subject, between the Same and the Other, between interiority and exteriority, between the ego and sociality; deconstruction, by the veering from the "I" to the "he," of the very structure of the alternative between the two levels of textual meaning, the story and the discourse. For if the "he," as Blanchot says, is "the unillumined event of what takes place when one recounts . . . , the impersonal coherence of a story,"[23] the "I" is, on the other hand, the very proprietor of discourse. But what the text establishes is precisely not the distinction, but on the contrary the utterly parodic equivalence of the two levels: the *story*, here, of apprenticeship of the commonplace, is in reality but a fable of *discourse*. And, if the narrative, by the repetition of the event, of the place, demystifies the affirmation—in its role as common-place the affirmation, for its part, does not cease to disenchant the story, to shatter the immediacy and the very status of the narrative itself. Story and affirmation, narrative and discourse are therefore here, mutually, relays from one to the other, each subverting the authority of the other. If it is therefore true that the narrative, here, practices a sort of placing between quotes of the affirmation of romanticism, of its *topoi*, it is no less true that the discourse, as a force of the very masking of the cliché, shatters before the fact the realism of the narrative, with its pretension to transparency, transitivity and objectivity. If the narrative demystifies, decenters the discourse of the subject, it can only be, in its turn, through the equivalence of the "he" and the "I," a reference to the explosion of the subject itself: a reference, in other words, to the urgency of the expression and of the discourse exactly at its cleavage, in its lack of authority. Thus erasing the reassuring distinction between story and discourse, Flaubert questions himself at once with regard to the limits of the narrative order, and to the mystifications of the discursive order. What *November* tells us is, precisely, that telling is neither so simple nor so natural, that telling cannot simply happen on its own: the story is a convention, the story is also a discourse, a rhetoric, subject to mystifications, to the red herrings of clichés. That explains why Flaubert, who put the finishing touches on realism, so desired to be disengaged from it himself. For he saw only too well — even if unconsciously — in the ideal of *mimesis* the lure of bourgeois ideology seeking to secure itself by the appropriation of a pseudo-objectivity, a pseudo-transitivity, as if the acts, the events were closed, defined, substantivated, intelligible, as if it were possible to appropriate for oneself the meanings of words and their referential power, as if the representation of meaning could truly assure an intelligibility of the consummation of meaning, as if the significance of clichés could be homed in on, delimited, fixed once and for all.

Not so; for Flaubert, the only undisputable reality is the part of the illusion conveyed by language, the utterly linguistic power of the referential illusion. A referential illusion common, moreover, to both realism and romanticism: one believing in the representation of society, the other in that of subjectivity. For Flaubert, however, this double illusion of representation comes down to the same result, to the very structure of the marker within language. If, in displacing himself from the "I" to the "he," Flaubert erases his signature, puts himself in quotes together with his romanticism, his realism — his recognition of the social and institutional value of the word — consists only in the gesture itself of the total and generalized putting in quotes, which implies the italicizing of the notion of reality itself.

The discovery outlined by *November* is precisely to have understood and made understandable, regarding the cliché, not the circumstantial position of citation, but the structure of citationality itself: the constitutive loss of the origin and of the context, which is the basis of all signs. The strength of the text is not, thus, the placing in quotes of a particular expression, but rather the placing in italics, if one may say so, of expression as such, of meaning as such.

Neither romantic nor realist, neither "I" nor "he," neither discursive nor narrative, Flaubert diverts signs, sets them adrift in their space of play, space with neither center nor truth, space, precisely, of interference, of the between. By the very incoherence of its style, by the obvious and explicit displacement of its elocutory solicitations, by the interference and intercommunication of its heterogeneous registers, *November* is a modern text; and perhaps more modern than *The Sentimental Education*.

November, after the fact, becomes a sort of commentary on a future writing: commentary on the displacement which, under the sign of Flaubert, will take place in language. More than any other, Flaubert well understood that the novel is precisely that which is repeated, understood in its very principle of repetition, principle of iteration and at the same time of otherness. Flaubert therefore understood, in other words, that modernity, *par excellence*, is the place of the other: the place of blindness and of incomprehension.

But the question of the very modernity of Flaubert becomes, as a result, naïve, a trick question. For if the modern text is that which, by its iteration of the stereotype, rejoins difference, the text which decenters and deconstructs itself in order to differ from itself, what have we done, in declaring *November* a modern text, if not to have instituted it, on the contrary, as an illusion of identity? An identity that resembles *us*? To judge Flaubert as modern is perhaps to say, simply, that Flaubert has *seduced* us with his language; that Flaubert has led us to believe that we resemble him, that he resembles us, that we meet in the common-place: "*I was therefore what all of you are*, a certain man who lives, sleeps, eats, drinks, weeps, laughs, well closed-in on himself, and finding in himself, wherever he betakes himself, the same ruins of hopes struck down as soon as they are raised, the same dust of crushed things, *the same byways a thousand times traversed*, the same unexplored deaths, terrifying and boring" (p. 252). "I was therefore what all of you are." But we know already, and by way of Flaubert himself, that a common-place — be it that of reading — is not the same as we think it to be, but other. Flaubert, henceforth, is *our* common-place. And *his* modernity is none other, doubtless, than precisely that distance at which we always trail behind ourselves.

Notes

1. [Translator's Note: Throughout Felman's text, the terms *lieu commun, cliché*, and various forms of the word *stereotype* occur. Whereas *commonplace* seems more frequent as an adjective in American English than as a substantive, her constant playing on it both as cliché and as location held in common provides the rationale for my choice of words. Where the sense of place as location seems to require particular emphasis, I have hyphenated the word. All translations from works cited are my own.]

2. Letter to Louise Colet, December 17, 1852 in Geneviève Bollème, editor, *Extraits de la correspondance [de Gustave Flaubert], ou préface à la vie d'écrivain* (Paris: Seuil, 1963), pp. 96–97.

3. *Exégèse des lieux-communs* (Paris: Gallimard, 1968), pp. 33–34.

4. *L'Innommable* (Paris: 10 / 18, 1972), p. 23.

5. Letter of December 2, 1846, in Bollème, p. 44.

6. This question appears all the more pertinent in that *November* formulates it explicitly: "Of what use to write this? Why continue, in the same doleful voice, the same funereal tale?," in Flaubert, *Oeuvres complètes* (Paris: Seuil, 1964), 2 vols., I, 253. Except when otherwise indicated, all references to the works of Flaubert are to this edition henceforth abbreviated *OC*.

7. "Théophile Gautier," in *L'Art romantique*, edited by H. Lemaître (Paris: Garnier, 1962), p. 673.

8. *Mémoires d'un fou*, *OC* I, 234 (emphasis added).

9. Cf. for example, Gautier, *Albertus* (1832); Musset, *Fantasio* (1834), *Les Confessions d'un enfant du siècle* (1836), etc.

10. Cf.: "I had so much read the word 'love' in the poets, and used to repeat it to myself so often to charm myself with its sweetness, that with each star sparkling in a blue sky on a mild night, at each murmur of the current along the shore, . . . I would say to myself: 'I love! oh! I love!' " (p. 250).

"There was . . . for me one word which seemed beautiful among human words:

adultery. . . . A singular magic perfumes it; all the stories one tells, all the books one reads, all the gestures one makes say it and comment on it eternally . . ." (p. 257).

"*Certain words overwhelmed me, that of woman*, of *mistress* especially; I searched for the explanation of the first in books, in etchings. . . . The day when at last I guessed all . . . I felt a sense of pride in saying to myself that I was a man, a being organized so that one day I might have a woman for myself: the word of life was revealed to me" (p. 249; emphasis added).

However, the "word of life" — italicized, as it should be — is this not the cliché *par excellence*? Human life, like literature, is thus submitted to the conventional restrictions and inaugural — and arbitrary — constraints of signifiers.

11. The original French term is *fille publique*, or public woman, which expresses the same sort of commonality as common-place. *Call-girl* at least attempts to offer a similar general availability. [Translator]

12. Baudelaire, "Madame Bovary," in *Curiosités esthétiques, L'Art Romantique*, p. 644.

13. Cf. the narrator's conclusion, p. 268: "Without knowing one another, she in her prostitution and I in my chastity, we had followed the same path, ending at the same abyss."

14. Cf. p. 257: "I loved everything, even to the hard rocks on which I leaned my hands . . . and I thought then how sweet it was to sing canticles at night, on my knees, at the feet of a madonna who gleams in the light of the candelabras, and to love the Virgin Mary who appears to mariners, in a corner of the sky, holding the sweet infant Jesus in her arms."

15. "Le messager," in *Bulletin de la Société française de philosophie*, session of November 25, 1967, p. 37.

16. "*Un aller et un retour*" takes the commonplace French expression for round-trip and breaks it into its component parts. [Translator]

17. The words I have expressed here as "novelistic" and "romantic" — the latter in the literary sense — are romanesque and romantique, both of which commonly translate into English as romantic. [Translator]

18. Cf. the suggestive resemblance of this manner of dying to the death of the literary hero *par excellence*, Don Quixote:

> "Turning then towards Sancho, he [Don Quixote] added: "Forgive me, friend, the occasion which I have given you to appear as mad as I, in causing you to fall into the error in which I myself was, that is that there were and there are knights-errant in this world.
>
> — Alas! Alas! replied Sancho sobbing, do not die, my good lord, but follow my counsel and live many years more; for the greatest *madness* that a man can commit in this life is *to allow himself to go and die without anyone killing him, nor under any blows other than those of sorrow*." (*Don Quichotte*, Paris: Garnier-Flammarion, 1948, 2 vols., Fr. trans. by L. Viarot, II, 502; emphasis added.)

19. *L'Innommable*, p. 20.

20. *L'Entretien infini* (Paris: Gallimard, 1969), pp. 563–65.

21. Cf. G. Genette, "Silences de Flaubert," in his *Figures* (Paris: Seuil, 1966) pp. 223–43.

22. *L'Innommable*, pp. 5–6.

23. *L'Entretien infini*, p. 558.

Madame Bovary

[Review of *Madame Bovary*] Edmond Duranty*

Madame Bovary, a novel by Gustave Flaubert, shows obstinacy in description. It makes one think of a line drawing, to such a degree is it made with a compass and meticulous exactitude: calculated, worked over, everything at right angles, and totally dry and arid. We are told that the author spent several years working on it. Indeed its details have been set down one by one, each given the same value; each street, each house, each room, each brook, each blade of grass is fully described: each character when he arrives on scene makes preliminary remarks on a host of useless and uninteresting topics, merely for the sake of bringing out his level of intelligence. As a result of this system of obstinate description, the novel is presented almost entirely in *gestures*: not a hand, not a foot, not a facial muscle moves without two or three lines or more of description. In this novel there is no emotion, no feeling, no life, only the great force of an arithmetician who has calculated and assembled what there can be in the way of gestures, steps, and inequalities of terrain in *given* characters, events, and landscapes. This book is a literary application of the mathematics of probability. I am speaking here for those who have been able to read through it. The style is uneven, as always happens with a man who writes *artistically* without *feeling*: here imitation, there lyricism, never anything personal. — I repeat, always material *description* and never *impression*. It seems to me pointless even to consider the point of view of this book, which the aforementioned faults deprive of all interest. — Before this novel appeared, people thought it would be better. — *An excess of study* cannot take the place of the spontaneity which comes from feeling.

*Reprinted from George Becker, compiler and translator, *Documents of Modern Literary Realism* (Princeton, N.J.: Princeton University Press, 1963), 98–99. First published in *Réalisme* 5 (15 March 1857):79–80.

M. Gustave Flaubert
Barbey D'Aurevilly*

. . . *Madame Bovary* is a novel of manners, and of present-day manners, and even though the sentiment that here presents itself is horribly degraded by the corruption that invades a weak soul and that ends up destroying it as if by a slow rot, here it is a question of the heart of a woman, and the imagination expects something other than a surgeon's hand, impassive and bold, which reminds one of the hand of Dupuytren[1] poking about in the heart of his Pole when he had thrown his sternum back upon his face in the most astonishing of operations. . . .

M. Flaubert is a moralist, undoubtedly, since he writes novels of manners, but he is a moralist as little as possible, for moralists are affected somewhere — in their hearts or in their minds — by the things they describe, and their judgment dominates their emotions. M. Flaubert, on the other hand, has no emotions at all; he has no judgment, at least any appreciable judgment. He is an incessant and indefatigable narrator, he is an analyst who never loses his composure; he is a "describer" even to the most minute subtlety. But he is deaf and dumb to the effect of everything he tells. He is indifferent to what he describes with the scrupulousness of love. If they forged story-telling or plot-summarizing machines at Birmingham or Manchester in good English steel which functioned all by themselves according to unknown dynamic processes, they would function absolutely like M. Flaubert. One would feel in these machines as much life, as much soul, as much human visceral reaction as in the man of marble who wrote *Madame Bovary* with a pen made of stone like the knives of the savages.

Now certainly, M. Gustave Flaubert is too intelligent not to have in him firm notions of good and evil; but he invokes them so seldom that one is tempted to believe that he in fact doesn't have them, and this is why when his book was first read there was such a great, resounding cry of immorality which, actually, was a calumny. No, the author of *Madame Bovary* was not at all immoral. He was only insensitive. . . . An extremely peculiar sort of originality! There are novelists who love their heroes, who exalt them, who justify them or who pity them. There are others who detest them, who condemn or curse them, and this is yet another way to love them. But all or almost all of them have some emotional reaction to the types[2] they have created. Human nature is loath to have a subject in hand without feeling some passion for or against. But M. Flaubert escapes from this custom which seems a law of the human spirit. Still young for so much coldness, he makes his debut resembling nothing so much as the elder Goethe. He proves that one can embrace a type in one's thought, carry him perhaps years in that intellectual cohabitation which sets most

*From *Les Oeuvres et les Hommes*, tome 4, "Les Romanciers," 1968 (first published 1865), 61–76. Translated for this volume by Robert Steele, Michigan State University. Reprinted by permission of Slatkine Reprints, Geneva, Switzerland.

spirits aflame, then drop him from one's brain, organized, living, without having been moved one single time by the nature that one has given him or the destiny that one has made for him. The *Madame Bovary* of the novel lacks maternal feeling, and it is one of the characteristics of her type. Very well! M. Gustave Flaubert is the Mme Bovary of his book. He is to his singular heroine what she herself is to her child. Will someone say this is a strength? We believe it is poverty.

Such is the radical defect of a work which recommends itself by qualities of a great power, but which criticism was duty bound to point out immediately, before any detailed analysis, because this defect affects the totality and the foundation of the work itself—because this weakness of sensitivity, of imagination, and I will say more, of moral and poetic sense, recurs on each page and stamps the entire work of M. Flaubert with a frightful dryness. As far as we are concerned, we are aware of no literary composition which reveals a truer talent which is at the same time more devoid of enthusiasm, emptier of heart; of a crueler cold-bloodedness. Except for a barely visible twist of irony—is one even sure it is there?—associated with the thought of the novelist and then nearly always when one would prefer him to be serious and sincere—for example, when he gives the details of the religious education of his Mme Bovary, the work offers to the spirit only a discouraging barrenness, despite the vividness of its sorrow and of its style. The interest one takes in it is the interest of a poignant curiosity soon satisfied, but as for the charm that makes one recollect the book in daydreams, the charm that belongs properly to art, even in its most terrifying compositions, the man of talent who has written Mme Bovary doesn't have the supreme sorcery it requires. Will he have it some day? They say M. Flaubert is in the middle of his life. From the vigor of his observation, one feels that he has *waited* for himself, which is a heroic feat in a time when everyone is in such a hurry. We have much faith in those men who have mastered their faculties and have forced them to be silent for a long time. Silence is the father of thought. But is charm voluntary? Can it be conquered through meditation or study? And if M. Flaubert had had the gift for it, wouldn't he have shown it in this first work, the fruit of youth brought to maturity, and would we be reduced to regretting its absence?

II

Madame Bovary is an accurate, well-conceived, and fresh idea. It is not a novel such as we always produce in the first part of our life, for as the novel is most often personal observation applied to matters of sentiment, we all want to believe that we are more or less experienced in matters of the heart. How many people there are for whom the novel that they write is only a confession in the third person! When tragedies were in fashion, writing a tragedy was only a literary pretension, but writing a novel is a literary pretension doubled by another much more profound. They are the memoirs of fatuity. Flaubert's *Madame Bovary* is not at all the memoirs of his fatuity. Personality may have its place here, for one is not sufficiently aware of how much the personality of a man is near him when one believes it most distant; but M. Gustave Flaubert belongs to the true race of novelists: he is an observer more occupied with others than with himself. Having lived for a long time in the provinces, he found more apparent there than in Paris, where it exists also, although it is less complete, a kind of woman forgotten by Balzac. And he has put himself to the task of painting her in infinite detail in a consummate study. It is merely the average woman of declining civilizations, that woman who is, alas! (it makes one tremble) the average woman in societies without beliefs, that type of feeble being without great passions, without the stuff of the great virtues or the great vices, inclining at random toward good or toward evil, according to circumstances, and who, practical and chimerical at the same time, ruins herself by reading the books she reads, by the influences and suggestions of the intellectual environment she has created for herself; for this environment leads her to consider with horror the other environment in which she is obliged to live. Certainly, this is a reality, if ever there was one, which ought to have tempted the pen of a master. By tackling it with the firmness and precision of his manly spirit, M. Flaubert has shown that, if he is not yet a master, he can become one.

In fact, with the understanding of a profound artist, he has placed his Madame Bovary, so unexceptional by nature, against the background best suited to emboss the contours of what was common in her, and to accentuate most energetically the outlines of her type. He has made her the daughter of a well-to-do peasant, who has given her just enough education to make a false "young lady" despise her good-natured but simple-minded father, should he have in his coarse hands the callouses caused by the handle of the plow or the oaken staff or should he make mistakes in French. He has married her to an imbecile who fails at everything, even at being grotesque, and who, since it is impossible for him to become a doctor, has reconciled himself to being only a local health official, a sort of paramedic, clumsy and groping. Bovary is one of those men for whom the best women would be pitiless: all the more reason for Emma Rouault to be! He is Jocrisse[3] disguised as a member of the bourgeoisie — a Jocrisse who is sober and tight-lipped with a hidden sentimentality. He loves his wife with that imbecilic affection one finds in sentimental literature, that sort of affection which certain lower species have for the higher species, which is a question of animal physiology much more than of moral sentiments.

Not content to have explained his heroine through her father, her education, her marriage, and especially her husband, M. Flaubert has established his Madame Bovary in a village in Normandy, right in the middle of a small-town society composed of the pharmacist, the village priest, the notary public, and the tax collector, and he has erected within eyesight, off in the distance, the chateau next door to any village, where the ancient races are presently expiring among the last scraps of fortune they have saved from the revolutions. This chateau, seen from a distance, must elicit in the mind of Madame Bovary many dreams and desires, but the author does not content himself with these vague fancies, with these curiosities which are incubated in a corruption whose principle is now dormant, but will soon awaken. He constructs his plot in a way that opens his chateau to his heroine and allows her to mingle one evening with the festivities and the luxury of a society only glimpsed in the romantic novels she has read. This evening at the chateau de la Vaubeyssard is, by the way, one of the scenes in the book where M. Flaubert has most shown his kind of talent, shrewd and blunt even in the nuances, which he grasps firmly and precisely, as a surgeon pinches veins. Before this scene, we have had foreshadowings, but the novel's central crisis must really be dated from this ball, where the eye begins to corrupt the soul and where the world outside enters in the heart of "Madame Bovary" never to leave.

There it awakens thirsts she will no longer satisfy, even when she slakes them. These men with unknown manners, who have wrinkled her dress while waltzing with her, have infected her with the plague of guilty desires and disgust for the life that she finds again on returning home. The yeast of the senses, tasted at this ball, ferments. . . . Her first thought, frankly adulterous, is of a notary's clerk, with pink cheeks, timid and curious, as naive as a sentimental ballad, but it is only a thought. This young man, whom the author will bring back later and who will be Madame Bovary's second lover, is replaced by a corrupt libertine, coarse, expert, and bold, with an equivocal, polished elegance, who was destined to triumph naturally over a woman like her, for in her isolation from the society that haunts her memory, it is this man who reminds her the most, on the surface, of the dandies of the chateau de la Vaubeyssard. He is only bourgeois but he is rich. He wears green velvet suits and soft boots, and he has something in him of the gentleman farmer, the horseback rider in a circus, and the parvenu. This man, elegant and lusty, habituated to fallen women, and basically only a fool, has found the doctor's wife pretty, and at first sight, during a country fair, he reels off to her all the stupidities and vulgarities which compose that easy thing of which men ought to be less proud: seduction. A few days later, Mme Bovary becomes the mistress of M. Rudolph Boulanger de la Huchette. They go horseback riding together through woods and isolated places. These assignations are provoked by the husband, who is happy to see his wife in riding costume, but they are not enough: Madame Bovary goes to see her lover secretly when Bovary is on his rounds.

The lovers settle down into the intimacy of adultery, which runs its course with all its depravations, wearying the man who has had enough after a few moments of ecstacy, and exalting the woman all the more.

Always literary, always preoccupied with great models, Madame Bovary soon exhausts the whole romantic wardrobe of the nineteenth century. She smokes, she wears men's vests, and ends up wanting to be carried off and to make her little trip to Italy, like anyone else. . . . Unfortunately at this point the false hero of the novel to whom she has given herself collapses. He has had enough of this fool. He refuses to encumber his life with an elopement with a married woman who talks of taking her daughter with her, and he jilts her with insolent paternalism and the prudence of a wise man who is protecting the income from his investments. Floored by the cowardice of the man she loves, Madame Bovary is at the point of dying from a brain fever caused by abandonment, sorrow, disappointment, shame. But this first love, which leads her down the first few steps of the staircase of infamy, throws her onto the next, from which she will roll down to the last.

And she will not raise herself back up again, because the novel has to reach its conclusion, because women like Madame Bovary never stop at a second love. They don't poison themselves. They continue to live, to give themselves, to take themselves back, to corrupt themselves voluptuously each day more and more through contact with ignoble caresses, and to express more and more in their own person the terrible saying of Diderot: "It is farther for a woman from her husband to her first lover than from her first lover to her tenth." The notary's clerk, M. Léon, this bourgeois cherub, who had poured into Madame Bovary's breast the first burning impurity, has left Yonville and is finishing his studies at Rouen. Madame Bovary is convalescing, having vainly sought a consolation and a strength in a religion which Flaubert (he must be, unless I'm wrong, an unbeliever) shows us through a ridiculous and stupid village priest. She meets this young man, whom she had formerly loved and desired, at the opera where her husband takes her to distract her; the two lovers, no longer novices, take up again with each other suddenly and furiously, their fury caused by the regret of not having seized each other sooner. This second love, admirably described by M. Flaubert, who is a veritable nosologist of corruption, is very different from the first because of all the vices the lovers have acquired, all the cowardly habits they have contracted. Madame Bovary, whose needs for voluptuousness reawaken more ravenous from their languors in the breast of suffering, begins again with Léon the intimacy she had enjoyed for a while with Rodolphe. Only she wants it more complete, deeper, better hidden, less breathless, and in order to achieve that she slithers through all the contortions, all the abominations of adultery, the intrigues, the lies, and the betrayal! She convinces Bovary, for he is perpetual consent itself, to send her to Rouen every week to take music lessons, and these lessons are only a pretense to live secretly with Léon. More audacious because she is a woman, and because given an equal amount of corruption the woman is always more advanced and more hardened, she drags Léon along as she had been dragged along by Rodolphe. She is the man of this new intimacy.

Léon is a mediocre soul, a variety of coward who indeed has his merit after M. Boulanger de la Huchette. The life he shares with this mistress, demanding in passion, demanding in caprice, and, to top it all off, demanding in the refinements of material existence, obliges him to expenses which threaten his savings and compromise his future. He worries about that sometimes. She notices and makes fun of him for it. She feels for him a little of that contempt under which she has buried Bovary in her. heart, but this contempt, which profanes love, does not extinguish it. She who, as wretched as she is, is worth more than the men who have soiled her, knows how to ruin herself and ruin her husband without letting a trace of it appear on her face when she offers it to the kisses of her weak lover! She borrows, in fact, she spends, she buys on credit, she abuses the power of attorney that Bovary has trusted her with, and when everything is gone, devoured, swallowed up, when there are no more resources, when the health officer's furniture must be auctioned off, she slips furtively to the pharmacist's, swallows arsenic by the handful and dies; fortunately, one must add, because if she hadn't poisoned herself on that day, another day she would perhaps have poisoned her husband, like Madame Lafarge.

III

Here, disentagled from the thousand subplots that are attached to it, mixed with it, and which complicate it, is the plot of M. Flaubert's novel. The great merit of this novel is in the central figure, who represents all the ideas of the book and which, although ordinary, ceases to be so by the depth with which she is understood and treated. Madame Bovary, studied, scrutinized, detailed as she is, is a superior creation; she alone earns for her author the title of novelist. We say "she alone"; for the rest of the book we have our reservations. The provincial society with which M. Gustave Flaubert has surrounded his Madame Bovary is not the same sort of bold and learned creation. That society is not lacking in truth, undoubtedly, but it is a lesser truth, and an observer with the acuity of M. Flaubert was obliged to produce more than that. His pharmacist Homais, who has been praised overmuch, is a special variety of the eternal M. Prudhomme,[4] the universal type whose ghost floats above all present-day thinkers, who have so little aptitude for depicting the comic of the nineteenth century. His village priest M. Bournisien is only a hastily sketched caricature. If this character represents hatred toward the clergy, hatred expressed in this way is innocent and does not offend us. We don't need to pardon it. But if he is an exceptional figure, an individual like all those which M. Flaubert has grouped around his health official and his wife, we say that it is not depicting a society from the point of view of art to repeat in all the costumes the same imbecile, and that here again is manifest the absence of powerful variety that the great novelists ought to make abound in their works.

As to style, by which one is a painter, by which one lives in the memory of men, that of *Madame Bovary* belongs to a literary artist who has his own language, brilliant, sparkling, and of an almost scientific precision. We have said above that M. Flaubert had a pen of stone. This stone is often a diamond; but diamonds, despite their brilliance, are hard and monotonous when it is a question of the "spiritual" nuances of a writer. M. Flaubert has no spirituality. He must be a materialist in doctrine as in style, because such a nature could not be inconsistent. It has been poured into the mold in a single stream, like Venetian crystal. What M. Flaubert is anywhere, he is everywhere. His style, like his power of observation, has the most astonishing feeling for detail, but for that tiny, imperceptible detail that everyone forgets, and which he perceives by a singular microscopic conformation of his eye. This man, who sees like a lynx into the shadowy soul of his Madame Bovary, and who gives us the exact account of the spots which are turning blue like bruises here, black as sin there, this beautiful fallen peach, with deceptively velvety contours — this man is an entomologist of style who would describe elephants in the same way that he would describe insects. He makes life-size engravings shaded with tiny dots in which nothing merges and everything is separated. Certainly, this method of depiction requires a sure hand, but breadth is worth more than fineness of detail. So many subtle observations end up putting spots before one's eyes! The light begins to flicker on all these superfluous little lines of shading, on all these contours made shockingly perceptible by the overly well defined relief of the drawing, in the same way that light flickers when it is reflected by the prisms of precious stones and dazzles us. Pursuing detail so inveterately destroys the very effect planned by the writer; M. Flaubert ought to be careful of that! Perhaps he has a superb future, but his success of today forces criticism to tell the truth with greater rigor. He is a large talent inclining toward small things, and he might lose himself in them, get swallowed up, as if he himself were little!

[Editor's Note: The following was added by Barbey D'Aurevilly after the publication of Flaubert's novel *Salammbô* in 1862.]

The future which I was pleased to predict for M. Gustave Flaubert has not materialized. After years of staggeringly extensive studies and bone-breaking effort, the author of *Madame Bovary* has only been able to produce *Salammbô* — a book that is difficult to classify, since it is neither a novel nor a history. *Salammbô* — for which the author's friends have pulled the ropes in all the belltowers so long that they have broken and [the bells] can no longer be heard — *Salammbô* has fallen definitively into the most deserved neglect. There she joins the *Incas*:[5] two books of the same sort, given the difference in centuries. There is so little of the Gustave Flabuert of *Madame Bovary* in *Salammbô* that I hold him for dead, and consequently, unless there is a miracle, unable to be reborn. The habitual procedures of a writer reveal the nature of his spirit. Those of M. Flaubert — who paints with an awl — are so dry, that one deduces without astonishment the fundamental aridity of a man who has no longer anything living or observed to say after *Madame Bovary* — probably derived from personal experience. I ask him to pardon the brutality of the term: M. Flaubert has impressed me as no longer having anything in his guts. There are two sorts of intellects: the Intuitives, the Diviners, and the Inventors, who even from the bottom of a sack would invent, divine, and see; and the Describers, for whom it is necessary that life come to the aid of thought, and who, were it not for the fact that they had encountered certain events and persons, would not have a single idea at their service. . . . Might M. Gustave Flaubert be among these last? I fear that he is.

Notes

1. Baron Guillaume Dupuytren, 1777–1835, was a famous surgeon and a pioneer of anatomical pathology [Editor].

2. I have decided to leave the word "type" consistently as it stands in the original for the benefit of those who wish to refer Barbey D'Aurevilly's remarks to the Balzacian concept of the type. Occasionally, as here, "character" might provide a less jarring translation [Translator]. See Honoré de Balzac, *La Comédie Humaine* (Paris: Gallimard, 1976–80), 11 vols., I, 18; and Balzac, "Lettres sur la littérature, le théâtre et les arts," in *Oeuvres complètes*, edited by Marcel Bouteron and Henri Longnon (Paris: Conard, 1912–40), 40 vols., XL, 320. Balzac claimed that each subject had only one possible form, and that the writer had to have the vision of the ideal model or type for each of his creations [Editor].

3. An easily led simpleton in early theater [Translator].

4. A character created by Henri Monnier, whose name in French has become proverbial to refer to a person who pronounces pompous banalities with great self-satisfaction [Translator].

5. *Les Incas* (1777) is an obscure historical romance by Jean-François Marmontel (1723–99), the chief contributor to the *Encyclopédie* [Editor].

Madame Bovary: Flaubert's Anti-Novel

Jean Rousset*

AN ASPECT OF FLAUBERT'S TECHNIQUE: POINT OF VIEW

We hear a lot today about the *anti-novel*. The expression was already in use during the seventeenth century: Sorel[1] applied it to the novels in the tradition of *Don Quixote*, written in reaction against the Romanesque excesses of current fiction. Sartre was instrumental in bringing the term back into fashion when, in his preface to Nathalie Sarraute's *Portrait of a Man Unknown*,[2] he wrote: "The anti-novels keep the appearance and outline of ordinary novels. . . . But they do so in order to undermine the genre all the more effectively: they set out to undo the novel on its own terms; while seemingly constructing one, they destroy it before our eyes. . . ." This, he adds, indicates that "the novel is reflecting upon its own nature."

Extending the meaning of the term somewhat further, we can say that the anti-novel occurs whenever the novel loses faith in itself, becomes critical and self-critical, wishes to break with the established norms of the medium. A "crisis" of the novel then takes place; today we have a crisis of the fictional character, of its "psychology," even of the subject-matter. If by "subject" we mean the narrative, the plot, the sum of events that take place in the novel, it becomes clear that this "subject" tends increasingly to stand apart from the actual work, or even to disappear altogether. Robbe-Grillet recently admitted as much: "In my first book, *The Erasers*, there still was a conventional plot, imitated, in fact, from *Oedipus the King*. But it did not concern me in the least; I was not interested in making it consistent or plausible. Nor should the readers of *Jealousy* ask themselves whether or not the book contains autobiographical elements; this time, they have good reasons not to do so for, in this novel, nothing—or almost nothing—happens. . . ."[3]

Well before Robbe-Grillet and Nathalie Sarraute (different from each other as they are), Gide had his spokesman and protagonist Edouard say in *The Counterfeiters:* "My novel does not have a subject"; and George Moore used to warn Virginia Woolf.[4] "Mrs. Woolf, take my word for it, you'll never be able to write a good novel entirely without a subject." Such indeed was her dream, and who would deny that she made it come true?

Can we go back even further? The naturalists seem to be making similar claims, as when Goncourt tells Huret:[5] "Although more novels are

---

*Reprinted from *Madame Bovary*, by Gustave Flaubert, A Norton Critical Edition, Edited by Paul de Man, with the permission of W. W. Norton & Company, Inc. Copyright © 1965 by W. W. Norton & Company, Inc. Pages 439–57. Translated by Paul de Man.

being sold than ever before, I am convinced that the novel is a used up, dying genre. It has said all it had to say. I have done all I could to kill off the 'Romanesque,' all that has to do with adventure and sentiment for its own sake, to replace it by a kind of autobiography, memoirs of people to whom very little happens."[6] However, what is being eschewed here—and will also be rejected, in very similar terms, by Zola and Huysmans—is the plot and the fiction of earlier novels rather than the subject, the reference to the real world—a part of the novel that the naturalists were far from ready to relinquish. Yet there were readers, at the time, who complained that novels lacked subject-matter entirely, exactly as impressionistic painters were being blamed for making pictures without a subject.

In this context, one feels compelled to stress the importance of Flaubert, the pure novelist critic, brought up from infancy on that greatest ancestor of all anti-novels, *Don Quixote*. His ambition, expressed when he starts *Madame Bovary*, is well known: "What I deem beautiful, what I would want to do, is a book about nothing, a book without reference outside itself . . . a book that would be almost without a subject, or in which the subject would be almost invisible, if such a thing is possible" (January 16, 1852). And, a little later: "If the book on which I am working with such difficulty can be brought to a successful conclusion, its existence will at least have proven the following two truths which I consider to be self-evident: first, that poetry is entirely subjective, that, in literature, there is no such thing as a beautiful subject—hence, that Yvetot will do just as well as Constantinople; and that, consequently, it makes no difference what one writes about" (June 25 / 26, 1853).

This century-old declaration of war against the intrinsic importance of the subject[7] clearly shows that the novel was felt to be in a state of crisis and revolt well before 1950. When today's "new novelists" are up in arms against the "traditional novel," they are attacking a novel that was itself rebelling against its predecessors. Differences exist, not only between the products of this rebellion but also, less obviously, between the models that are being rejected: the non-subject of one generation often becomes the subject to be rejected by their successors [sic].

This does not prevent Flaubert's experiments from being particularly meaningful for us today; he is the first in date of the non-figurative novelists. The subject—and the psychology—of *Madame Bovary* certainly still play their part, albeit a muted one, in the concert of the novel, which could not exist without them. Yet, we have the right, and perhaps the duty, to ignore them and to echo Flaubert's statement to Goncourt: "As for the story, the plot of a novel—I couldn't care less." We can add to this the very modern-sounding statement of beliefs: "The works of art that I admire above all others are those in which there is an *excess of Art*. In a picture, it is Painting that I like; in a poem, Poetry."[8] One could complete the statement: and in a novel, it is technique and style. Flaubert himself seems to invite us to read *Madame Bovary* as if it were a sonata. Thus we might escape the reproach he addressed to the greatest critics of his own time: "What shocks me in my friends Saint-Beuve and Taine is that they do not pay sufficient attention to *Art*, to the work in itself, to its construction, its style, all that makes up its beauty. . . ."[9]

Flaubert does not explicitly mention a principle of composition which must have concerned him to the highest degree: the "point of view" from which the novelist considers the events and the characters described in the novel. Is it the impartial and panoramic view of the ideal witness? One would expect this to be the case, remembering the author's declared intention in *Madame Bovary* to make himself as impersonal and objective as possible. This was, moreover, the usual technique in Balzac's novels. But Flaubert has no faith in impersonal knowledge. No such thing as objective reality exists for him; every vision, every perception is someone's particular illusion; there are as many "colored glasses" as there are observers. Does not this challenge the privileged position of the all-knowing author, endowed with divine and absolute vision?

I. AN INTRODUCTORY CHARACTER: CHARLES BOVARY

The general organization of the book comes as a surprise: the main character is absent from the beginning as well as from the epilogue of the novel. This anomaly leads us directly to the problem of points of view.

The organization of the novel, which gives Charles Bovary a central position at the beginning and at the end, had been planned from the very first scenarios on. The only change that took place along the way is the growing importance of Homais in the final pages. These two characters are presented from the outside and from afar, almost as if they were things, opaque in their lack of self-awareness. The novel is thus framed by two episodes in which the point of view is very definitely that of the bystander watching the scene from a distance and from above, altogether detached from the inner motivations of characters which he treats as if they were puppets. At the one end, Charles first enters the field of our vision when he appears in the classroom observed by that curiously neutral "we" that will soon vanish from the novel; at the other end of the book, in a symmetrical construction so effective that it more than justifies the change in the original outline, we have the triumphantly grotesque exit of the pharmacist. At the two gates of his work, as he meets and as he leaves us, Flaubert has concentrated a maximum of sad irony and sarcasm, because these are the places in which his observation is most remote from its object. Thus the novel first moves from the outside inward, from the surface to the heart, from detachment to involvement, then returns from the inside to the periphery. Flaubert's first glance at the world always remains aloof, and only records the outside, the crust, the grotesque aspect of the mechanical gesture.[10]

But soon enough he penetrates beneath the surface. Homais remains seen from the outside throughout, thus making it possible to use him for the concluding passage, but the same is not true for Charles. From the start, while he holds the center of the stage for a relatively long time, the author draws nearer to him and takes the reader with him. The puppet becomes human: a brief flashback tells us about his birth, his childhood and adolescence, thus opening the way for a more sympathetic insight. It is nevertheless with some feeling of surprise that we suddenly find ourselves intimately close to him, sharing in his reverie: "On the fine summer evenings . . . he opened his window and leaned out. The river . . . flowed beneath him . . . Opposite, beyond the roofs, spread the pure sky with the red sun setting. How pleasant it must be at home! How fresh under the beech tree!"[11] One almost suspects a mistake on Flaubert's part: such nostalgic dreams before the window, such reveries directed towards open space, are usually associated with his heroine. He could not resist this slight token of identification, this brief moment during which he espouses the point of view of his character. As a temporary protagonist, Charles is allowed some of the benefits of this position. But the moment of insight is brief; the author at once withdraws again to the proper distance. The first drafts reveal that Flaubert had originally planned several pages of memories and dreams; he suppresses most of them, for they would definitely have made the character too close, too intimate. Yet he was unable to describe Bovary purely as if he were a mere object. Perhaps he didn't want to. The actual function of Charles Bovary in the novel and the explanation of his dominating presence in the introductory section can now be stated.

It is through Charles's eyes that we will first come upon Emma. Charles will be used as a reflector until the moment when the heroine, having been gradually introduced and then accepted, will occupy the front of the stage and become the central subject. But, like her future husband, she must first appear in the humbler guise of a character seen from the outside, as if she were a mere inanimate thing. Unlike Charles, however, the eye that perceives her is not critical, but dazzled, and the sensibility that reflects her image is familiar to us; the reader has even been allowed a glimpse of its inner workings, especially on the occasion of the doctor's early-morning visit to the Bertaux farm when, half asleep, we share in his split, double perceptions, just before Emma comes on the scene. Flaubert then uses Charles to introduce Emma, and to make us see her as she appears to him; we adopt strictly his point of view, his narrow field of vision, his subjective perception, as we follow him step by step in his discovery of an unknown woman. The author relinquishes the privileged position of the all-knowing novelist and gives us instead an image of his heroine that remains deliberately superficial and incomplete, in the sense that it records only successive and fragmentary impressions.[12]

Charles arrives at the farm: "A young woman, in a blue merino dress, with three flounces, appeared on the threshold . . ." A blue dress is what he notices first of all, is all that he shows us. One page later, he notices the whiteness of her nails, then her eyes; somewhat later still, on talking with her, he notes the "fullness of her lips." When she turns her back on him, her hair on her neck swings in a movement "that the country doctor noticed there for the first time in his life." Instead of the full-sized portrait that exists out of time, and records what the author knows and perceives, as Balzac or, before him, Marivaux, would have given us, Flaubert draws a portrait composed of gradually emerging fragments — he lets such a portrait come into being from the pointillist[13] observations of a character who is emotionally stirred and involved. Other encounters with Emma will add further touches, always similarly scattered, as they originate in the confused and troubled consciousness of a man who is falling in love.

At times, Flaubert's first drafts allow us to recapture exactly his efforts to seize this vision and to render it faithfully. We have him writing, for instance, in his earliest version: "She wore neither shawl, nor cape, her white shoulders had a pink glow."[14] This is a beautiful impression of the effect of light in a kitchen on a summer day, but much too subtle for Charles Bovary. Retreating as author, Flaubert suppresses the passage and replaces it by an observation in keeping with the character behind which he is hiding: "He could see little drops of perspiration on her bare shoulders." One should add, however, that Flaubert doesn't rigorously adhere to the necessity of reflecting the limitations and distortions of his characters; he was still rather remote from Faulkner who locked himself hermetically within the interior monologue of a half-wit. Whether from lack of consistency or because he refuses to be over-systematic, Flaubert at times fills out Charles's usual perceptions, just as he sometimes puts in Emma's mind reflections or shades of irony that couldn't possibly be hers. The result is frequently a compromise in which it is difficult to discriminate between the contradictory view-points of the outside observer and the inner eye. Flaubert will not hesitate to commit the "error" for which Sartre so bitterly criticizes Mauriac (as if Mauriac were the first guilty of moving freely in and out of the consciousness of his characters):[15] "As for Charles, he didn't stay to ask himself why it was a pleasure to him to go to the Bertaux," or else: "Was she speaking seriously? Emma probably didn't even know herself. . . ."

There can be no question, however, that throughout the prologue Charles is deliberately used as a center and as a reflector. He is never absent, and Emma is seen only through his eyes. All we know about her is what he finds out; the only words she speaks are those addressed to him. We don't have the slightest idea what she really thinks or feels. Emma is systematically shown us from the outside; Charles's point of view demands this. In this respect, Flaubert adheres strictly to his method. He even provides us with an extreme example: at the moment when the young girl makes the ominous decision to marry, a decision on which her entire miserable destiny and, therefore, the substance of the book hinges, the novelist hides her out of our sight; her conversation with her father, her inner reactions, and her answer are recorded indirectly and at great distance by Charles who is hiding behind the hedge and waiting for the window-blind to be pushed open against the wall. Only much later, when Flaubert moves closer to her and unlocks her thoughts, a set of refractions and juxtapositions will reveal something of what she thinks of Charles and her marriage, of her expectations, of what went on in her during that half hour. For the time being, however, she remains an opaque character contemplated from afar by Charles Bovary. All we know of her is what he knows – the outline of a face, a few gestures, a dress.

Soon enough, we discover what hides behind this surface and what kind of human being this young woman actually is, for the point of view is about to change. But Charles himself will never discover much more; to him, she will always remain that unknowable quantity that she will soon cease to be for us. He will never find out what hides behind this veil, for he totally lacks the novelist's power to penetrate into her inner self. From Chapter V on, the angle of vision slowly starts to revolve; from pure object, Emma becomes subject, the focus shifts from Charles to her, and the reader penetrates into a consciousness which, up till then, was as closed to him as it was to Charles.

This is probably the deeper reason for the country doctor's central position in the first chapters, as well as for the rigorous adherence to his point of view, including the occasional and surprising plumbing of his intimate self. Not only does it allow the reader to meet Emma first through a sensibility that is itself immersed in the flux of time; more than that, this organization of the perspective allows him to experience from the inside the type of knowledge that Charles will always possess of his wife. Thus prepared, the reader will remember it later, when Emma will have moved to the center, and this recollection will illuminate and enrich the fictional universe in which he immerses himself.

II. THE ART OF MODULATION

From Chapter VI on, Emma glides to the center of the novel, a place which she will never leave, except for some brief interruptions. There is nothing unusual about this. Balzac, master of the total and panoramic point of view, often chooses a central character, such as, for instance, Rastignac,[16] and organizes the action around him. Flaubert's originality resides in his combining the author's point of view with the heroine's. His perspectives alternate and interfere with each other, but the subjective vision of the character always predominates. His technical problem is to achieve the shifts in point of view and the transitions from one perspective to another without interrupting the movement, without disrupting the "tissue of the style."

Consider, for example, the transition from Charles to Emma, the gradual introduction, by almost unnoticeable steps, of the heroine's point of view. The point of departure and final destination of his itinerary are marked by the return of the same object, observed by two different sets of eyes: the garden of Tostes. "The garden, longer than wide, ran between two mud walls . . . to a thorn hedge that separated it from the field. In the middle was a slate sundial. . . ; four flower-beds . . . Right at the bottom, under the spruce bushes, a plaster priest was reading his breviary." This is a straight-forward catalogue, an objective inventory of surfaces and materials, drawn up as by an outside observer,[17] altogether detached — without any anthropomorphic participation in things, as Robbe-Grillet would put it. The reason for this objectivity stems from the fact that Emma, when she is entering her new house, is still an utter stranger to whom Flaubert has not yet given us any access whatsoever. Thirty pages later, Emma's initiation accomplished, we come upon the same little garden, seen this time through the subjective glance of the disenchanted heroine, reacting fully to all the elements of stagnation, decline, and decay that reside in things: "The dew had left on the cabbages a silver lace with long transparent threads spreading from one to the other. No birds were to be heard; everything seemed asleep, the espalier covered with straw, and the vine, like a great sick serpent under the coping of the wall, along which, on drawing near, one saw the many-footed woodlice crawling. Under the spruce by the hedgerow, the curé in the three-cornered hat reading his breviary had lost his right foot, and the very plaster scaling off with the frost, had left white scabs on his face."

In the interval between the two passages everything has changed, not only in the situation and the mood of the heroine, but in the reader's position toward her as well. A skillful revolving movement has shifted the point of view, and the center of vision now gradually coincides with Emma's. We get a first glimpse into her dreams, followed, in flashback, by an analysis of the developments that lead to her present sensibility. Flaubert's hand is very apparent throughout; at this point, none of these insights could have been Emma's own. Then comes a more revealing insight in her dreams of another honeymoon: "She thought, some times . . ." leading to the long reverie under the beech trees which is by now altogether subjective and richly endowed with all the characteristics of Flaubert's inner ecstasies.[18]

Henry James, speaking of one of his novels, mentions "a planned rotation of aspects"; the expression could very well apply to Flaubert. It designates a subtle art of modulation in varying the point of view, an art of which Flaubert is a true master and which he puts to constant use. For if it is true that Emma never ceases to stand at the center of the novel, Flaubert nevertheless substitutes at times, for a brief moment, the outlook of another character. Such shifts are no easy matter to negotiate for an author who detests any trace of discontinuity, and wishes to avoid, at all cost, the tricks and manipulations of the novelist-stage director which abound in the first version of *The Sentimental Education*. When Flaubert relinquishes Emma's point of view in favor of that of Charles or Rodolphe, or gives the front of the stage for a moment to a minor character, he uses something resembling a closed-circuit system, without interrupting the flow of the narration. An example will show how the method works.

In the third chapter of Part II, immediately following the arrival at Yonville, Emma enters her new house; the reader goes with her, feeling "the cold of the plaster fall about her shoulders like damp linen. . . ." At this point, the novel has to impart miscellaneous bits of information about recently introduced characters such as Léon and Homais. Flaubert has to move away from the heroine without breaking the thread. He uses Emma's own outlook: "The next day, as she was getting up, she saw the clerk on the Square . . . Léon waited all day, etc. . . ."; the point of view has glided towards the clerk, where it stays for a while. From the clerk, whom M. Homais "respected for his education," we move almost imperceptibly over to the pharmacist, his habits, his attitude towards the new doctor, thus allowing a smooth transition to Charles. "Charles was depressed; he had no patients. . . ." Yet, in compensation, he rejoices in his wife's pregnancy. This glance cast by Charles on his pregnant wife closes the circle, returns us to Emma, happily concluding the full circuit of alternating viewpoints: "He looked at her undisturbed . . . Emma at first felt a great astonishment." Moreover, by juxtaposing the thoughts of Emma and Charles, Flaubert shows how distant they are from each other. He may, at times, deliberately forego his gradual transfers in order to reveal, as by a sudden gap, this divergence of their outlooks, the infinite distance that keeps them apart, even when they are sitting or lying side by side: "He saw himself dishonored . . . Emma, opposite, watched him; she did not share his humiliation, she felt another. . . ." But, as a rule, Flaubert puts a great deal of care in his art of modulation. Thus when Rodolphe and Emma end their last nocturnal dialogue, which the reader has experienced through the consciousness of the young woman:

> " 'Till tomorrow then!' said Emma in a last caress.
> And *she watched him* go.
> He didn't turn around . . . He was already on the other side of the river, walking fast across the meadows.
> After a few moments Rodolphe stopped. . . ."

Again, carried by Emma's eye, the reader leaves her for the object of her contemplation and joins Rodolphe; he hears him think and sees him write the letter that puts an end to the affair.

This art of modulation, this concern with smooth and gradual transition,[19] reflects in a distinctive manner Flaubert's general effort towards what he calls *style*. He conceives of style as a binding agent which reduces the diverse to the homogeneous. He strives for a unity of texture, as tight and even as possible, in order to create continuity: "Style is made of continuity, as virtue is made of constancy."[20] When he criticizes a poem by Louise Colet or Leconte de Lisle,[21] his strictures are aimed at unevenness of tone or of color. In his eyes, what makes for the quality of a work are not the pearls but the thread that holds them together, the uniform movement, the flow. Rereading the parts of *Madame Bovary* on which he has been working, he writes to Louise Colet: "I reread all this the day before yesterday, and I have been horrified by its inadequacy . . . Each paragraph is good enough by itself, and I am convinced that some pages are perfect. But just because of this, *it won't do*. It is a set of well-turned, static paragraphs which do not dovetail with each other. I'm going to have to loosen up a lot of screws and joints. . . ."[22] Those articulations will become the main concern of the artist; they must be made strong and flexible, while remaining invisible. Flaubert applies the mortar with infinite care, and he is not less careful in wiping away the last trace of its presence: "I've had to remove a lot of mortar that was showing between the bricks, and I had to rearrange the bricks to hide the joints from sight."[23]

Flaubert's imagination has always been captivated by the sight of large rocks, by vast arrangements of stones. At the end of his fine essay on Flaubert, Jean Pierre Richard shows how the deep fluidity of Flaubert's being leads him, in his creative effort, to strive for the firmness of rocks and stones; this sedimentation will be considered successful provided that the original plastic and humid mass is not allowed to dry up altogether. Flaubert remains faithful to himself when he defines his picture of "beauty" as being an entirely smooth surface, a *naked wall*. The term appears in a letter from 1876, but it goes back to a memory of his youth: "I remember how my heart beat and what pleasure I felt on looking at the wall of the Acropolis, a naked wall . . . I wonder whether a book, regardless of what it has to say, could not produce a similar impression? Is there not an intrinsic quality, a kind of divine power, in the precision of the construction, the economy of the means, the *polish of the surface*, the harmony of the whole. . . ?"[24] Elsewhere he writes: "Prose must stand erect from end to end, like a wall. . . ." What fascinates Flaubert in the picture of the wall is the homogeneous block, the compact, immobile, uninterrupted mass, the "great uniting line," the perfection of continuity created, as we have seen in the modulating passages.

This ideal of the "straight line" and of massive construction does not exclude variations of tonality and of movement in the inner texture of the novel, zones of greater or lesser intensity that determine the rhythm, the pulsation of the book.

In this respect, and without leaving the questions of point of view and field of vision with which we have been concerned, we should notice the important part that windows play in *Madame Bovary*. Léon Bopp has observed the importance of the frequent presence of the heroine before open windows. This allows for striking effects of depth perspective and panoramic vision, corresponding to phases of maximum subjectivity and extreme intensity.

III. WINDOWS AND PANORAMIC VISION

Maria, in the story *November*,[25] spent whole days at her window waiting, keeping a vigil over the empty space in which a customer might appear, or an event occur. The window is a favorite place for certain Flaubert characters who, though unable to move by themselves, are nevertheless swept away by the current of events. They are frozen by their own inertias while their minds wander forever. Caught in the closed space in which their souls dry up, they welcome the window as an escape which allows them to expand into space, without having to leave their chosen spots. The window combines open and enclosed space, represents an obstacle as well as an escape, a sheltering room as well as an area of endless expansion, a circumscribed infinity. Flaubert's main characters who, as Georges Poulet has so well shown, are always absent from where they live and present where they do not, vacillating between contraction and expansion, are bound to choose for their dwelling places borderline entities which allow for escape in immobility; no wonder they select windows as the ideal locale for their reveries.

Already in *Par les Champs et par les Grèves*[26] the following passage appears: "Ah! air! more air! give me space in which to breathe! Our oppressed souls are stifled and dying near the window. Our captive minds turn and turn upon themselves, like bears in cages, bumping against the walls that enclose them. Let my nostrils at least breathe in the scent of all winds that encircle the earth, and *let my eyes escape toward all the horizons*."[27]

Emma Bovary, another captive locked within the walls of her cage, finds before her window an "escape towards all horizons": "She often stood there." In Tostes, she stands at the window to watch the rain fall and the monotonous round of the village days go by; in Yonville, the notary clerk as well as Rodolphe are first observed from a window; standing in the garden window, Emma hears the ringing of the angelus bells that will awaken a mystical longing in her, drawing her gaze upwards to lose itself among the clouds or among the meanderings of the river; the attic-window gives her the first dizzy temptation toward suicide; and after her illness, when she resumes contact with life, "they wheeled her arm chair by the window overlooking the Square. . . ." They are the windows of despair and of dreams.

On the other hand, we find in the novel closed windows, with all curtains drawn during the rare moments when Emma is no longer alienated from herself or from the place where she lives and, consequently, feels no need to scatter herself into the endless infinity of dreams. Instead, in the early and happy moment of her passions, she makes herself into the center of all things, as in Rouen, with Léon, "in the carriage with drawn blinds . . . more tightly closed than a tomb," then in the hotel room where they live locked up all day long "all curtains drawn, all doors locked . . . in a hothouse atmosphere," as one of the early scenarios expresses it. The same had happened with Rodolphe when Emma, at the onset of their affair, paid him surprise visits at la Huchette, in the room half-darkened by "the yellow curtains along the windows." But this first passion is generally a passion in the open air, in garden or forest, where there are no windows at all. Flaubert thus contrasts the nature of the two lovers, while remaining faithful to the thematic meaning of the windows in his novel.

In conjunction with their special significance for Flaubert's characters, the windows provide the novelist-director with interesting technical opportunities in staging and ordering his scenes. Flaubert uses them frequently to vary the narrative perspective and to engineer interesting optical effects. The brilliant "symphonic" passage of the Agricultural Fair at once comes to mind, in which the point of view is that of the two future lovers, watching from the window on the second floor of the town hall. The panoramic view here offers a double advantage: in the first place, it reinforces the author's ironical detachment towards the goings-on below and towards the budding idyll that he treats in juxtaposition to the fair; more important still, it reflects the upward motion, the more elevated note struck at the moment of Emma's entrance upon the life of passion. The tone is picked up in the following episode: the same panoramic vision is used again a little later, during the horse ride when Rodolphe completes the conquest begun on the day of the fair. Arriving at the top of a hill, Flaubert gives us a panoramic outlook over the land similar to the one that Emma gains, at this same moment, over her life: "There was fog over the land. Hazy clouds hovered on the horizon between the outlines of the hills; others rent asunder, floated up and disappeared. Sometimes through a rift in the clouds, beneath a ray of sunshine, gleamed from afar the roofs of Yonville, with the gardens at the water's edge, the yards, the walls and the church steeple. Emma half closed her eyes to pick out her house, and never had this poor village where she lived appeared so small." The beginning of her love is marked by a rising above the habitual level of existence; the place where this existence occurred must first vanish before her eyes: Yonville must shrink away into a distance made infinite by the bird's-eye perspective, in order to make room for the imaginary space in which her love will take place, associated here with the image of evaporating water: "From the height on which they stood, the entire valley seemed an immense pale lake sending off its vapor into the air." At the moment when the author casts over the world the all-embracing glance of his heroine, as she is carried upward by her rising exaltation, the village and its houses have become a shapeless mirage, suspended in mid-air.

A few pages farther, on the evening of the same day, Emma dreams of this new life that dawns upon her. As if the high view of the afternoon had completely entered the inner landscape of her soul, she still thinks in terms of height and infinity, united against the lowliness of her common existence: "She was entering upon a marvelous world where all would be passion, ecstasy, endless rapture. A blue space surrounded her, the heights of sentiment sparkled under her thought, and ordinary existence appeared only intermittently between these heights, dark and far away underneath her."

Flaubert has made a different use of the same hilltop above the village, at a moment that is not less decisive, though oriented in the opposite direction. Madame Bovary has seen Rodolphe for the last time and she returns to Yonville, utterly dejected and about to kill herself. Instead of the ascent towards the ecstasy of passion, we now have the descent towards suicide. During this hallucinated walk at nightfall, we meet her at the top of a hill, the same perhaps as before. Suddenly, she is shaken out of her spellbound state:

> It all disappeared: she recognized the lights of the houses that shone through the fog.
> Now her plight, like an abyss, loomed before her . . . she ran down the hill . . .

The return from the world of the imagination to the world of reality is now a falling towards the village; this time, the village appears out of the fog instead of hiding beneath it; it is a descent into the abyss.

Thus, in two passages which, though quite far apart, are the symmetrical opposites of each other, Flaubert has placed his heroine, at the onset and at the end of her love-quest, in the same dominating position and has made her command the same panoramic outlook. It is up to the attentive reader to notice the structural link that unites the two episodes and to discover the wealth of meaning added by such a tightly controlled construction. One should compare to this another diptych, combining this time the use of the window with that of the carriage (which will play such an important part in the *Sentimental Education*): the two views of Rouen, on the arrival and at the departure of the stage coach, during Emma's Thursday encounters with Léon. We are given one more panoramic view: "Thus seen from above, the entire landscape seemed motionless like a painting. . . ." And here again, the landscape, at first frozen, will start to move, to vibrate and to expand under the impact of an imagination driven by impending passion. There is one important difference, however: instead of appearing remote and hidden by a veil that makes it shrink into near oblivion, the dwelling place of her desire will now, in a reverse optical illusion, appear out of the mist and start expanding into an immense capital — the only entity large enough to contain the ever widening space she projects before her: "Her love grew in the presence of this vastness, and filled with the tumult of the vague murmuring which rose from below. She poured it out, onto the squares, the avenues, the streets; and the old Norman city *spread out before her like some incredible Capital, a Babylon into which she was about to enter."*

Windows and panoramic views, spatial reveries, opening up into infinite perspectives, make up the crucial centers around which the plot is organized; they are points of highest resistance that stop the flow of the narrative. They coincide with the adoption of a most unusual point of view: the author relinquishes his traditional godlike rights and leaves room instead for a totally subjective vision. He places himself behind his heroine and looks entirely through her eyes. Such moments occur at significant points in the book. They are unevenly distributed; entirely lacking during the periods of action, when the play of passion is acted out, they are more frequent during periods of stagnation and suspended waiting. So for instance at Tostes, after the invitation to the ball, when for the first time we see Emma, at the end of the evening, open the window and lean out.[28] From then on, in Tostes as well as in Yonville, the reverie will never cease, till the moment when she embarks upon her great adventure, returns to her husband, rejects him again after the clubfoot episode, prepares her elopement, gets involved in her financial dealings with Lheureux. After these chapters of action and accelerated movement, the end of the affair with Rodolphe brings back a slower tempo, a new period of stagnation and inertia. Again, this change of pace is introduced by a window opening up before the heroine; this time, however, the window is already a tragic one, suggesting the dizziness and loss of consciousness that is a prefiguration of the end. She reads Rodolphe's letter near the attic window, "opposite, beyond the roofs, the countryside stretched out as far as the eye could reach. . . ." She is about to return to a world of regrets and frustrated desires, in which she will try to expand beyond the limits of her confinement, to "float" in the airy realm which is that of her reverie and of her panoramic visions: "she was right at the edge, almost hanging, surrounded by vast space. The blue of the sky invaded her. . . ."[29]

Those repeated flights of reverie before the open window are always followed by a fall, a return to earth: " 'My wife! my wife!' Charles called . . . and she had to *go down* and sit at the table!" The book, like the inner life of the heroine, consists of this rhythmical succession of flights and falls. Thus, at the beginning of Chapter VI of the second part, the open window through which the ringing of the angelus is heard leads to a flow of memories and to an ascent into a weightless, suspended state expressed by images of flight, of swirling feathers: "she felt limp and helpless, like the down of a bird whirled by the tempest"; then, on returning from church, "she let *herself fall* into an armchair," recaptured by the heavy and confining world of the room, by the monotonous weight of time, by the opaque presence of creatures who "are there" as if they were pieces of furniture: "the pieces of furniture seemed more frozen in their places . . . , the clock went on ticking . . . little Berthe was there, between the window and the sewing table . . . Charles appeared. It was dinner time. . . ." Trying to reestablish contact with daily life, after the moments of escape towards the beyond of the windows, is always an act of falling, a falling back into confinement.

The same double movement recurs at other crucial passages, such as the scene at the Agricultural Fair. Emma, stirred by a smell of perfume and the "distant" sight of the stage coach, unites in a kind of ecstasy lovers and experiences of the past before she returns downward, to the crowd on the square and the official oratory. Or again, in another ecstasy of a similarly erotic nature, the scene at the opera in Rouen, which heralds the beginning of the affair with Léon as the preceding one began the affair with Rodolphe. The box from which Emma looks "from above" over the stage is an exact equivalence of the window, a new amalgamation, a synthesis of confinement and expansion towards a space on which an imaginary destiny is being acted out. This time, it is not her own destiny that is being played out, but somebody else's being performed for her benefit; yet it doesn't take her long to recognize her own plight, to identify with the main feminine part, to join her in her desire to "*fly away* in an embrace" and to see another Rodolphe in the tenor part: "A mad idea took possession of her: he was looking at her right now! She longed to run to his arms . . . , and call out 'Take me away!' . . . The curtain *fell* . . . and she *fell back* into her seat. . . ." The sudden collapse of the dream and of the aerial perspective is followed after the flight, by the inevitable letdown. On this occasion, Flaubert stresses at once the heaviness of the air and the confinement of the space: "The smell of gas mingled with the people's breath and the waving fans made the air even more suffocating. Emma wanted to go out; the crowd filled the corridors, and she fell back in her armchair with palpitations that choked her."

One cannot fail to see in this sense a foreboding of Emma's last request when, during her death-struggle, gasping for air, she begs: "Open the window . . . I am suffocating." In her life, every ecstasy is followed by a smaller version of death; her actual, ultimate death harmoniously blends with the prefigurations that prepared it.

Moments of reverie, during which Flaubert's point of view comes closest to coinciding with that of his heroine and which allow us a glimpse into Emma's intimate self, abound in the slowest-moving parts of the novel, during the periods of inertia and spleen when time seems to stand still. They constitute the most original and striking aspects of the novel, the ones, also, that are most typical of Flaubert. During those moments, Flaubert relinquishes, to a considerable extent, the objective vision of the universal observer.

On the other hand, at times when the action must move forward, when new facts or characters have to be introduced, the author reclaims his sovereign rights and resorts to a panoramic perspective. Restoring the distance between himself and his characters, he can again show them from the outside. This happens, as we have shown, at the beginning and at the end of the novel, or in the opening chapters of a new part. Fresh beginnings demand the presence of the novelist-director, who sets the stage while introducing the cast of characters: so it is at the beginning of Part II, the big scene in the inn at Yonville or, in the introduction of Part III, the conversation between Emma and Léon in a Rouen hotel room, the rendezvous at the cathedral, the coach ride through the streets of Rouen. During the coach ride Flaubert takes advantage of the momentary distance that separates him from his heroine to achieve a surprising effect: the new lovers are in the coach, all curtains drawn, but the reader is not allowed to join them. In the foregoing pages, he was allowed no insight into their souls, but he could observe gestures and attitudes, catch the meaning of words that were spoken; here even this privilege is taken from him — he can see nothing at all, and has to be satisfied with following the carriage from afar as it meanders through the streets. During this decisive episode, he finds himself confined to the narrowest point of view possible, that of the indifferent citizens of Rouen, for whom this woman is a total stranger. When she finally emerges from the carriage, he sees her in this very light: "a *woman* got out, walking with her veil down and without looking back." The effect is all the more uncanny since the reader has been allowed earlier intimate glimpses of Emma's soul, and this close knowledge makes it easy for him to guess what goes on behind the lowered veil.

A similar effect recurs somewhat later in the book, when the author adopts an equally distant point of view to narrate Emma's desperate call on Binet: the scene is shown through the eyes of the two prying neighbors as they watch through the attic window. We can hardly hear a word, we watch from afar; gestures and attitudes have to be guessed and interpreted — it is like a scene from a silent movie. One may assume that Flaubert, who has kept us in very close contact with his main character and made us share in her drama from the inside, feels so certain of our participation that he allows himself this sudden withdrawal to show us, for one brief moment, the heroine as she appears to the alien eye of the outside judge and observer. Immediately afterwards, we briefly lose sight of her altogether. The two gossips watch her disappear down the street in the direction of the graveyard, and we can only wonder with them what Emma is about to do. Then in a new and abrupt reversal, the novelist suddenly takes us back to Emma as she visits the nurse, letting us into her consciousness. Those violent manipulations of the reader, echoing the pathos that abounds in this part of the narrative, are the more effective since, at all other times, Flaubert, modulating and gliding from scene to scene in almost imperceptible transitions, has taken exactly the opposite approach.

In Flaubert's novel, the point of view and the subjective vision of the characters play a considerable part, at the expense of straight-forward factual reporting. As a result, the importance of the slower movements increase as the outside impartial observer relinquishes his privileges, to a greater or lesser degree.[30]

This slowness of tempo combined with the use of inner perspective constitute the novelty and the originality of Flaubert's novels. He is the novelist of the inner vision and of a slow, almost stagnant action. Admirable and distinctive as those qualities are, Flaubert himself nevertheless discovers them only gradually by trial and error, more by instinct than by design, and not without some serious misgivings. We read in his letters that there is no "action," no "movement," "fifty pages without a single event." His concern about the shape his novel is taking (almost in spite of itself) stems from the awareness of his difference from his predecessors. He is thinking primarily of Balzac, for whom all is action, drama, and suspense. Then he resigns himself: "One must sing in one's own voice: and mine will never be dramatic or seductive. Besides, I am growing more and more convinced that all this is a matter of style, or, rather, of appearance, a way of presenting things."[31] The best he can do is to try to maintain a balance between action and inaction, between facts and dreams: "It will be a difficult task to make an almost equal division between adventure and thought."[32]

Fortunately for us, he will never quite succeed in this.[33] The dreamy nature of his heroine and the natural bent of his literary talent pull in the same direction. The nature of Flaubert's genius is such that he prefers the reflected consciousness of an event to the event itself, the dream of passion to the actual experience, lack of action and emptiness to presence. This is where Flaubert's art really comes into its own. What is most beautiful in his novels bears little resemblance to ordinary fiction. It is found not in the events—for, in his hand, they tend to crumble and disappear—but in what lies between events, those wide empty regions, the vast areas of stagnation in which no movement occurs. To succeed in charging emptiness with so much existence and substance, to conjure up such fullness out of nothing, is the miracle.[34] But this reversal has still another consequence: in an objective narrative written in the third person, it magnifies the importance of the character's point of view and stresses the optics of his "thought"—the stage on which everything that matters takes place.

Flaubert is the great novelist of inaction, of ennui, of stagnation. He didn't know it, or didn't know it clearly, until he wrote *Madame Bovary*; he found out in the process, and not without some anxiety.

In so doing, he revealed (or confirmed) what is perhaps a law of literary invention: creation implies insecurity; whatever is new disturbs, and the first gesture of the innovator is a gesture of refusal. Yet it is this hesitant and tentative inquiry that leads the innovator to his real self. He comes to know himself for what he is in the act of composing. And this confirms another law: even with as deliberate a writer as Flaubert, as convinced as he was that everything could be made a matter of plan and of conception, true invention takes place in the course of the actual writing;

the work completes its own conception in the concrete acts that make it come into being.

Notes

1. Charles Sorel (1600?–74), author of *La vraie histoire comique de Francion*, is considered to be one of the founders of the realist novel in France [Paul de Man].

2. The leading existentialist philosopher, author, and critic Jean-Paul Sartre was interested in the experiments of Nathalie Sarraute in trying to bring the novel back to a more essential reality by stripping it of conventional forms of plot, dialogue, and description. With Alain Robbe-Grillet, Nathalie Sarraute is the leading representative of the so-called "new" French novel [Paul de Man].

3. *Prétexte*, 1 (January 1958; new series): 100.

4. André Gide (1869–1951) and Virginia Woolf (1882–1941) both experimented boldly with the traditional forms of the novel, especially by juxtaposing different events and loosening the conventional narrative sequence [Paul de Man].

5. Edmond de Goncourt (1822–96) was the elder of the two Goncourt brothers, authors of naturalistic novels and of a famous journal. Jules Huret was a journalist whose interviews with prominent writers produced important documents on the history of nineteenth-century French literature [Paul de Man].

6. Jules Huret, *Enquête sur l'évolution littéraire* (Paris: Charpentier, 1891), p. 168.

7. We can go even further back in time to quote Mme de Lafayette, who describes *La Princesse de Clèves* as a non-Romanesque novel, because in it she relinquishes the trappings of earlier novels: "It contains nothing adventurous or strikingly unusual; so it is not really a novel, but rather a memoir . . ." (Letter to Lescheraine, April 13, 1678).

8. Flaubert, *Correspondance*, 9 vols., in his *Oeuvres complètes* (Paris: Conard, 1910–54), 28 vols., vols. II–X. Henceforth referred to by volume and page number only, as here: IV, 397. Letter to Amédée Pommier, September 8, 1860.

9. Flaubert, *Lettres inédites à Tourgueneff* (Monaco: Editions du Rocher, 1946), p. 15 (February 1869).

10. See, for instance, the arrival in Egypt, described by Flaubert in II, 119, 121–22. Letter to Louis Bouilhet, December 1, 1849. "I climbed to the crow's nest and saw this ancient Egypt . . ." (p. 121).

11. Gustave Flaubert, *Madame Bovary* (New York: W. W. Norton, 1965), p. 7.

12. Although Stendhal's and Flaubert's methods are entirely different and unrelated, one should consult George Blin's admirable study, *Stendhal et les problèmes du roman* (Paris: Corti, 1954), particularly the second part.

13. The pointillist technique in painting, whose main representatives were Seurat and Signac, proceeded by juxtaposing small dots in primary colors; the technique can be said to be analogous with the selection of minute details in Flaubert's description of character [Paul de Man].

14. Flaubert, *Madame Bovary. Nouvelle Version*, edited by Jean Pommier and Gabrielle Leleu (Paris: Corti, 1949), p. 166. Henceforth abbreviated "Pommier-Leleu."

15. The allusion is to an early article by Jean-Paul Sartre, entitled "M. François Mauriac et la liberté" (*Nouvelle Revue Française*, February, 1939), reprinted in Sartre's *Situations I* (Paris: Gallimard, 1947), pp. 36–57.

16. Rastignac, who appears throughout Balzac's *Human Comedy*, is the central figure in *Old Goriot* [Paul de Man].

17. In the first draft one reads at this point: "A third party, who would have observed them facing each other . . ." (Pommier-Leleu, p. 182).

18. This is beautifully analyzed by Georges Poulet in "Gustave Flaubert: The Circle and the Center," pp. 392–407 in Flaubert, *Madame Bovary* (New York: W. W. Norton, 1965).

19. Cf. for instance: "I think I made a great step forward, namely in the *imperceptible* transition from the psychological to the dramatic part . . ." (emphasis added). III, 423. Letter to Louise Colet, 1854.

20. III, 401. Letter to Louise Colet, December 18, 1853.

21. Flaubert's long-time mistress and confidante was also a poet of sorts, though certainly not of the calibre of Leconte de Lisle (1818–94), who was the leader of the Parnassian school of poetry [Paul de Man].

22. III, 92. January 29–30, 1853.

23. III, 264. Letter to Louise Colet, July 2, 1853.

24. VII, 294. Letter to George Sand, April 3, 1876.

25. *Novembre* is a 120 page-long story written in 1842, when Flaubert was 21 years old, remarkable because it already contains so many of the stylistic and thematic devices of the later master [Paul de Man].

26. A journal kept by Flaubert and his friend Maxime Du Camp during their 1847 hiking trip through the Touraine and especially through Brittany [Paul de Man].

27. *Par les champs et par les grèves, Oeuvres complètes*, XIII, 125–26 (see note 8).

28. In this passage, Flaubert had made sizeable deletions: the walk of the woman at dawn, in the park, and her prolonged contemplation of the countryside through colored window panes (Pommier-Leleu, pp. 216–17). It is a great pity that Flaubert chose to discard these passages, although, understandably enough, he considered them important. The latter is a perfect illustration of subjective vision: seen through differently colored panes, the landscape changes not only in color, but also in shape, in mood, even in structure. Emma's world will similarly be seen colored by the different shades of her passion.

29. The first draft reads: "She was going to float in the void, in order to annihilate herself . . ." (Pommier-Leleu, p. 444).

30. For a further development of these observations, see the outstanding passages in Erich Auerbach's *Mimesis* showing how it is Emma who sees, while it is the author who talks, reprinted in ["The Realism of Flaubert"], pp. 383–92 in Flaubert, *Madame Bovary* (New York: W. W. Norton, 1965).

31. III, 86. Letter to Louise Colet, January 15, 1853.

32. III, 394. Letter to Louis Bouilhet, December 10, 1853.

33. In comparing the scenarios with the final texts, one notices that, far from adding more action to his novel, Flaubert rather tends to make it sparser: in the first scenarios, Emma became Léon's mistress before embarking on the affair with Rodolphe; similarly, in the *Éducation*, he had first planned that Mme Arnoux would become Frédéric's mistress. See Marie-Jeanne Durry, *Flaubert et ses projects inédits* (Paris: Nizet, 1950), pp. 137ff.

In the first version of the *Éducation sentimentale*, Henri and Mme Renaud elope and live in exile the life of their dreams; in *Madame Bovary*, Flaubert does away with the voyage and has Emma embark only on imaginary trips; the event is replaced by the dream of the event.

34. "Nothing happens, but that nothing has become a heavy, oppressive, threatening something" (Erich Auerbach, p. 389 [see note 30]).

Flaubert's Presuppositions   Michael Riffaterre*

Intertextuality in fiction is the key to the novel's significance. The significance system consists in the relationship between the writer's idiolect and the sociolect, which latter belongs to both reader and writer. Only the writer knows the idiolect's sign system thoroughly. It is up to the reader to evaluate, categorize, and interpret this sign system by detecting its references to the sociolect, by listening to the *voix de l'autre* [voice of the other] or sorting out the *texte de l'autre* [text of the other] or *le discours social* [social discourse], in Claude Duchet's phrase, and this through, and in spite of, the idiolect's interferences.[1] In short, the reader is able to interpret the text only by way of the intertext. To my mind, the real problem is understanding what makes interpretation mandatory rather than a matter of free choice. A related problem is to find out how the reader manages to pinpoint the locus of the intertext: even if he does not accomplish this, something within the text drives him on to track down and make out the shape of the missing piece of the puzzle.

The answer, the factor that guides the reader and dictates his interpretation, seems to me to be presupposition.[2] That is to say, the implicit and requisite preceding conditions of an explicit statement. In the novel, specifically, presuppositions have explicit corollaries on the surface of the text — metonymies. These figures refer to sign complexes that they substitute for and repress, as it were, pushing them back into intertextual latency.

A quotation, for instance, may seem merely to presuppose the text it is culled from. In fact, however, it presupposes a particular use of the quotation, a context-bound quoting behavior. The quotation therefore derives the significance it has in the novel from an interpretant, halfway between the quoted text and the quoting text. This interpretant is encoded in the sociolect.

There is such a quotation in the opening scene of *Madame Bovary*. You will recall that young Charles Bovary's awkwardness has set off riotous hilarity among his new classmates. Confused and rattled, he yet cannot bring himself to part with his complicated headgear.

> "What are you looking for?" asked the master.
> "My c-c-c-cap," said the new boy shyly, . . .
> "Five hundred verses for all the class!" shouted in a furious voice, stopped, like the *Quos ego*, a fresh outburst.[3]

In *Quos ego* we recognize — or at least Flaubert's contemporaries recognized — a phrase from Vergil's *Aeneid*. The allusion is to the scene where the Winds — children of Aeolus — throw the sea into turmoil and

*From *Diacritics* 11 (1981):2–11. Reprinted by permission of the author and of the Johns Hopkins University Press.

threaten to sink the Trojan ships; Neptune rises from the briny deeps and puts an end to their mischief with these two words alone — he does not even have to complete the menacing command, *Quos ego* — just two personal pronouns: *Quos*, those who(m) and *ego*, I. Presumably, those who dare to stir up my waters, *quos*, them will I (*ego*) punish or destroy. The merest beginning of the sentence is enough to scare off the Winds. A famous example of ironhanded dominion, but above all a famous quote because it exemplifies the ultimate in rhetorical efficacy, concision triumphant, and a figure called *reticence* or *aposiopesis*. The speaker breaks off in mid-sentence: this both conveys his supposed excitement, and annihilates his hearers by hinting that what he was about to declare is too overpowering to put into words. Vergil's phrase has served imitators from Boileau and Racine down to Flaubert and beyond. The nineteenth century Larousse, however, calls attention only to the many parodies of Neptune's two-word blast, and concludes: "The *quos ego* of Neptune is the expression of supreme dissatisfaction on the part of a superior."[4]

Here, quite obviously, the quotation fits the context. Obeying typographical rules, the Latin is quoted in italics. In his provocative paper on Flaubert's manipulations of italics, Duchet seems to think this particular quote, at least, merely conforms to usage: says he, it reflects the mentality of a sort of elementary school elite, calling as it does upon the schoolboy's store of classical learning (Duchet, p. 153). But Duchet also points out that although there may be nothing here to modify any character delineation or alter its meaning, such passages do indicate that there is present in the text what has already been spoken in and by the sociolect: *une référence extra-diégétique, un hors-texte du texte, le déjà-là, le déjà-parlé de la société du roman* (Duchet, p. 151) (an extra-diegetic reference, an *hors-texte* of the text, the already-there, the already-spoken of the novel's social world). If, on the other hand, the characters *are* contaminated here by the quotation from the sociolect, they are made to look like the reality of the reality-reflection that is the sociolect, to look like a product of the sociolect. What I should like to add is that the mechanisms of the text are more complex than those of a mere literary allusion, and that they extend far beyond the passages underscored by italics.

First of all, the text here seems to do no more than quote Vergil. If that were all there was to it, the presupposition would be the same as in Vergil — a threat so dread it works without having to be fully pronounced. We should have a parody, a spoofing translation of a classroom scene into epic code. It would have to be interpreted as Flaubert's own joke, and diversely evaluated: an idle jest, perhaps, perhaps a heavyhanded one. This would only confirm the disquiet of those readers who think this introduction does not quite fit the novel, that it is a sort of weakening, a sudden show of vulnerability in an objective author who wishes to remain invisible but is betrayed by a moving memory from his own childhood rather than his hero's.

But what is quoted here is the quotation of a quotation, another text that includes the Vergil quotation as one of its own constituents. And within this other text the Vergil quotation is already one of the text's stereotyped components, a component whose meaning is governed not by the Vergilian meaning but by the quotation's role in a new representation. The quotation is thus not a sign standing for pedantry. It is already part and parcel of a stereotyped portrait of the schoolteacher as figure of fun. In the collection of satiric vignettes, *Les Français peints par eux-mêmes* (published with Gavarni and Henri Monnier illustrations in 1840), there is one *monographie*[5] on *Le maître d'études* where the harried teacher's uniform formulae are signs of the social outcast's sole claim to superiority: his status of classroom tyrant. The *monographie*'s words seem to have dictated Flaubert's passage: "God knows what prodigious quantity of imitations of the famous *quos ego* he performed calling to order *The first person who talks.* . . . and he stops, sure of its effect; or equally, *a hundred lines* and he does not name the one he means to warn, so that thanks to this adroit reticence each student sees the formidable hundred lines of verse suspended above his head."[6]

Note *reticence*, the very name of the trope supremely exemplified ever since Quintilian by *quos ego* (Quintilian, *De institutione oratoria,* 9.2.54). The description of the teacher and his suspense strategy are both derived from the definition of the trope. Nothing could be clearer than that the system determining both descriptive and narrative sequences is discursive, verbal, rather than referential. Thus Flaubert's quotation is quoting not Vergil but the descriptive system of the word *teacher,* one of whose components is borrowed from Vergil. Further, this system is not just a fragment of discourse, a prefabricated text: it is composed of elements already marked. In our particular case they are already comical so that the reader reads into Flaubert an embedded semiotic system. Whence a different interpretation. *Quos ego* is not a questionable joke of Flaubert's, but a faithful rendition of a kind of score well established in language, a score whose accuracy as representation is therefore guaranteed by the sociolect. Far from being *hors d'oeuvre,* the scene is an overture, for this score actualizes a structure that is to inform significance of the novel again and again throughout its length.

Significance flows from the defeat of Neptune himself, defeat of his all-powerful trope by the weakest of adversaries, by the innocent bumble-bee of a boy, a well-meaning kid named Charles. The boy is turned thereby into the epitome of the spoiler, of the square peg in the round hole. And the farcical clincher here is the tyrant's overthrow by this hapless David of the classroom: the teacher has to mop his brow — gesture of the harassed boss undone by the naïvest underdog in so many low comedies, of the big cat of animated cartoons undone by a puny mouse.

What the quotation presupposes is an intertext of a norm. What it entails is a sequence of variations on Charles' perennial contradiction: innocence and destructiveness; the sequence in which the future Charles is to bungle the surgery that was to establish his fame, irritate his wife most acutely whenever he tries hardest to please her, at his every step produce the reverse of what he intends — the misery of well-intentioned negativity.

The italics merely point to words whose presuppositions enable the reader to make the connection between text and intertext. But these italics are by no means necessary for the presupposition to be perceived or for the connection to be made: at most they are a deixis of interpretation, somewhat akin to the *points d'ironie* [irony marks] that Balzac aspired to introduce into the typographical arsenal. But irony is only a special intertextual case. More generally, metonymy, as I have suggested, is the connecting link between novel and intertext: the instant the reader grasps the fact that the metonym is a fragment, a fraction therefore presupposing a whole, metonymy becomes a reference to the complex to which it owes its meaning, that is, a descriptive system either available to our linguistic competence, or actualized within another text.

Let us verify this by the system most central to *Madame Bovary*, the representation(s) of the adulteress. This representation might be studied as a theme. The thematic approach, however, cannot tell us why a given actualization of a theme is effective and convincing. Whereas presupposition offers an explanation, since it is by presupposing that a verbal sequence compels the reader to compare text and intertext. Presupposition creates a logical need for gap-filling. The intertext that responds to this need actualizes the semes of a kernel word, first in the shape of a sentence, then as a system of representations. Everything, in the system organized around this verbal nucleus, derives from the single matrix sentence. Instead of trying to hypothesize the matrix, I will apply this moral pronouncement of Proudhon (entered under *adultère* in the first volume of Larousse, published in 1866, nine years after the novel): *l'adultère est un crime qui contient en soi tous les autres* [adultery is a crime which in itself contains all others]. No phrasing could be apter for generating the descriptive system in question here; the whole novel can be shown to derive from that system. It is significant that one initial nudge should set in motion the entire causal concatenation, from one single transgression on through all species of disorders, to the final ineluctable retribution. That one lone transgression should suffice demonstrates the power of one lone taboo: no woman shall be free. The weakness of her sex makes it necessary that she be held in connubial bondage: once unshackled, the wife must and will fall prey to the evil temptations her nature makes her incapable of resisting. There is no incident in the long chain of events that is not contained in the very kernel of the system. Once again, I shall quote from *Les Français peints par eux-mêmes*, this time from a piece on *la femme adultère* (1841). The essay offers what looks like an exhaustive catalogue of all possible choices the adulteress may make in the course of her shady career. The author is one Hippolyte Lucas, a forgettable writer whose very anonymity seems to make him the voice of the sociolect: *"Adultery! . . . a word which is rarely pronounced, even these days, when the thing is so wide-spread, and one that is even taken as a sign of ill-breeding, but that we may be allowed to use. This word, the despair of worldly people, ought to gratify etymologists. No expression better conveys its idea. Adultery comes from a Latin verb that signifies alter, and nothing in fact more alters things and feelings* [*Les Français*, vol. 3, p. 265].

Nothing could be clearer: one word's ultimate presupposition, its etymology, entails the whole fictional text. Our spokesman for society expatiates: *Once started down this tortuous path, a woman cannot stop herself* (p. 267). A further rule must be observed if the system's well-oiled wheels and cogs are to get going: the deduction of entailment from presupposition must be exemplary. Opposition or distance between the two poles of this diegesis must therefore always tend towards a maximum polarization: hence the *monographie's* insistence that the first fatal step leads inevitably to the last fatal leap. These inseparable and complementary poles thus set the limits of the fictional space extending from an imaginary or metaphorical transgression (wicked thoughts nurtured by immoral and forbidden readings) to the most definitive of all actual or literal transgressions — the one that drags the heroine out of existence, and out of the text, simultaneously putting an end to what can be lived or to what can be told in words. The adulteress either commits suicide or sinks into prostitution. As for the first metaphorical step, I might call it fictional without any play on words, since the errant wife is stepping out of bounds when she secretly indulges in the reading of scandalous novels and in a daydreaming identification with the women who slink about the Never-Neverland of wish-fulfillment. This peculiar susceptibility to the printed word is perhaps more generally assumed to be an attribute of Woman, rather than just Adulteress: throughout the Romantic era, a woman is one who reads novels as a substitute for active living; she regresses into moral and legal minority the moment she marries. I hardly need point out that *Madame Bovary* is a fiction about the dangers of fiction.

A second presupposition of *adulteress* is a negative husband: he must be a good man, good as a human being (otherwise if he were bad, his badness would mitigate his victimization by the wife); but he must be a frustrating mate: *La faute (de l'adultère) en est . . . à l'imbécillité des maris* (Ibid.) (The blame for the adultery lies . . . with the imbecility of husbands). *Imbécillité* here may be taken in extreme cases in its strong primary acceptation. What is implied, then, is that the husband is sexually inadequate. This failure unleashes the female predispositions that are as much a presupposition of the word *woman* as is her vulnerability to reading: *Woman, thy name is Lasciviousness*. If the husband plays an aging David to her young Abishag, or an Abelard to her Heloise, as our essayist puts it metaphorically, then the husbandless bride will *cut the Gordian knot with Alexander's sword* (p. 269). The full weight of implicitness charging these images with innuendo, the pent-up power packed into the presupposition is palpable. Now I realize that this version of the frustrating male is not the one Flaubert selected. Charles does have what it takes to keep his female satisfied, if only she would give him a chance. But the point is that so strong is the presupposition of Woman's natural lubricity, *any* frustration at all will set it off. The more general ill consequence entailed by the husband's presupposed deficiency is *ennui*. Boredom, we know, and its other face—the vision of escape—*is* the solution Flaubert chose.

The result is the detailed and suspense-laden actualization of this essential seme of woman: her unbridled sexuality. Witness the *monographie* ticking off the stages in the progress of the disease, from *femme sensible* (one lover) to *femme galante* (more than one). Ill repute forces the victim "to go hide her shame in some great city where for lack of any natural support she ends by lowering herself to the condition of a kept woman [*une femme entretenue*]" (more than one lover, plus financial backing) (p. 267). And then the grand finale: "unless suicide triumphs over prostitution."[7]

The intensifying drive of the salacity sequence best testifies to the generative power of presupposition: the steps traced in the *monographie* prefigure Emma's descent into Hell. First, a sense of shame, or of anxiety: in Emma's case, the silent witness of the drafts, and in the printed version, the dismal sounds that scare her, following her first tryst with Rodolphe. Then the rapid development in Emma of a brazen, Machiavellian (the *monographie*'s very word) (p. 265) gift for dissembling: she weaves all sorts of lies and pretexts for getting off to Rouen. And finally, the lurid apotheosis: "this divinity of the household will be transformed into a dishevelled bacchante, while her husband consumes his days and nights in long work so that she can have a decent existence; she will give herself over to the prodigal joys of the courtesan" (p. 266).

I will not labor the point by quoting the scene where our Yonville Messalina disrobes in a rage of sexual frenzy, with her girdle-laces whistling like serpents—a revealingly "mad" hyperbole. What proves the existence of a model, a paradigm, is the sexual rewrite of the extreme unction scene, where the dying Emma kisses the image of Christ in an unambiguous climax—a translation into sexual code of the ultimate pathological consequences flowing from the initial given. Similarly, another "sick" end product of intertextual presupposition, Balzac's old miser Grandet on his deathbed grabbing the golden crucifix, translates into *greed* code the accelerating-fall structure.

I cannot emphasize enough how powerful the logic of entailments is, how necessary the complete unfolding of the sequence of tragic aftereffects following upon the adulteress's transgression. So necessary, indeed, that the rejected alternative, the prostitution ending, refuses to go away altogether. It hovers about, but with the suspense of the choice rejected, the temptation spurned. Hence a partial re-heroization of the fallen heroine. I am thinking of how Emma calls to the *notaire* for help, and of the ambiguous last interview with Binet (a scene without ambiguity when read by a witness like Madame Tuvache).[8] Better still some readers are so alive to the lure of the more melodramatic outcome, that they improve on Flaubert: the *Madame Bovary* entry in Larousse's *Grand dictionnaire* (1867) cannot resist playing out the alternative unactualized by the novel. The suicide is appropriate, but it makes the denouement too physical, that is, "too true to realism," realism being misunderstood as a preference for material description exclusive of moral considerations. The dictionary goes on to offer a rewrite of the denouement: "instead of poison, shame was necessary. Madame Bovary . . . ought to have dragged out the rest of her days working the banal corner of some disreputable block."[9]

Thus do the entailment paradigms operate to contaminate the entire text they produce. Consequently the text does not come to a finish until after every component of the descriptive and narrative complex has been affected. So with the final result of the alteration implicit in the word *adultery*, or in its etymology (again, when I say "etymology," I am referring to a meaning to be found elsewhere, a semantic key to the text, retrievable in the intertext of the kernel word's origin, an interpretation of discourse to be provided by the intertext of another language). Adulteration presupposes the presence of a purity to be destroyed. The purity topically ascribed to the married woman, her sanctity as a mother, this purity is that of the family of which she is the priestess. By her act, then, she destroys what in her keeping was holiest, the children. Sometimes she gets herself an abortion "happy . . . if the womb that bears them does not become their tomb"; but if she lets them live, she ignores them: "the same indifference, the same neglect rules over all," (*Les Français*, p. 266) and the unfortunate progeny are handed over to the grudging care of a nurse. Which scenario, as we know, Emma Bovary follows to the letter.

This need for the derivation to be exhaustive in order to be exemplary, this need for the text not to stop until the last consequences have been drawn, only this need can satisfactorily explain why a novel ostensibly about Emma Bovary should go on long after she is dead and buried, and go on not to relieve those she has wronged but to extinguish them.[10] Charles and her daughter are not secondary characters, they are her corollaries, the victims crime presupposes, the spoilable objects an exemplary corruption demands. This is the satisfactory explanation, because it rests upon the generative power of the entailment; the ending must be complementary or corollary to the beginning.

The text's saturation by the enthymeme-like descriptive system, the text's paranoia, we might say, is the narrative aspect of the presupposition's semiotic process. At the descriptive level the process results in a uniform marking of such words in the text as are also words of the system: this marking reflects their value, their symbolism, for instance, within the system. A change does occur, however; within the system these words are metonymic of the kernel lexeme, of the presupposing lexeme. In the text, on the contrary, they are free of the grammatical constraints imposed upon them by the system, and free of their kernel-lexeme metonymy: they become its metaphors. Take the celebrated *fiacre*, for example. This hackney coach is not of Flaubert's invention, it is a prop borrowed from the adulteress system: honesty in a wife presupposes she has no secrets from her husband and so she is at liberty to use his carriage and horses as she pleases. Infidelity calls for secrecy and requires a cabman who does not know her. Our *monographie* pictures *le fiacre aux stores baissés* [the carriage with blinds drawn] carrying her to her clandestine rendezvous. This *fiacre* cancels out the meaning of the family-conveyance and posits intrigue; in fact it is so well established as a metonym of wifely treason that when Balzac's virtuous Mme Jules takes a hackney in *Ferragus*, she is at once convicted of infidelity in the eyes of an observer [Balzac, *La Comédie humaine*, Pléiade, vol. 5, p. 23]. The use of the *fiacre* in Flaubert is certainly much more serious or more to the point: to transform a vehicle *to* sin into a vehicle *of* sin is to go way beyond the sociolect. As far as literary scandal is concerned, the scene we are bound to imagine going on inside fully explains why *La Revue de Paris* dropped the episode from the serial publication of the novel.[11] But what I contend is that it might not have occurred to Flaubert to use a hansom cab as a kind of *maison du berger* of illicit love, had it not been for the preliminary marking of *fiacre* as a metonym of adultery. Above all, this marking protects the reader against the temptation to question the verisimilitude of the whole pro-tracted encounter; as a vehicle it may not be very practical for committing the act in; as a word it extends the adultery isotopy on into the descriptive code. As a word *fiacre* translates into urban discourse, into the discourse of an urban setting (*Cela se fait à Paris* [It's done in Paris], says Léon, more aptly than he may intend), the rustic metaphor for dalliance that riding-into-the-woods with Rodolphe constitutes. *Aller se promener au bois* [take a ride in the woods] and *prendre le fiacre* [take the cab] are for a woman cliché metaphors for having an affair.

Now, what I have just said about markings and metaphorical trans-fers applies as well to symbols: we feel, for instance, that there is more to certain key episodes than meets the eye; but linear reading does not yield a satisfactory meaning. We fail to grasp their symbolic significance unless we make a detour through the intertext. Presuppositions then lead us on to the correct interpretation.

During Emma's death agony, a blind beggar appears: a case in point. Critics all agree he is symbolic, but they do not agree of what: Fate,

Damnation, Hell, or quite simply Reality.[12] For anyone in Emma's predicament, they are synonymous anyway. The particular significance of the beggar's song is more opaque:

> Often the heat of a summer's day
> Makes a young girl dream her heart away.

Emma raised herself like a galvanised corpse, her hair streaming, her eyes fixed, staring.

> To gather up all the new-cut stalks
> Of wheat left by the scythe's cold swing.
> Nanette bends over as she walks
> Towards the furrows from where they spring.

"The blind man!" she cried.
And Emma began to laugh, an atrocious, frantic, desperate laugh, thinking she saw the hideous face of the poor wretch loom out of the eternal darkness like a menace.

> The wind blew very hard that day
> It blew her petticoat away.

A final spasm threw her back upon the mattress. They all drew near. She had ceased to exist [p. 238].

Years ago D. L. Demorest (in *L'Expression figurée dans l'oeuvre de Flaubert* [Geneva: Slatkine reprints, 1931] pp. 466–69) suggested that the song symbolizes, word by word, step by step, the course of Emma's life and demise. He did not say just how. I propose to read it as a metaphor of Emma's degradation: a sexual one and therefore most apt. The position of the short-skirted girl is explicit: prone, hence revealing, a commonplace of voyeurism. The tricks of the wind are also explicit; they expose the girl's flesh, play the role of sexual aggressor. An ironic image and one with many salacious variants in folksongs about catching girls in the bushes or rolling them in the hay. Now the obscenity of the gesture presupposes that a skirt is not for lifting, while the skirt presupposes the woman. The decent woman is one whose skirt is unliftable; in skirt code, sexuality is skirt-lifting, and the metonym for a loose woman is a liftable skirt. All points well exemplified in French *gauloiserie*.

Now recollect that the first time Emma hears the song, it is quoted "Often the warmth of a summer day / Makes a young girl dream her heart away. / And all the rest was about birds and sunshine and green leaves" [p. 193]. An incomplete quotation, a summary far from accurate, a misleading paraphrase of the complete text. But that was before the Fall, before the first lover, before the fatal first misstep. Now we know the real text, the literal truth. Emma knows, she laughs bitterly, and dies. My interpretation: there are two readings of a song symbolizing Emma in her own eyes (and inviting the reader to see her as she sees herself). The first, the innocent reading, is Emma fantasizing, Emma wallowing in the idealized love affairs detailed for her in silly *romans pour dames*. The second reading, postlapsarian, a metatext of the prostitution denouement, gives us sex despoiled of its sublimations, a stark depiction of the heroine as slut: in brief, the coarse carnality no longer hidden behind the veil of self-delusion, or if you prefer, a *roman réaliste*. Any possible reservations about my *skirt* presuppositions would surely give way if I could produce a virtuous *unliftability* intertext presupposed by the sinful liftability. Well, I can. Better still, my proof comes equipped with the kind of stylistic features that demonstrate that no reader can help noticing its import and that the writer, or first reader, was well aware of the potentialities of the *text vs. intertext* polarization. My evidence is the phrase *jupe insoulevable* [unliftable skirt]: *insoulevable* is one of Flaubert's rare coinages, if not his only one — and he would not have departed from the sociolect's accepted lexicon without good reason. What is more, the phrase occurs in a passage of *L'Éducation sentimentale* that stands in direct semiotic opposition to our death scene: the meeting between Frédéric and Madame Arnoux in the country. Here is his best opportunity to bed her at last, but the lady's chastity remains impregnable: "This dress, blending with the shadows, seemed huge to him, infinite, unliftable; and precisely because of that his desire redoubled."[13] Then Madame Arnoux reminds him she is another man's wife. Curtain. I could not have dreamed up a neater symmetry [liftable/unliftable] nor could I have dreamed up a more perfect moral correspondence: metonymy for the wife who resists temptation to unfaithfulness: [huge dress . . . unliftable]; metonymy for the wife who falls: [a petticoat that blows away].

This on metonymy, brings me back to my opening remarks. Significance, that is, the text seen as one signifying unit (as opposed to meaning, where such units are infratextual — lexical or phrastic), significance depends upon the presuppositions contained in certain words. These words are metonymic (they function *like* metonyms: for example, they are quotations; or they *are* metonyms). The role of metonymy in the novel is well recognized as far as its diegetic and descriptive functions are concerned: metonymies transform *topoi* into a narrative, and metonymies are the raw material of mimesis, especially of realism.

We still have to find out how metonymy is able to turn into metaphor or symbol — an apparent paradox. The answer, I suggest, is to differentiate semantic and semiotic, meaning and significance. In the linearity of the text, in the verbal sequence, metonymy remains metonymic: that is its meaning. Its significance, contrariwise, shows itself in the intertextual reference: metonymy becomes the substitute for the intertext, thus assuming the symbolic function.

Notes

1. Claude Duchet, "Discours social et texte italique dans *Madame Bovary*" in *Langages de Flaubert*, ed. Michael Issacharoff (Paris: Minard, 1976), pp. 143–63; cf. Duchet's "Significance et in-signifiance: Le Discours italique dans *Madame Bovary*" in *La Production du sens chez Flaubert*, ed. Claudine Gothot-Mersch (Paris: Union Générale d'Éditions, 1975), pp. 358–78.

2. See Jonathan Culler, "Presupposition and Intertextuality," *Modern Language Notes* 91 (1976): 1380–96; Marc Angenot, "Présupposé, topos, idéologème," *Etudes françaises* 13, nos. 1–2 (1977): 11–34; Michael Riffaterre, "La Trace de l'intertexte," *La Pensée* 215 (1980): 4–18.

3. *Madame Bovary*, ed. and trans. Paul de Man (New York: Norton, 1965), p. 3. Translations of *Madame Bovary* are from this edition and will be referred to in the text by page number. Other translations are my own. Vergil *Aeneid* 1.135 is quoted; on the structure of quotation, see Antoine Compagnon, *La Seconde Main* (Paris: Seuil, 1979), 49–92.

4. Pierre Larousse, *Grand Dictionnaire universel du dix-neuvième siècle*, s.v., "*quos ego*," vol. 13 [1875].

5. *Monographie* was the French nineteenth-century literary genre also known as *physiologie*; see Fritz Nies, *Genres mineurs: Texte zur Theorie und Geschichte nichtkanonischer Literatur* (Munich: Wilhelm Fink, 1978), pp. 111–12.

6. Eugène Nyon, "Le Maître d'école," in *Les Français peints par eux-mêmes*, preface by Jules Janin, 8 vols. (Paris, L. Curmer, 1840), 1:339. The collection includes pieces by Balzac, Théophile Gautier, Charles Nodier, and others reprinted from various periodicals.

7. In Eugène Sue's *La Famille Jouffroy* (1854), a noble countess, first unfaithful, at the last a common drunken whore murdered in a brothel, exemplifies the alternative solution. Emma may have been spared simply because Flaubert preferred to maintain the provincial setting. Cf. Mlle Leroyer de Chantepie, Flaubert's epistolary confidant, who, despite her feminism, writes of Emma: "She must either become a courtesan or die" (26 February 1857, in Flaubert, *Correspondance*, 2 vols., ed. J. Bruneau [Paris: Pléiade, 1973], 2:686).

8. *Madame Bovary*, p. 223 (" 'Women like that ought to be whipped,' said Madame Tuvache").

9. Cf. Alfred August Cuvillier-Fleury's review of the novel, quoted in René Dumesnil's edition of *Madame Bovary*, 2 vols. (Paris: Belles-Lettres, 1945), 1:clxvi.

10. Critics have suggested that the novel goes on because it actually focuses on Homais and the triumph of mediocrity (e.g., Victor Brombert, *The Novels of Flaubert* [Princeton, N.J.: Princeton University Press, 1966], pp. 89–90; R. J. Sherrington, *Three Novels of Flaubert* [Oxford: Oxford University Press, Clarendon Press, 1970], p. 143).

11. See the references to the episode during the Flaubert trial: Dumesnil, ed., *Madame Bovary*, 2:219, 250.

12. See P. M. Wetherill, "Madame Bovary's Blind Man: Symbolism in Flaubert," *Romanic Review* 61 (1970): 35–42; and, completed by M. Aprile, "L'Aveugle et sa signification dans *Madame Bovary*," *Revue d'Histoire littéraire de la France* 76 (1976): 385–92.

13. *L'Éducation sentimentale*, ed. René Dumesnil. 2 vols. (Paris: Les Belles Lettres, 1942), Part 2, Chapter 3: vol. 1, p. 254.

Salammbô

Flaubert and the Question
of History

Eugenio Donato*

One of the most striking characteristics of Flaubert criticism is the uneven way in which it has treated his various works, practically dividing the corpus of his writings in two. On the one hand, there are works which have attracted a relatively inordinate amount of attention, namely *Madame Bovary* and *L'Éducation sentimentale,* which are supposed to illustrate, according to a myth initiated by the naturalists but rejected by Flaubert, the latter's "Realism." On the other hand, there are *Salammbô, La Tentation de saint Antoine,* and *Bouvard et Pécuchet,* neglected by the critics in spite of Flaubert's conceiving *Salammbô* in dialectical opposition to *Madame Bovary,* his claim that the *Tentation* was his life work and finally the importance he gave to *Bouvard et Pécuchet,* his last and unfinished work. Among the many consequences of this division of the Flaubertian corpus, not the least significant is the classification of *Salammbô* and the *Tentation* as romantic works exemplifying Flaubert's hapless quest for a temporal as well as a spatial exoticism. Such a classification makes Flaubert's so-called "realism" a self-fulfilling prophecy, for it generates an opposition whereby *Madame Bovary* and *L'Éducation sentimentale* are novels of a successful mimetic "here and now," while the *Tentation* and *Salammbô* represent their author's misconceived quest for an exotic "there and then." It is through the explicit or implicit acceptance of this dichotomy that *Salammbô,* from Sainte-Beuve to Lukács and beyond, came to be treated as an "historical novel," and the problems of history with respect to the texts of Flaubert came to be localized upon that single novel. In this paper I shall argue that the opposition between a Flaubert centered upon a contemporary reality and a Flaubert in quest of an exotic bygone Orient is untenable, and that if there is a problem of "history" with regard to *Salammbô,* that same problem touches upon Flaubert's total literary production.

In spite of their irreducibly divergent esthetic and critical ideologies, Sainte-Beuve's and Lukác's objections to *Salammbô* are remarkably simi-

*From *MLN* 91 (1976):850–70. Reprinted by permission of the Johns Hopkins University Press.

lar. Both reproach Flaubert's novel with being simultaneously *too* exotic and *too* contemporary. The reproach is always one of excess: on the one hand Flaubert has chosen a subject that is too oriental and too archeological; on the other, his main characters, and in particular the character of Salammbô, resemble too closely contemporary characters and heroines of romantic novels.

For Sainte-Beuve, if the historical novels implied, by definition, the "re-creation" of a past, such a past should not be temporally or spatially too remote from their author; hence, for the French critic, Walter Scott was writing about the Scottish middle ages from a privileged position not granted to Flaubert writing about Carthage in antiquity: "Walter Scott, the master and the true founder of the historical novel, lived in his Scotland, [only] a few centuries, a few generations away from the events and characters he traced for us with so much life and verisimilitude,"[1] whereas in Flaubert's novel, "There is, between it [Antiquity] and us — an abyss. Scholarship, which can bridge that gulf, at the same time dampens and kills our enthusiasm. . . . You can reconstitute Antiquity, but you can't bring it back to life" (p. 435). The subject matter of *Salammbô*, as well as its geographical setting, are in fact so remote that Sainte-Beuve claims to fail to understand how anybody could possibly be interested by them: "How do you expect me to get interested in that lost war, buried among the passes or the sands of Africa. . . . What do *I* care about the duel between Tunis and Carthage? Tell me about the duel between Carthage and Rome, that's another matter! I pay attention to it, I get involved" (p. 437). Yet for Sainte-Beuve, if the subject matter of the novel deals with a war far too remote to be of interest to the nineteenth-century reader, the main protagonist is on the contrary too contemporary; in opposition to the archeological setting of the novel the character of Salammbô is "a sentimental Elvire who has one foot in the Sacré-Coeur" (p. 417).[2]

Lukác's critique is close enough to Sainte-Beuve's to puzzle the reader into asking himself what might be the function, here, of Lukác's Marxist epistemology, which does not seem to displace the formulation of the problem left to us by Sainte-Beuve. For Lukács too, the novel remains a "frozen, lunar landscape of archeological precision"; as for Salammbô herself, she provides ". . . a heightened image, a decorative symbol, of the hysterical longings and torments of middle-class girls in large cities. History simply provided a decorative, monumental setting for this hysteria, which in the present spends itself in petty and ugly scenes, and which thus acquired a tragic aura quite out of keeping with its real character. The effect is powerful but it shows that Flaubert, because of his embitterment with the shallow prose of his time, had become objectively untruthful and distorted the real proportions of life."[3]

The nature of both Sainte-Beuve's and Lukác's objections is easy to perceive. Both in fact assume a purely mimetic view of narrative; both assume that the function of literature is to represent a "reality" and hence to be "true." It matters little that Sainte-Beuve expects the novel to represents what he calls "soul," "nature," "life" — "There is something you call the soul of a work" (p. 429); ". . . if everything you describe were true, copied after nature, I would become interested in it . . ." (p. 437); "Let us return to life, to what is in the domain and within reach of all, to what our age desires the most and which can move it sincerely or enchant it" (p. 442) — and that the Marxist critic wishes the novel to represent "the real social-historical and human driving force" which is the cause of conflict, or human motives which "spring organically out of a concrete social-historical basis" (Lukács, p. 148). What both Sainte-Beuve and Lukács expect and demand from fiction is the presence in representation of what each considers to be an "ultimate reality"; the objects may be different, but not the metaphysical imperative for fiction to obliterate representation by placing in front of the reader something other than itself. In the last analysis, both the romantic Sainte-Beuve and the Marxist Lukács criticize Flaubert in the name of the same metaphysics.

That Sainte-Beuve's and Lukács's critiques are similar and stem from the same metaphysics of presence[4] with respect to fiction is made all the more evident by the fact that basically Flaubert did not deny Sainte-Beuve's charges but rather their pertinence. He admits that his novel is a mixture of old and new: "God knows how far I carried scruples regarding documentation, primary sources, interviews, journeys, etc. . . . Well, I consider all that as quite secondary and subordinate. Material truth (or what people identify as such) should be no more than a springboard that helps you to rise higher. Do you think I'm dumb enough to be convinced that I created a genuine reproduction of Carthage in *Salammbô*, and an exact picture of Alexandrianism in *Saint Anthony*? Not at all! But I'm sure of having expressed the *ideal* people have of them today,"[5] and in his answer to Sainte-Beuve he states, "*I* wanted to seize hold of a *mirage* by applying the devices of the modern novel to Antiquity."[6] Flaubert's insistence in his reply to Sainte-Beuve on the authenticity of the archeological background of *Salammbô* is in the same vein as his answer to Froehner, who had questioned its exactitude. But for Flaubert one must not confuse the fictional aspects of the novel with their antiquarian underpinnings; the "material truth" is quite distinct from the "devices of the modern novel," and their conjunction produces not the presentation of a "reality" but the transcription of a mirage. If fiction in Flaubert's expression is a mirage, it does represent "something," but the metaphysical status of that which is represented, both as object and as presence, is at best dubious. Flaubert admits also that the character of Salammbô does not represent an authentic Carthaginian woman, but then insists that nobody could represent one because it is impossible to know an Oriental woman. On the other hand, Salammbô does not represent a contemporary type of woman either, but a type best examplified by Saint Theresa: "As for my heroine, I'm not defending her. According to you she resembles "a sentimental Elvire," a Velléda, a Madame Bovary. Not at all! Velléda is active, intelligent, European. Madame Bovary is driven by manifold passions; Salammbô, on the contrary, is fixated on a single obsession. She's a maniac, a kind of Saint Theresa. Never mind! I'm not so sure she's real; for neither I, nor you, nor anyone, no ancient and no modern, can know the woman of the East, for the reason that it's impossible to keep company with her" (S / G, p. 356). Salammbô, then, is either pure surface, pure representation, or, if she represents "something," that "something" is, again, neither ancient nor modern, neither Oriental nor nineteenth-century French. If we are to accept Flaubert's characterization of his novel we can better understand the perplexity and irritation of both the romantic and the Marxist critics faced with Salammbô. The nature of representation brought into play by the novel is not simply one of presence and identity, its textual surface does not dissolve in front of a simple "reality"; what shimmers behind the mirage, both the archeology and the feminine typology, escapes the possibility of being simply identified with either Carthage or nineteenth-century France as epistemological objects.

For both Sainte-Beuve and Lukács, then, the nature of representation in Salammbô is problematical. The Carthaginians are too distant to be "real," the Orient too exotic to be "real," Salammbô too contemporary to be "real." The insistence of both critics on a metaphysically rooted epistemology stops both of them short from asking what might have been a far more pertinent question, namely, why did Flaubert choose Carthage and the Orient? Instead of insisting on the question of what Carthage and the Orient represent, they might have displaced their inquiry to the question of what Carthage and the Orient could signify for the nineteenth-century author of Salammbô.

If it is a commonplace to state that Flaubert had a need to pursue a quest for exoticism as a reaction to what he considered to be the drab reality he portrayed in Madame Bovary, more rarely is the question asked as to what constitutes a possible otherness to his actual environment, or, more generally, what form such an escape might take. In a temporal context, for example, it is not the Carthage of the Punic Wars that appears to be for Flaubert the ideal period to live in, but perhaps the Rome of the Empire. In a letter to Louise Colet, for example, he writes: "What I wouldn't give to see a Triumph, what I wouldn't sell in order to enter Suburre some evening when the torches were burning at the doors of the brothels and tamborines thundering in the taverns! As if our past wasn't enough for us we ruminate on that of all humanity and we delight in that sensuous bitterness. After all, so what! That's the only place you could live! That's the only place you could think of without scorn and pity!"[7] More specifically, in a letter to Alfred Le Poittevin he writes:

I've reread Michelet's *Roman History*. — No, Antiquity makes me dizzy. I lived in Rome, surely, in the time of Caesar or Nero. — Have you sometimes thought about an evening Triumph when the legions were returning, perfumes smoking around the victor's chariot, captive kings walking behind, and then that old circus! That's where one has to live, you see. That's the only place you can get air and you get a chestful, of that poetic air, like on a high mountain, so much that your heart pounds. Ah! One day I'll drink a snoutful of Sicily and Greece. Will you be with me then when I tell you: old man, buy your rifle and order a light vest from your tailor, will you answer: let's go and long live the Muse."[8]

Before proceeding any further, a remark is in order. From the last quote it should be apparent that Flaubert's nostalgia for a given antiquity cannot be dismissed as simple exoticism. Antiquity belongs to a complex metaphorical network which has, among other functions, that of metaphorically staging Flaubert's own act of writing. In the letter to Alfred Le Poittevin, the quest for antiquity is presented as equivalent to a quest for altitude. I have shown elsewhere that the quest for altitude is a spatial metaphor for a quest for an absolute difference which would make a textually unmediated representation possible. I have also tried to show how the quest for altitude and difference has to fail, and how for Flaubert the quest for altitude has to end in spatial mediocrity, the metaphorical characteristic of the nineteenth-century prose writer, for whom representation has of necessity to be a textually mediated operation.[9] The temporal quest for antiquity is in fact analogous to the spatial quest for altitude: "What makes figures from Antiquity so beautiful is that they were original: that's everything, to derive from oneself. Nowadays, how much study you have to undergo to free yourself from books, and how much you have to read! You have to drink in oceans and piss them out again."[10] In another letter he writes:

> What artists we would be if we had never read anything except what was beautiful, never seen anything except what was beautiful, never loved anything except what was beautiful; if some angel watching over the purity of our pen had from the beginning put us out of reach of harmful relationships, if we had never spent time with imbeciles or newspapers! The Greeks had all that. They were in a *visual* setting that nothing can restore. But it's insane to try to step into their shoes. In the North you don't need short tunics, but fur overcoats. The forms of Antiquity do not suffice for our needs and our voice is not made to sing those simple tunes. Let's be as artistic as they, if we can, but differently from them. The human consciousness has broadened since Homer's day. Sancho Panza's belly is making Venus' girdle split.[11]

Let us note in passing how the temporal opposition of antiquity and modernism is isomorphic to the spatial opposition of a southern Orient and a northern Europe. The nostalgia for antiquity, then, is a nostalgia for an absolutely original, unmediated form of writing.

This, of course, is not the case for either the Carthage of *Salammbô* or the Egypt of *La Tentation de saint Antoine*. Between them and Flaubert stand the archeological museum and the library of erudition, and it is only through the Museum and the Library that the modern writer can have access to them. The writing of *Salammbô* and *La Tentation de saint Antoine* is for Flaubert a conscious and willed textual operation, rather than a quest for exoticism. It is, then, in relation to the metaphoric networks which they emblematize that we must try to situate the temporal and spatial characteristics of Egypt and Carthage.

Usually Polybius is quoted as the main historical source for *Salammbô*, and no doubt with regard to the plot of the novel that is exact; yet Polybius is really the result of a choice on Flaubert's part, and it is in Michelet, his other source, that we stand a better chance of finding what had attracted him to Carthage in the first place.

For Michelet the confrontation between Rome and Carthage is first and foremost a war of Races, and in that war one of the races will be obliterated:

> It's not without reason that the memory of the Punic Wars has remained so popular and so alive in the memory of men. That struggle was to decide not only the fate of two towns or of two empires; it was a question of knowing to which of the two races, Indo-Germanic or Semitic, would fall the mastery of the world. . . . On one side, the heroic spirit, that of art and legislation; on the other, the spirit of industry, navigation, commerce. Everywhere these two enemy races met and attacked each other. In the primordial history of Persia or Chaldea, heroes ceaselessly do battle with their industrious, perfidious neighbors. The latter are artisans, blacksmiths, miners, magicians. They love gold, blood, pleasure. They erect titanically ambitious towers, hanging gardens, magical palaces, which the warriors' swords scatter and erase from the earth. The struggle recurs along all the coasts of the Mediterranean, between the Phoenicians and the Greeks. Everywhere the latter take over the counting-houses and colonies of their rivals in the East, as the Romans will do in the West. Great Carthage remained, an empire far more powerful than the Phoenicians'; Rome annihilated it. Then something was seen unique in history, an entire civilization vanishing at a stroke, like a falling star."[12]

What characterizes the Carthaginians is the fact that they are an impure race, wherein sexual and genealogical differences are abolished: "That impure race, fleeing before Sesostris' sword or the exterminating dagger of the Jews, found itself backed up against the sea, and took the sea as its homeland. Only the unbridled license of present-day Malabar can evoke the abominations of those Phoenician Sodoms. There, generations swarmed without belonging to any particular family, each not knowing his father, being born, multiplying at random, like insects and reptiles, which swarm over their burning strands after a rainstorm. They themselves said they were born of the clay" (Michelet, p. 441). When the Carthaginians face the mercenaries, they are confronted by another racially undifferentiated group of individuals: "The first punishment of Carthage, after the shameful treaty of the Egatian Islands, was the return of its armies. Back upon her fell those bands without a country, law, or God, that impious, bloodthirsty Babel that she had thrust upon the other nations. Let us enjoy the spectacle of this just expiation at leisure" (Michelet, p. 453).

It is evident, then, that what Michelet reads in the confrontation of Carthage and the mercenaries as an episode of the Punic Wars is an event *at the end* of a given history, where abolished differences [*sic*] meet abolished racial, genealogical, and linguistic differences and destroy each other, that is to say, erase the differences between each other.

If we were to transpose Michelet's characterization into Flaubert's problematic, in what seemed to be an absolute temporal difference the original term is similar to the end term. The temporal difference between Carthage and nineteenth-century France is a pseudo-difference based upon a primary identity. The perception that the France of Flaubert is at the end of a history of which Carthage is supposed to represent if not the beginning, at least a more primitive or even original moment, is illusory. Carthage itself is at the end of a history.

It remains for us to show that the second term of the pseudo-difference, i.e. nineteenth-century France, is not only similar to the first term, insofar as the first term is also at the end of history, but that each of them is at the end of history, so to speak, *sui generis;* that nineteenth-century France is at the end of its history in the same way that the Carthage of the Punic Wars was at the end of its own history, and that what originally appeared as temporal difference is nothing but the mirage created by a textual interplay of identity and indifference.

As described by Flaubert, being at the end of history is more than simply being at one extremity of a temporal sequence. The end of history is in fact for Flaubert a historical period characterized by a nihilistic apocalypse. In that sense, nineteenth-century France is for him at the end of time in the same way that Carthage was for Michelet. In a letter to Princess Mathilde he writes: "I feel the ending of the world. Whatever may happen, all that I loved is lost. We are going to fall, when the war has ended, into an execrable order of things."[13] In another letter to his niece, he writes: "We are close to the beginning of the end!"[14]

In a letter to Madame Régnier, this feeling for the end of history coincides, as for Michelet, with the sense of the end of a race: ". . . That's it! We are spectators of the end of the Latin world. Farewell, all that we love! Paganism, Christianity, boorishness ["muflisme"]. Such are the three great evolutions of humanity. It is disagreeable to find oneself in the last."[15]

To George Sand, he writes: "The wars between the races will perhaps begin again. Before a century has passed, you'll see several million men slaughter each other in one sitting. The entire Orient against all Europe, the old world against the new."[16]

The race, then, that will be the victim of this new war of races is going to be the Latin race; "The Latin race is in its death throes. France will follow Spain and Italy, and loutishness ["pignouffisme"] is beginning. What a collapse! What a fall! What wretchedness! What abominations!"[17] Again, in a letter to his niece he writes: "Come what may, the world I was part of has had its day. The Latins have had it! Now it's the Saxons' turn; they'll be devoured in turn by the Slavs. And so forth."[18] Even if there were no war to abolish races, races would disappear in any case, for races are not intrinsic essences but only differential properties, and the most characteristic element of the end of times is the abolishment of differential traits: "Oh! Race, how I believe in it! But there are no more races! Aristocratic blood has been exhausted; its last droplets have probably coagulated in a few souls. If nothing changes (and that's possible), within perhaps fifty years Europe will languish in vast shadows and those dark ages of history, where nothing shines, will return."[19]

I have argued elsewhere[20] that for Flaubert, the end of history means a general collapsing of all differences — racial, social, political — into mediocrity, mediocrity being understood literally as the property of being in the middle, that is to say, of not sustaining any differential space or opposition. Socially, for example, the damning thing about the bourgeois is not that they are bourgeois, but that the bourgeois as the middle term between aristocratic and working classes is all that there is left:

> . . . the only thing to learn from the present régime . . . is that the idea of the People is as worn out as that of the King. So let's put the worker's smock and the monarch's purple together, and throw both of them into the latrines to conceal conjointly their stains of blood and mud; they're stiff with them.[21]

> The Socialists are no better than the Bourgeois, or rather, there's nothing else but Bourgeois.[22]

> But I think one truth emerges from all that: it is that you have no need for the common herd, the numerical element of majorities, approval, consecration. '89 dismantled royalty and nobility, '48 the middle class and '51 *the people*. There's *nothing* any more, except a base and stupid mob. We have all sunk to the same level in a shared mediocrity.[23]

My purpose in this context is not to discuss Flaubert's political views. Suffice it to say that for him the future of history is uniquely and strikingly characterized by uniformity, honogeneity, and mediocrity: that is to say, by the absence of all differences: "The world is going to become damn stupid. From now on for a long time to come it's going to be really boring. It's just as well we're living now. You wouldn't believe that we chat a lot about *the future of society*. For me it's almost certain that it will be, sooner or later, regimented like a high school. The underlings will order you about. Everything will wear a uniform."[24]

To return to Carthage, it should be apparent by now that Carthage, the Punic Wars, and the revolt of the mercenaries do not offer to Flaubert a historical reality which differs from the perception of his own, but on the contrary, one that is remarkably similar.

History, for Flaubert, is periodical, and it is its periodicity which makes for the possibility for periods which are temporally distant to be similar to each other. Thus history is punctuated at regular intervals by periods of agony: "Perhaps we need barbarians. Humanity, that eternal old man, receives blood transfusions from its periodic death agonies. How base we are! And what a universal decrepitude!"[25]

What is important, of course, is not only the fact of the similarity of Carthage to Flaubert's perception of his contemporary reality, but also that the categories which subtend this similarity describe as well the metaphorical network in terms of which he stages, for the nineteenth-century writer, the act of writing.

For Flaubert the perception of history is itself an historical problem. It is only in periods at the end of history that one perceives history historically, so to speak:

> Wretches that we are, I think we have a lot of taste because we are profoundly historical, because we are open to everything, and because we place ourselves within the perspective of our object in order to judge it.[26]

> The sense of history dates from yesterday, and perhaps it's the best thing about the nineteenth century."[27]

The perception of Carthage as history belongs to the nineteenth century, and as such partakes of the problematic of the end of history. Therefore the perception of Carthage as different is only the result of the sameness which makes a sense of history possible in the first place. It is not the author of *Salammbô*, but the critics, who view it as exotic and who deny its fundamental historicity, who are the victims of a romantic epistemology.

An identical consideration governs for Flaubert the question of style: "To write *the mediocre* well and to ensure that at the same time it preserves its appearance, its outline, its very words, that's devilishly hard."[28] The contemporary artist cannot escape the imperatives of a mediocre style; the problem for the modern writer is to manipulate the imperatives of a mediocre style to produce out of mediocre sameness the effect of difference as a stylistic and optical artifact.

I should like to illustrate this proposition with an example which goes beyond Flaubert. When the latter read Zola's *Nana*, he was terribly taken by it and in particular by its ending. In a letter to Zola, Flaubert wrote: "If I had to record everything in it that's special and strong, I'd write a commentary on every page! The character depiction is marvellously true to life. *Authentic* expressions abound; at the end, Nana's death is worthy of Michelangelo" ["*Michelangelesque*"].[29] What can Flaubert mean by "*Michelangelesque*," since Michelangelo, along with Homer, Shakespeare, and Rabelais, represents artists who, in Flaubert's literary ideology, were capable of having access to the sort of original difference which is denied to the modern artist?

The most important metaphor that Flaubert uses to signify the accomplished mediocrity of the end of history is that of rottenness and decomposition. Under the pressure of time and history, a final rotting and decomposition reduces everything to a uniform, homogeneous, repulsive medium, into which individuals and civilizations are bound to be drawn. An individual's existence is a continuous process of decay: "As if all the rottenness and all the infection that preceded our birth and that will recapture us at our death weren't enough, during our lives we are only successive, alternating, and overlapping corruptions and putrefactions."[30] From birth to death the process is linear and irreversible: "How nothingness invades us! Hardly are you born, than you begin to rot, so that life is only one prolonged battle against decay, which steadily triumphs more and more until the conclusion, death. There, decay reigns supreme."[31]

But in all of our singular instances, the process of corruption is the individual emblem of the movement of history: "We are dancing not on a volcano, but on the plank of a latrine which seems to me rather rotted. Presently society will go drown in nineteen centuries of shit."[32] The artist and the writer, who is himself submerged in the process, can only write and compose with the secondary derived corrupted materials that have been handed down to him:

> But finally mustn't one be familiar with all the chambers of the heart and the social organism, from cellar to attic, and not even forget the toilets, especially not forget the toilets! A marvellous chemical process unfolds in them; there fruitful decomposition occurs. Who knows to what excremental juices we owe the scent of roses and the taste of melons? Have they reckoned how much degradation you have to contemplate in order to form a spiritual greatness? How many nauseating miasmas one must swallow, how many griefs endure, how many tortures suffer, in order to compose one decent page? That's what we are, we writers, winegrowers and gardeners. From the putrification of humanity we derive delights for it, we make bouquets of flowers grow upon displays of wretchedness.[33]

It is, then, with the belated corrupt refuse and excrements of history that the writer creates his fictions and illusions.

Let us return to the ending of *Nana*. In the striking final passage of the novel, Zola describes the decomposing cadaver of Nana:

> Nana remained alone, face-up, in the candle light. She was a charnel heap, a mass of secretions and blood, a shovelful of rotted flesh thrown there, on a pillow. Pustules had invaded her entire face, one touching the next, and, withered, shrunken, muddy gray, they seemed already like mold on the earth, on that formless jelly where you could no longer make out the features. One eye, the left one, had completely disappeared beneath the boiling purulence; the other, half open, was sinking, like a black, decayed hole. Pus was still running from the nose. A reddish crust starting from one cheek partly covered the mouth, drawing it into an abominable laugh. And on that horrible, grotesque mask of the void, the hair, the beautiful hair, remained as radiant as sunlight, flowed like rivulets of gold. Venus was putrefying. It seemed that the virus she had caught in the gutter, on the corpses she had allowed into her intimacy, that ferment with which she had poisoned a nation, had just risen back up to her countenance and had devoured it.
>
> The room was empty. A great, desperate breath rose from the boulevard and swelled the curtains.
>
> — To Berlin! To Berlin! To Berlin![34]

This remarkable passage could not escape the notice of Flaubert. Nana's cadaver emblematizes the metaphor of decomposition, which undoes her body but also shows her function in the general decomposition of society. Finally, the decomposition of the body of Nana coincides with the beginning of the Franco-Prussian War, which for Flaubert was the one most important event in the beginning of the end of history and the return to barbarism.[35] We begin to guess what Flaubert might have meant by characterizing the passage as *Michelangelesque*. The differential element is not at the origin; on the contrary, the passage is different in the way it follows the movement of decomposition to the emblematic end of history. What remains untouched in the decomposing body of Nana is her hair, metaphorized as the sun and as gold. For Flaubert, the sun is also one of the metaphors of an absolute which does not fall victim to the process of corruption; it is the metaphor of the ontological status of a difference that cannot be reduced to identity, of an otherness which cannot be reduced to sameness. Such a sun is, of course, *not perceptible* — "Heraclitus blinded himself the better to see that sun which I'm talking about"[36] — and hence it is inconceivable that it could be objectified in a linguistic representation. For Flaubert, "Higher than life, higher than happiness, there is something blue and incandescent, a great motionless, subtle sky of which those radiations that reach us were sufficient to bring worlds to life. The splendor of genius is only the pale reflection of this hidden Word."[37] Hence the "light" by which we "see" is not that of the sun, but that of some of its pale metaphors, such as candlelight or gaslight: "We have gas lighting in our brains!" In relation to this particular metaphoric network, Zola's "And on that horrible, grotesque mask of the void, the hair, the beautiful hair, remained as radiant as sunlight, flowed like rivulets of gold" is all the more remarkable, inasmuch as by placing the metaphor of the sun as the immutable element amid an extreme decomposition, it constitutes a second-degree emblem of the nature of the literary work in Flaubert's conception of it. Flaubert, in fact, simply appropriated Zola's metaphor; in a letter to Maupassant, written the day after the letter to Zola congratulating him on *Nana*, he states: "Poetry, like the sun, puts gold on the dunghill."[38]

The thesis that Flaubert's "Oriental" novels are dictated by a romantic quest for the exotic, for a world temporally and spatially different from the European bourgeois world in which he lived, associates together indiscriminately the historical element of antiquity with the geographical component of the Orient. The two in fact are neither similar nor quite symmetrical. The question of what the Orient means for Flaubert is too complex — and probably too heterogeneous — to admit a simple answer. In what follows I should like briefly to isolate some of the components that go into the making of what is labeled, conveniently but inaccurately, "Flaubert's Orient."

At first it would appear that the Sun resides in the Orient. The Sun, absent from the Northern fogs, the Sun, absent from belated European history, is in the Orient a presence: "What a sun! What a sky, what terrain, what an *everything*!"[39] ". . . and then the sun! the sun! And a vast boredom that consumes everything."[40] What this Sun illuminates is not the bookish, costumed Orient imagined in Europe. Flaubert in fact denounces the latter: "Until the present day, the Orient has been understood as something sparkling, screaming, passionate, abrupt. People have seen in it only dancing-girls, curved swords, fanaticism, sensuality, etc. In short, we have not gone beyond Byron." What the Sun in fact makes possible is the last scene of *Nana* — not as textual allegory, but empirical reality —

> On the contrary, what I love in the Orient, is that grandeur which is unaware of itself, and that harmony of disparate things. I recall a bather who had a silver bracelet on his right arm, and on the other, a vesicant. There's the real Orient, and consequently, the poetic one; scoundrels in rags, wearing epaulets and completely covered with vermin. So leave the vermin alone; they make golden arabesques in the sunlight. You'll tell me that [the famous courtesan] Ruchiouk-Hânem's bedbugs lower her in your eyes; but that's just what charms *me*. Their nauseating odor mingled with the scent of her skin trickling with sandalwood perfume. I want there to be an element of bitterness in everything, an inevitable blast of the whistle in the middle of our triumphs, and desolation itself in enthusiasm. That reminds me of Jaffa, where, upon entering the city, I breathed in the smell of lemon trees and corpses both at once; the caved-in graveyard revealed half-rotted skeletons, while the green trees'

golden fruit swayed above our heads. Don't you feel how complete such
poetry is, and that this is the great synthesis?

The Orient is actually made up of the simultaneous conjunction of the
different, the permanent, the original, and the rotten, the corrupt, as
everyday occurrences. In other words, the Orient presents the monstrous
as real rather than as a textual construct. The important thing to
underscore, however, is that inasmuch as difference in the Orient is given
as empirical reality, it cannot be reinscribed in a linguistic representation.
One can see the poetry of the Orient, one can live the poetry of the Orient,
but one cannot write the poetry of the Orient. In the letter that I have just
quoted, Flaubert proceeds to write: "Ah! How I would like to be a scholar!
And what a fine book I would compose with the title: *The Interpretation
of Antiquity!* For I am sure of being part of tradition; what I add to it, is
the modern sensibility." But this brings us back to the historical problem of
writing history, which obliterates the difference offered by the Orient. A
book entitled *The Interpretation of Antiquity* would only reveal an
archeological Orient seen through the mediation of books, and if one were
to add to it "the modern sensibility," what one would have is something
resembling *Salammbô* rather than a representation of what the Orient *is*.
When Flaubert proposes to write a book about the Orient *qua* Orient as
opposed to an historical archeological Orient, the subject he proposes to
deal with is not the Orient but the disappearance of the Orient: "If I were
younger and if I had money, I would go back to the Orient to study the
modern Orient, the Isthmus of Suez Orient. A major book on that subject
is an old dream of mine. I would like to depict a civilized person becoming
a barbarian and a barbarian becoming civilized, to develop this contrast
of two worlds ending up by blending together."[41]

The fact is that for Flaubert the Orient is in its agony and soon it will
disappear as Orient — if it has not already done so. To Théophile Gautier,
whose quest for the exotic could not have been unknown to Flaubert, he
writes: "In a little while from now the Orient will cease to exist. Perhaps
we are the last to contemplate it. You don't realize how much is already
soiled: the Turkish soldiers have trouser straps! I've seen harems board
steamboats" (see note 39). And to Baudry he writes: "I think that the
Orient is even sicker than the West."[42] It is thus, in the logic of Flaubert's
system, that the Orient will survive only in its Sun, that is to say, the
Orient will no longer be perceptible as different:

> Soon the Orient will no longer exist except in the sun. In Constantino-
> ple, most of the men are dressed like Europeans; they perform operas
> there; there are reading rooms, milliners, etc. A hundred years from
> now, the harem, gradually invaded by the society of Frankish women,
> will collapse under its own weight, aided by serialized journalism and
> popular theater. . . . Soon the veil, already becoming thinner and
> thinner, will leave women's faces, and Mohammedanism will take flight
> with it altogether. Each day there are fewer pilgrims to Mecca. The

> Moslem priests are getting drunk like the Swiss. People are discussing
> Voltaire! Everything is falling apart here, as it is in our own country.[43]

Even eroticism in the Orient becomes mediated by trite European romantic representations and texts: "In another brothel we screwed some
passable Greek and Armenian women. — The house was run by a former
mistress of our servant. It was like home. On the walls there were
engravings of love scenes, and episodes from the life of Héloïse and
Abélard with captions in French and in Spanish. — Oh Orient, where are
you? — Soon it will be only in the sun!" If the spectre of Voltaire returns, it
is because Voltaire is the metaphoric name of history: "So Mohammed falls
too and without having had his Voltaire. The great Voltaire is time, the
general wearer-out of all things."[44] And so in the end the Sun of the Orient
will withdraw, leaving only the corruption of history.

　　If, in the works of Flaubert, one were to search for an emblematic
juncture of the corruption of space integrated into the movement of
history, one could probably find no better example that that of Jerusalem,
which offers the pitiful spatial example of the temporal corruption of the
center and origin of at least one history: "Jerusalem is a boneyard
surrounded by walls. — Everything is rotting there, dead dogs in the
streets, religion in the churches: (a powerful idea). There are quantities of
turds and ruins. . . . The Holy Sepulcre is the agglomeration of every
possible curse. In such a small space there is an Armenian church, a Greek
one, a Latin one, a Coptic one. All that insulting each other, cursing each
other from the depths of the soul. . . ."[45] And yet it is such an historical
ruin that in the last analysis offers a center from which Flaubert can
write: "The sweepings of all the old religions that you find in Syria is
something unheard of. — There I was at my center. There'd be enough to
work on for centuries."[46]

　　In conclusion, the temporal and spatial situation of the author of
Salammbô and *La Tentation de saint Antoine* is thus similar to that of the
characters in the novels. Their temporal relationship is one of proximity
and similarity rather than one of distance and difference. The opposition
that would sustain the accusation of exoticism which Sainte-Beuve and
Lukács leveled at Flaubert is in fact subverted by the latter. In Flaubert's
choice of Carthage, what might appear at the outset as a desire for an
otherness defined as difference is dictated by the necessity of finding an
otherness which could be a form of sameness. What does appear as
different is, in fact, an effect, an optical illusion, a mirage. Flaubert
writes from the standpoint of the end of time — to write at the end of time
means to write from a position of mediocrity, which in turn implies
writing in such a way that representation does not have a direct unmediated relation to an object. *Salammbô*, like *La Tentation de saint Antoine*,
is written with an accumulation of "notes upon notes, books upon books,"

"booking to the point of indigestion." The function of art is, of course, to create the *illusion* that the language of fiction is the language of its object, that *Salammbô* is the language of Carthage and *La Tentation de saint Antoine* is the language of fourth-century Alexandria, and that Carthage and Alexandria exist as linguistically reachable objective entities. The quest for exoticism and for a lost object is not, then, what determines the writing of fiction: rather, well-constructed fiction is an optical machine that produces the exotic, the distant, and the different as illusion or mirage. Constructed illusion is the only form of metaphysical reality-sustaining representation that Flaubert subscribed to: "I believe only in the eternity of a single thing, that is, *Illusion*, which is the real truth. All the others are only relative."[47] The function of art is to create such illusions: "The chief quality and the goal of Art is *illusion*."[48] The presumed realism of Flaubert — if there is such a thing — can only stem from an assumed identity of illusions. Art creates illusions, but these illusions are not illusions of some presumed sort of reality. The optical illusions of art are only illusions of other optical illusions, for ". . . our joys like our misfortunes are only optical illusions, effects of light and perspective."[49]

If there is a nostalgia in Flaubert, it is not a nostalgia for a lost object but rather, as we saw earlier, for a language and a mode of representation that would have an original and linguistically unmediated relation to its objects. Nevertheless, Flaubert also knows such a language to be unobtainable. If it were not, one could look at the sun and name the sun.[50] Yet in the northern fogs, at a belated time in history, one cannot look at the sun or name it by its proper name. As one can guess, Flaubert sees his destiny as temporally and spatially bound to the northern fogs of late history: "I carry always with me in my deepest self something like an aftertaste of the medieval melancholia of my country. It smells of fog, of the plague brought back from the Orient, and that falls to the side with its carvings, its stained glass and its leaden gables, like the old wooden houses of Rouen."[51] Bound by such constraints, the writer has no other alternative but to construct linguistic optical machines which could create the metaphorical illusion and mirage of twenty-five candles shining like a sun:

> What artists those Ancients were! And what languages those languages were! All the ones that we will be able to make, well, they'll never be worth the former. That's where you have to live. That's where you have to go. — To the sunlit land, to the land of Beauty. People who understand material existence, when it's raining in the winter, close their shutters, light twenty-five candles, build a great fire, fix a bowl of punch and lie down on tiger skins to smoke cigarettes. — You have to take that in the moral sense, and as the Persian proverb says, "block the five windows so that the house can see more clearly." An ant, what does the world matter to me? Let it spin as it pleases, I'll live in my little house that I'll cover with a tapistry of diamond dust.[52]

Or, as Flaubert would remind us, "The pitiable inadequacy of language!
To compare stars to diamonds."[53]

Notes

1. Article on *Salammbô* dated December 22, 1862, in *Oeuvres complètes de Gustave
Flaubert* (Paris: Club de l'Honnête homme, 1971–76), 16 vols., II, 435. Subsequent references
to this volume will be identified in the text by page number only.

2. "Elvire" was the fictional dedicatee and love object of several of the *Méditations
poétiques* (1820) by the Romantic poet Lamartine. For generations of French people she was
the embodiment of a passionate, star-crossed lover [Editor].

3. György Lukács, "*Salammbô*," in R. Giraud, editor, *Flaubert: A Collection of
Critical Essays* (Englewood, N.J.: Prentice-Hall, 1964), pp. 145, 147.

4. The "metaphysics of presence" presupposes a given order of meaning as existing in
itself, as fundamental rather than derivative and conditional. See Jonathan Culler, *On
Deconstruction* (Ithaca, N.Y.: Cornell University Press, 1982), pp. 92–96 et passim [Editor].

5. Flaubert, *Oeuvres complètes* (Paris: Conard, 1910–54), 28 vol. *Correspondance*, 9
vol., henceforth cited by Roman numeral for the volume and Arabic numeral for the page,
corresponds to volumes II–X. Here VIII, 374. Letter to Léon Hennique, February 2–3, 1880.

6. *Salammbô*, edited by E. Maynial (Paris: Garnier, 1961), p. 355. Henceforth cited in
the text as S / G.

7. Flaubert, *Correspondance*, edited by Jean Bruneau, (Paris: Gallimard, 1973 –), [2]
vols., I, 437. February 1847. Subsequent references to volume one of this edition will be cited
as B.

8. B, p. 266.

9. See Eugenio Donato, " 'A Mere Labyrinth of Letters': Flaubert and the Quest for
Fiction / A Montage," *MLN*, 89, vi (December, 1974): 885–910.

10. II, 409.

11. III, 281.

12. Jules Michelet, *Oeuvres complètes*, edited by Paul Viallaneix (Paris: Flammarion,
1971–). [20 volumes planned]. *Histoire Romaine*, II, 440–41.

13. VI, 171. October 23, 1870.

14. VI, 196. January, 1871.

15. VI, 201. March 11, 1871.

16. VI, 137–38. August 3, 1870.

17. VI, 184. Letter to George Sand, October 30, 1870.

18. VI, 163. October 5, 1870.

19. III, 129. Letter to Louise Colet, March 25–26, 1853. In his original footnote 12,
Donato observed: "I am aware of the implicit anachronism in quoting texts written by
Flaubert well after *Salammbô* in order to illustrate the textual dialectics of the earlier novel.
The late texts — in particular those after 1870 — are consistent with a philosophy of history
that Flaubert upheld throughout his life. From the quotes [identified in the present notes 13
through 18] it should be obvious that they are interchangeable with statements by Flaubert
contemporary with or preceding *Salammbô*. Again, I have chosen for simplicity's sake to do
the demonstration with *Salammbô*, but the same argument could be developed with *La
Tentation de saint Antoine*, the third version of which is contemporaneous or posterior to
some of the quotes [i.e., 1869–72]." My objection would not be that these quotations are eight
years later than the publication of *Salammbô*, so much as that they all come from an eight-
month period that corresponds to the Franco-Prussian War and the humiliating defeat of

France that dismayed Flaubert. The passages identified in notes 19 through 23, however, bear out Donato by showing Flaubert's pessimism unchanged from 1853 to 1878 [Editor].

20. See Donato's article cited above, note 9, and his essay on "The Museum's Furnace" that concludes the present volume [References given by Donato].

21. III, 211. Letter to Louise Colet, May 26–27, 1853.

22. Flaubert, *Correspondance: Supplément.* 4 vols. (Paris: Conard, 1954), IV, 105. Letter to Mme Brainne, August 15, 1878.

23. III, 349. Letter to Louise Colet (1853?).

24. B, p. 645. Letter to Louis Bouilhet, June 27, 1850.

25. III, 11. Letter to Louise Colet, September 1, 1852.

26. loc. cit., note 24.

27. IV, 380. Letter to Jules and Edmond de Goncourt, July 3, 1860.

28. III, 338. Letter to Louise Colet, September 12, 1853.

29. VIII, 386. February 15, 1880.

30. B, p. 418. Letter to Louise Colet, December 13, 1846.

31. III, 145. Letter to Louise Colet, March 31, 1853.

32. B, p. 708. Letter to Louis Bouilhet, November 14, 1850.

33. III, 407. Letter to Louise Colet, December 23, 1853.

34. Emile Zola, *Nana*, in his *Oeuvres complètes*, edited by Henri Mitterand. 15 vols. (Paris: Cercle Du Livre Précieux, 1966–69), IV, 347–48.

35. In some ways such a reading of Flaubert repeats that of D. H. Lawrence in *Phoenix: More Uncollected Writings* (New York: Viking Press, 1968), p. 358, and in *Phoenix: The Posthumous Papers* (New York: Viking Press, 1936), p. 312.

36. III, 399. Letter to Louise Colet, December 14, 1853.

37. III, 389. Letter to Louise Colet, November 29, 1853. The sentence quoted immediately below is from the same page.

38. VIII, 397. February 16, 1880.

39. B, p. 663. Letter to Théophile Gautier, August 13, 1850.

40. III, 136. Letter to Louise Colet, March 27, 1853. The following quotation comes from the same page, as does the next, continuing to p. 137.

41. VIII, 94. Letter to Mme Roger des Genettes, November 10, 1877.

42. B, p. 654. Letter to Frédéric Baudry, July 21, 1850.

43. B, p. 730. Letter to Louis Bouilhet, December 19, 1850. The following quotation comes from the same page.

44. Flaubert, *Voyage en Orient*, in his *Oeuvres complètes* (Paris: Club de l'honnête homme, 1971–76), 16 vols. X, 591.

45. B, p. 665. Letter to Louis Bouilhet, August 20, 1850.

46. B, pp. 696–97. Letter to his mother, October 7, 1850.

47. B, p. 429. Letter to Louise Colet, January 15, 1847 (?).

48. III, 344. Letter to Louise Colet, September 16, 1853.

49. B, p. 419. Letter to Louise Colet, December 16, 1846.

50. I am referring here to the problem of proper nouns and the metaphoricity of language as developed by Jacques Derrida in "La Mythologie blanche" in his *Marges* (Paris: Éditions de Minuit, 1972).

51. II, 348. Letter to Louise Colet, January 16, 1852.

52. B, pp. 435–36. Letter to Louise Colet, February 2, 1847.

53. Flaubert, *Voyage en Orient*, p. 522.

Salammbô and Nineteenth-Century French Society

Anne Green*

One of the accusations most commonly levelled against Salammbô is that it is a novel of escape whose historicism is evidence of a deliberate attempt by Flaubert to isolate himself from contemporary problems. György Lukács claims that Flaubert set out "to reawaken a vanished world of no concern to us," a world which would have no connection, direct or indirect, with his own; Victor Brombert says that Flaubert is interested in history only in so far as it implies absence and distance, or a closing-in on itself; Dennis Porter argues that Salammbô is a fictional dead-end where history is used for purely aesthetic purposes; and Albert Thibaudet calls it a novel deliberately detached from life where history is used as a distancing effect in order to present "a chunk of the undiluted past, a kind of dead star like the moon." Jean-Paul Sartre sees this kind of escape into the past as a characteristic response of Flaubert's — headlong flight into a long-vanished world is his only recourse when real life threatens.[1]

It is certainly true that Flaubert delighted in history and derived enormous pleasure from reading accounts of life in the distant past: but to suggest that Salammbô is simply the indulgence of an escapist imagination is grossly to underestimate the significance of this complex novel. We have seen how Flaubert painstakingly scanned hundreds of volumes of historical source material and then, from the vast amount of documentation, began to select a comparatively restricted range of detail to be included in the finished work. Faithful after a fashion to historical truth (his inaccuracies are generally sins of omission rather than of commission), he knew that he had probably done as much research into the history of Carthage as anyone else in France; he could be confident that the reading public would not be offended by blatant errors or anachronisms. It could pass as a historical novel set against a convincingly accurate background of the Mercenary wars. But if this were all, Salammbô would deserve the comparative neglect into which it has fallen. Flaubert, however, has attempted something far more ambitious. Like any great novelist, he challenges the way in which the reader sees the world around him: he offers a new perspective. If that perspective were limited to a remote and almost forgotten civilisation its interest would indeed be slight, as hostile critics were quick to point out. Instead, however, Flaubert is making a statement which is as applicable to the time at which he was writing as it is to ancient Carthage. In order to appreciate the novel fully, we must

*From Flaubert and the Historical Novel: "Salammbô" Reassessed (New York: Oxford University Press, 1982), 58–72. Reprinted by permission of Oxford University Press.

consider it in relation to the social and political climate in which it was written.

Why, first, did a novel portraying Carthage at the height of its decadence, threatened by barbarian hordes, suggest itself to Flaubert's imagination? His claim that he simply wanted to escape from the horrors of the present is clearly only part of the truth, for those aspects of contemporary French society which he found so distasteful emerge even more vividly in *Salammbô*. Their presence is far from being the "modernisation" which György Lukács roundly condemned as resulting from a failure of imagination on Flaubert's part.[2] It is not that Flaubert is so emotionally and intellectually a product of nineteenth-century France as to be incapable of avoiding anachronistic modernisms. Rather, he has chosen to examine, in an unfamiliar context, some of his own feelings and anxieties about contemporary France.

During the first part of the nineteenth century comments on conditions in France followed two opposing tendencies. On the one hand there were frequent expressions of faith and pride in the country's economic development and in technological advances which inspired confidence in future progress: on the other, there were accusations of decadence. As the century advanced, it was the awareness of the symptoms of decadence which gained ground. By 1852, Frédéric Ozanam, one of the foremost Catholic historians of the period, was writing that the best minds of his time believed in the decadence of France and felt that the idea of progress had become totally discredited.[3] And of course Flaubert in his *Dictionnaire des idées reçues* ["compendium of commonplaces"] shows just how commonplace this view of contemporary society had become: "AGE (our) — Inveigh against it. Complain that it's not poetic. Call it a period of transition, of decadence."[4]

Significantly, critics of this phenomenon often looked to the great cities of antiquity at the period of their decline as a shameful model of what was happening to France. When Eugène Pelletan vehemently attacked what he saw as the mediocrity, greed and moral turpitude of Parisians, the venality of the Press, and the vulgarity of literature in Second Empire Paris, he called his book *La Nouvelle Babylone*; Thomas Couture's painting *Les Romains de la décadence* was the sensation of the 1847 Salon; Taine likened Paris to Alexandria and Rome in his *Essai sur La Fontaine*; and Edgar Quinet, one of the more alarmist commentators on the state of the nation, gave dire warnings of disaster for France unless the country could rouse itself out of its moral and political apathy and avoid sharing the fate of the Rome of the late Empire. Like Babylon, Rome and Alexandria, Carthage was repeatedly evoked as just such a warning— Balzac, Janin, Mercier, Beauchesne, Bertin, Lecouturier and Berthet were among those who pointed to the fall of Carthage as a gloomy portent of the future of Paris.[5]

Others found more specific parallels. In 1840 Guizot pleaded the cause of peace with the words: "You want to act like Romans, and you have the constitution of Carthage!" When Guizot was subsequently appointed Minister for Foreign Affairs, Pierre Leroux recalled that remark, and commented that Thiers' "belligerent *eunuchism*" had simply given way to Guizot's equally ineffectual "pacifist and legislative *eunuchism*."[6] It goes without saying that in *Salammbô*, also, the eunuchs represent the passivity and quiescence of one element of a highly civilised society, and that the Carthaginian eunuchs were historically authentic. Flaubert has included them not merely to provide a touch of exotic local colour but as an imaginative symbol which already carried similar political connotations for his own period.

By 1862 it was a commonplace opinion that France was in a state of degeneration — after her accumulation of power and prestige during the Napoleonic period, an apparently inevitable decline seemed to have set in. The rot was spreading from within. Commentators were predicting the destruction of France in terms which again anticipate *Salammbô*: Paris, the capital of a nineteenth-century late Empire in moral and spiritual decline, was in danger of being destroyed by barbarians who would emerge from within France herself.[7] The words "barbarian" and "barbarousness" were frequent in polemical writing of the mid-century, a scornful label applied to any faction in society which seemed to contradict the values of the polemicist. As in *Salammbô*, where men of widely differing nationalities, creeds and motives are united under the term "Barbarians," so in the mid-nineteenth century the word was applied to almost anything that was seen as a threat.

Yet the terms were not always used pejoratively. There were some who welcomed the power and vitality inherent in any group capable of disrupting the status quo. Michelet, for example, noted that the rise of the working classes was often compared to a barbarian invasion and he seized on the analogy with enthusiasm. "*Barbarians!* Yes, that is to say, bursting with renewed vigor, living and rejuvenating. Barbarians, that is to say travelers en route toward the Rome of the future."[8] Leconte de Lisle's *Poèmes barbares*, too, express admiration for those distant, primitive, passionate and violent times, and Flaubert, while sharing the common belief that France was in a precarious position, in danger of being toppled back into an uncultured, savage and barbaric state, nevertheless also admired the energy and intensity he associated with "barbarousness."

His comments on the 1848 revolution in his notes for *L'Éducation sentimentale* indicate the ambiguity of his attitude — on the one hand the fabric of French civilisation is threatened with destruction: "New barbarians beneath whose blows the family, religion, freedom, the homeland, all civilisation risked perishing." Yet he also suggests that this can have a cathartic effect: "Relief as after a barbarian invasion."[9] Although in letters to friends Flaubert often complained that France was passing through a phase of outright barbarity, at the same time he could also appreciate the need for some such savage upheaval to shake an otherwise dull society out of its complacent lethargy. "Perhaps we need barbarians," he wrote to Louise Colet in 1852: "Humanity . . . receives blood transfusions from its periodic death agonies."[10]

So in a social and political climate where France's future was constantly likened to the downfall of the great decadent civilisations of antiquity, where even inter-party wrangles were described in terms of the age-old struggle between the Orient and the Western world, between barbarism and civilisation, Flaubert's choice of subject for his second major novel inevitably suggests his concern with contemporary problems and gives the lie to the assumption that he merely wanted to escape from the present. To draw parallels between nineteenth-century France and a degenerate antique society was as commonplace as the prediction of a barbarian invasion, and to liken Paris specifically to ancient Carthage was nothing new. *Salammbô*, however, is the first sustained exploration of the similarities between these two societies.

In describing the decline of Carthage, Flaubert used the simple technique of accompanying the city's moral and political corruption with a gradually increasing physical corruption, a theme which runs through the whole book. It is first introduced at the feast, when, at the height of the orgy, panic spreads among the mercenaries as the rumour goes round that the Grand Council has poisoned them. This detail is of particular significance not only because it is the first intimation of a sickness both physical and moral which will gradually envelop the whole army; but also because it has a striking precedent in mid nineteenth-century France.

It was in 1848 that one of the worst cholera epidemics of the century hit France, claiming nearly twenty thousand victims in the capital alone and provoking bitter resentment at the government's handling of the situation. As in the previous severe outbreak of 1832, suspicions were rife — in 1832 all Paris police stations had received a circular from the Préfet de Police warning them that the "eternal enemies of order" were spreading a false rumour that the epidemic had been started deliberately by the authorities, who were using poison to reduce the population and divert attention from current political problems.[11] The *Salammbô* incident has no source in antiquity: it is only one of many instances of Flaubert's way of taking an observed response to a contemporary situation and then fitting it perfectly into his Carthaginian novel.

The insidious encroachment of sickness and corruption, of which the poison scare was only a foretaste, is accompanied by the buzzing of flies. They first appear clustering on the putrefying corpses of the lions which the mercenaries come upon when they first leave the city. It is at this point that the real sickness begins in the army: "They were, moreover, especially the men from the North, vaguely uneasy, disturbed, already ailing . . .

great mosquitoes whined in their ears, and dysentery began to spread through the army" (I, 702). Later when Spendius is haranguing the mercenaries, the manuscript bears a note to the effect that "from time to time he stopped to catch his breath; and you could hear only the buzzing of the flies."[12] Even in moments of apparent serenity Flaubert uses the buzzing of flies to indicate that all is not well. In the silence of the chamber where Salammbô is asleep, "a long mosquito was whining" (I, 720): the manuscript notes that there are flies buzzing in the temple of Moloch, attracted by the smell of meat (folio 197); and when Hamilcar returns to Carthage after his long absence, "in the silent rooms, all his memories buzz like flies."[13]

The whole course of the war is treated as a kind of creeping sickness — the barbarians fall prey to many different types of disease — "skin diseases," "nervous ailments," and so on, before the dreadful ending in the *défilé de la Hache*; Carthage itself resembles a city struck by the plague;[14] and even Salammbô's disguise as she crosses the desert to the mercenaries' camp accords with the prevailing situation: she is passed off as a sick boy travelling to a distant temple in search of a cure (I, 757). The corruption of Carthage itself is symbolised by Hannon's decaying body, carefully but ineffectually smeared with precious ointments and perfumes in an attempt to conceal the rot — a metaphor which recalls Gautier's poem "Paris" where he describes the French capital as "A society falling back into chaos, / With rouged cheeks and gangrene in its bones!"[15] In a sense the mercenary soldiers were right when they claimed to have been poisoned by the Carthaginians, since the corruption — the greed, the selfishness and ruthlessness — has spread to them. It is no coincidence that their skin diseases are said to be like Hannon's.

Flaubert's analogy between the moral corruption of Carthage and widespread physical sickness was one which had frequently been used to express uneasiness about the state of nineteenth-century French society, and accusations of corruption abounded. Writers often described corruption — whether in government or in the private sector — as a malignant disease spreading out from Paris. Balzac refers to Paris as "that great chancre they saw spread out beneath their feet, smoking and glowing with light, in the valley of the Seine," and Berthet has the Seine exclaim, "Oh! Who will free me from Paris, that ulcer on my flank?" in his poem "The Curse of Paris" (1852).[16] The opening speech at the Rouen reform banquet in December 1847, at which Flaubert was present, took "Corruption" as its main theme, and the announcement of the topic drew thunderous applause from the audience. Duvergier de Hauranne's address to the same assembly referred to the then existing electoral system as a kind of corruption spreading over France — nothing was being done to check the government's policies, he complained, "and while we wait, the tide is rising, the gangrene is spreading."[17] It was, as Flaubert himself described it later, "such a foetid age."[18]

Contemporary statistics show that it was during the period of revolution in the mid-century that the highest death rate occurred in France, with 36.7 deaths per thousand inhabitants recorded in 1849.[19] This figure was due in part to the cholera outbreak of 1848–49 which medical authorities attributed to polluted drinking-water and inefficient drainage and sewage. As a result the need for extensive civil engineering works was recognised and public controversy arose over the means of providing a sufficient supply of pure drinking water. Flaubert describes a similar predicament in *Salammbô*, where the lack of drinking-water is the cause of many deaths, both of Carthaginians during the siege, and of mercenaries trapped in the desert.[20] During the period that Flaubert was writing his novel, Haussmann's reorganisation of the water supply to Paris was arousing intense public interest, which focused particularly on one of his favourite projects — the construction, first proposed in 1854, of a 107-mile-long aqueduct carrying fresh water to Paris from the Somme-Soude springs. It is surely more than a coincidence that Flaubert should have introduced a great aqueduct into his novel, an aqueduct which, on his own admission, was a complete anachronism: "Confession! My *secret* opinion is that there was no aqueduct at Carthage at all, despite the present-day ruins of an aqueduct there . . . The memory of Belisarius cutting the Roman aqueduct of Carthage haunted me, and then it was such a fine way for Spendius and Mâtho to enter the city. Never mind! My aqueduct is an act of cowardice! I confess."[21] It is more than likely that the "act of cowardice" was suggested to him by the current interest in the great Paris scheme quite as much as by his recollection of the story of Belisarius.

Also at this time, Haussmann's plans for the redesigning and rebuilding of Paris were causing violent reaction in the French public. A number of novels written under the Second Empire are set against a background of the rapidly changing capital, and it is estimated that about ninety miles of new roads were driven through the city during Napoleon III's reign, transforming its appearance as well as the lives of thousands of people whose homes had to be torn down to make way for the new streets, open spaces and public monuments.

This is yet another feature of contemporary Paris which coincides with the Carthage of *Salammbô*: the face of Carthage is changing as quickly as the French capital, where crowded areas of medieval houses clustering round a network of narrow, winding alleyways were being cleared away under the Second Empire. As in Paris, the cramped, old quarters of Flaubert's Carthage are swept away, boundaries disappear, and the ancient walls are torn down so that their stones can be used to rebuild the ramparts. Other building is going on in the city — when Hannon reads out the list of government expenditures to the mercenaries, heading his account are sums spent on rebuilding temples and paving streets, and the novel dwells at length on descriptions of the architecture and topography of the city, and on the geometricality of its layout. But in

Carthage the superficial order and symmetry of the city cannot hide its moral and political disintegration.[22]

This is a contrast which is fundamental to the novel. The beautiful symmetry of the novel's structure as a whole effectively stresses the unease and disorder of the society about which Flaubert is writing, since this order and symmetry are constantly threatened, laying bare the flaws in an apparently highly organised civilisation. In spite of the oppositions which are repeatedly set up between the ordered Carthaginians and the disorganised barbarian rabble, these contrasts are temporary and shifting. When the mercenaries set up camp outside Sicca after the confusion of the banquet and the pell-mell departure from Carthage, the geometricality of their organisation comes as something of a surprise: "The Greeks arrayed their tents of hide in parallel lines; the Iberians placed their cloth shelters in a circle; the Gauls made themselves cabins of boards" (I, 702). And later, when the Carthaginians visit the mercenary camp, "instead of the confusion that they had imagined, everywhere there reigned a frightening order and silence" (I, 711). Similarly, the apparently random manoeuvres ordered by Hamilcar in the crossing of the Macar turn out to have a hidden order which wins through in the end. But more often the reverse is the case. The geometricality of the garden is soon destroyed and the internal dividing walls of Carthage are pulled down; and although Hamilcar, on his return by sea, passes through the outer harbour full of rotting flotsam into the yet incorrupted inner sanctum — the inner basin surrounding his island palace where the water is so pure that the white pebbles on the sea-bed are clearly visible — there is an indication, in the lucid, symmetrical description, that the distinction between the corruption outside and the still centre of purity will soon disintegrate. The process has already begun with the decay of the old triremes, unusable now with their rotting timbers and peeling paint. The order and symmetry of the positioning of the members of the night session, echoed by the geometrical architecture of the Temple of Moloch, is undermined by dissension among the Hundred, while the satanic figure of Spendius moves through the novel provoking disorder and delighting in the consequences. When we read in the final chapter that "everywhere you could feel order re-established, a new life beginning" (I, 794), we are ready to appreciate the irony: order is felt to have been restored, the veil of Tanit has been returned and the barbarians annihilated, but the reader has been made aware of the instability of such "order," and knows it cannot and will not last [for Imperial Rome will soon overwhelm Carthage — editor].

In May 1841 there appeared in the *Revue des Deux Mondes* a long and important article by Saint-Marc Girardin entitled "De la Domination des Carthaginois et des Romains en Afrique comparée avec la domination française." Like Guizot and Leroux, Saint-Marc Girardin was struck by the similarities between the Carthaginian and French attitudes to war, and it is possible that this article may have served, directly or indirectly, as yet another source for *Salammbô*: the parallels drawn between the French and Carthaginian colonisation of North Africa are closely argued and recur (although never explicitly) in the novel.

One of Saint-Marc Girardin's main points is that Carthage employed mercenaries from different countries in order to diminish the likelihood of conspiracies. Since the men had no ties of affection for the country that engaged them, sedition was not uncommon: but this was thought to be less dangerous than a revolt of a national army. All countries which have subsequently conquered North Africa have adopted the same strategy, he observes, and to prove his point he cites the latest statistics from the *Tableau des établissements français en Algérie* showing the number of native soldiers in the French army in North Africa. The other main point of comparison which he uses is the systems of land-ownership or of tribute-raising. He advocates the Carthaginian system whereby the colonisers owned and cultivated the land on the coastal strips but merely exacted tributes from inland towns. This was the system described by Polybius. In *Salammbô* Flaubert describes the cruelty and ruthlessness necessary for the successful operation of this scheme: "Carthage drained those nations dry. She exacted exorbitant taxes from them: and chains, decapitation, or crucifixion punished delays and even complaints. You had to grow what suited the Republic, provide what she asked. . . . Then, beyond the territories directly subject to Carthage, extended the domains of allies who paid only a moderate tribute; behind the allies roamed the Nomads, whom one could unleash on the former. Thanks to this system the harvests were always plentiful, horse-breeding skillfully done, the plantations magnificent" (I, 722). The system he describes is identical to the one which French colonisers were later to adopt in Algeria, and which Saint-Marc Girardin writes of approvingly: "Near Algiers, the Europeans own land, for there we can easily defend and cultivate the earth: and the higher administration was correct, I believe, in 1837, to annul a decree by General Damrément that forbade Europeans, in the province of Algiers, to acquire land. In the province of Constantine, on the other hand, which is an interior province, the Europeans are not allowed to own land. There, we are satisfied with governing and levying tribute."[23] That this article, drawing its parallels between the colonising policies of Carthage and contemporary France, should have been published in such a respected and widely circulating journal as the *Revue des Deux Mondes* is further evidence of the fact that in deciding to set his novel in ancient Carthage, Flaubert was choosing a background which for many of his readers must have held associations with specific aspects of their own society.

The associations are further strengthened when one considers the treatment of slaves by the two communities. On 26 May 1840, a commission was set up by royal command to look into the question of slavery in the French colonies, and the Act abolishing slavery was the first reform passed by the provisional government when it came to power in February

1848. Similarly, one of the first actions of Flaubert's mercenaries in Carthage, once they feel themselves to be in a position of strength, is to free the slaves from the dungeons. But in both cases the promised freedom is illusory. We know from contemporary reports (and Flaubert knew from first-hand experience) that although slavery had been nominally abolished, the inhabitants of many of the implanted villages in the North African colonies led lives of virtual serfdom. Millesimo, for example, was described by Flaubert on his return from Carthage in 1858 as: "A horrible town, all straight: a line of acacias in front of the low houses, little enclosures; it's the most ignoble aspect of civilisation . . . women, in the fields, plow or hoe wearing men's jackets and hats, Parisian janitors transported to Moorish lands, the scum of the poor districts beneath the African sun. And what wretchedness there must be there, furies, memories, and fever, pale, famished fever!" (II, 719).

The similarities between these politically inspired villages, created in the same spirit as the National Workshops, and the villages under Carthaginian control described in *Salammbô* will be discussed in the next chapter, but what is particularly relevant here is that although slavery had been officially abolished in the French colonies, the lives of people like the women Flaubert saw in Millesimo were unchanged. The government hailed its abolition of slavery as a symbol of the new freedom it would bring to society, and yet it was prepared to use the inhabitants of these implanted villages as slaves in all but name. The pattern of expectation and disillusion accompanying the 1848 revolution and described so tellingly in *L'Éducation sentimentale*, runs just as clearly through *Salammbô*, beginning with the symbolic freeing of the slaves: the course of the novel shows that this action is an empty gesture rather than a symbol of a new freedom. Flaubert suggests that in such a society there can be no real liberty. Behind the historically accurate account of the way in which each side eventually finds itself confined and besieged, he is drawing attention to man's perverse impulse to enslave himself to his own destructive greed and false ambitions. "There are so few people who love liberty these days!" he complained as he worked on *Salammbô*.[24]

The novel also reflects Flaubert's assimilation of current ideas on race and nationality. The manuscripts reveal how carefully he researched into the differences between men of various races—they abound in detailed lists of national characteristics, differences in dress, in behaviour, in weapons, together with notes on the origins of and relationships between different races. Worked into the finished novel these details serve to clarify the changing racial structures within Carthage. During its rise to power and prosperity the city has attracted men of many nationalities, from the Indians who ride the war elephants to the "men of the Caananite race" who have a monopoly of Carthaginian trade (I, 723). Gradually, the old social structure which had been based on a racial hierarchy breaks down (Flaubert had noted in a preliminary sketch that the different districts of the city had originally been built by different races, with Byrsa the oldest)[25] and instead gives way to a hierarchy based on wealth. A short passage at the centre of the novel describes how, in order to obtain stone for reinforcing the ramparts, Hamilcar orders the demolition of the old walls which had once separated the different racial groupings, and how, with the walls gone, "the differences in wealth, replacing the hierarchy of the races, continued to keep the sons of the conquered and those of the conquerors apart: so the patricians looked on the destruction of these ruins with irritation, while the plebeians, without really knowing why, rejoiced in it" (I, 741). In effect, Flaubert is here echoing Augustin Thierry's theories about the historical development of social structures, and showing how the class system within the city has formed along the same lines as the old racial hierarchy. In his comment on the patricians' discomfiture at the destruction of the dividing walls, Flaubert is clearly indicating the start of a class struggle, the beginning of the end of Carthage's established social hierarchy.

The mercenary army, on the other hand, is composed of small, clearly identified ethnic groups characterised by an intense energy and vigour, a primitive life-force that makes them capable of almost superhuman feats of strength and violence. Each group preserves much of its national identity, but, because of having lived and fought together for so long, these identities are beginning to merge. Religious beliefs spread from one group to another. Moreover the mercenaries' contact with the decadent luxuries of Carthage has a debilitating effect on them — as they leave the city to make their way through the hinterland Flaubert describes the "beginnings of an uneasiness motivated by the desert. The town has made them soft" (folio 178).

In *Salammbô* Flaubert can indulge his distaste for the milk-and-water contemporary man with his lack of drive and energy — men like Léon Dupuis and Frédéric Moreau who may well be sensitive and even moderately passionate individuals, but who nevertheless are incapable of sustained and vigorous action. In contrast, *Salammbô* shows scenes of unconstrained ferocity and intense passion in the confrontations between mercenaries and Carthaginians.[26]

In the first half of the nineteenth century many people firmly believed that the human race had degenerated from some primitive, superior stock, losing both physical and moral energy as time passed. As a nation became more civilised, so its vigour was thought to decline. This view is summed up in Leconte de Lisle's poem addressed "Aux Modernes" ("To Men of Modern Times"): "You live like cowards, without dreams or plans, / Older and more decrepit than the barren earth. / Castrated in the cradle by your times, that kill / All deep and forceful passions."[27] It was already a commonplace by the time that Flaubert was writing, yet for him the fascination of this primitive energy is an ambiguous one. For although Mâtho, for instance, is capable of phenomenal feats of strength and endurance, these often achieve nothing. One night he plunges into the sea and swims continuously for three hours until he reaches the foot of the Mappales cliffs, but this trial of strength merely results in bloodied knees and broken fingernails: he returns to the water and swims back. The energy of the mercenary army, too, is presented ambiguously. All too often it takes the form of unchannelled savagery, quite unlike the noble vigour of a stereotyped "primitive" as imagined by those who saw city life as an enervating influence.

Flaubert also seems to believe that something very like this primitive savagery soon manifests itself when men come together in large crowds. They are then particularly prone to violent changes of mood. Crowd behaviour and reaction in 1848 as described in *L' Éducation sentimentale* often follow a pattern very similar to their equivalents in *Salammbô*. In the later novel the crowd's respect and admiration for Professor Samuel Rondelot suddenly gives way to hatred and vituperation when they see him as a representative of authority, just as the mercenaries suddenly turn violently against Giscon whom they had welcomed with wild applause only moments earlier. In each case Flaubert portrays the same stupidity and fickleness and savagery of an angry crowd resorting to its ability to shout down opposition instead of putting forward a rational argument. The degeneration of dialogue into a meaningless animal noise is exploited in both novels. Examples from the barbarians are legion, but it is significant that this also happens at a dinner party given by Dambreuse, where an inane conversation ends with the exchange: "Ah! bah! — Eh! Eh!" (II, 66). Later, Frédéric leaves the political meeting at which he has tried to present himself as a candidate, while the crowd listens in uncomprehending admiration to a flow of Spanish. In describing crowd behaviour in *Salammbô* Flaubert is developing to the full a literary technique which he is the first to use to this extent. He treats the crowd as an entity, with all the characteristics of a hot-tempered, inconstant and unreflecting individual. Nevertheless, in the very spontaneity and impetuosity shown by large groups, he obviously saw traces of the kind of energy that he regretted had faded from contemporary behaviour — he was not being entirely facetious when he told Louise Colet that he liked the masses only when they were rioting.[28]

Flaubert's interest in questions of race and nationality was shared by a great many writers of the period. It was a time of unprecedented preoccupation with the physical characteristics of racial types in the belief that these would provide a key to a wider understanding of social dynamics. Interest in concepts of race had grown rapidly during the first half of the nineteenth century and left few areas untouched. Subjects as different as linguistics and natural sciences were affected: Dr. Gall's new science of phrenology enjoyed great popularity; and in the ecclesiastical field concern with distant races led to a surge of evangelistic missions. In a review of contemporary studies on the history of races written in 1848,

Alphonse Esquiros claimed that writers on race fell into two distinct categories—the physiologists, likes Serres or the Abbé Frère, who studied anatomical characteristics and tried to find connections between a nation's moral and intellectual progress and the development of the nervous system: and the historians, who looked on the ancient customs, language and literature of a race as the prime factor in understanding its distant past.[29] Among the latter were such distinguished historians as Michelet and Guizot, both of whom traced national characteristics back to a country's constituent races.[30] Augustin Thierry, who took these ideas further, based his theory of history on the intermingling of races. The origins of France's troubles could, he believed, be traced back to the moment when the barbarians infiltrated Gaul after the collapse of the Roman Empire in the sixth century, and it was in this clash of nationalities, with one people asserting its superiority over another, that Thierry saw the origins of the class struggle.[31]

One of the more controversial writers on the subject was Joseph-Arthur, comte de Gobineau, whose *Essai sur l'inégalité des races humaines* was first published in 1853–55. In this work he came to the conclusion that: "the ethnic issue dominates all other historical problems. It holds the key to them, and the inequality of the races whose co-operation creates a nation suffices to explain the entire chain of events forming its destiny."[32] Using this ethnological key to help him predict the future of France, Gobineau made a pessimistic forecast based on his theory of the inevitable debilitating effect of racial intermingling. The social changes he foresaw were not dissimilar to the changes Flaubert has shown to be taking place in Carthage: France, said Gobineau, is a great nation, conquering, expanding, wealthy and attracting foreign immigrants who settle there to enjoy the many advantages she has to offer. Gradually, then, her ethnic structure changes and her social structure comes to depend not on racial distinctions but on those of wealth and class. But as a hierarchy of class imposes itself and racial distinctions disappear, so the "pure" national stock becomes hopelessly diluted and weakened. Gobineau used the downfall of Carthage as an example to prove his theory: he saw Carthaginian civilisation as doomed from the outset because of the inherent political inferiority of the Phoenician race: "Insofar as they belonged to Phoenician stock, a stock whose political virtues were inferior to those of the races from which Scipio's soldiers came, the contrary outcome of the battle of Zama could not alter their destiny. Had they been fortunate one day, the next would have seen them succumb to revenge."[33] So the ultimate downfall of the civilisation becomes inevitable. *Salammbô* contains this same sense of the inevitability of Carthage's collapse, describing a civilisation which has passed its peak and is moving into the period of religious fanaticism, excessive luxury, immorality and decadence which Gobineau believed to be symptomatic of the last stages of national decline.

The changes taking place among Flaubert's barbarians also reflect contemporary ideas about the factors governing variations in racial characteristics. Hippolyte Taine's famous survey of the relationship between the development of a nation and the literature it produces was typical of current ideas in its definition of race in terms of innate, hereditary qualities which are modified by environmental factors.[34] When a race migrates, Taine argued, the change in climate necessarily affects its corporate intellect and its social structure—an idea which is illustrated by Flaubert's barbarian groups who find themselves outside Carthage, far from their countries of origin, and bewildered by their strange new environment. Living in clearly defined ethnic groupings at the beginning of the novel, the barbarians are shown gradually to lose their individuality as they re-adapt to their alien surroundings and assimilate new beliefs: "Camp, for most of them, replaced their homeland" (I, 787). In the context of contemporary ideas on race which Flaubert has used in his novel, the merging of nationalities among the barbarians marks the beginning of the long process of civilisation. The Carthaginians, on the other hand, have almost reached the end of that process and are soon to disappear. The implications for the nineteenth century are obvious. As Flaubert commented to Louise Colet, "there are no more races! . . . If nothing changes (and that's possible), perhaps within fifty years Europe will languish in deep shadows."[35]

Clearly, then, we cannot take at face value the letter to Mlle Leroyer de Chantepie which is frequently quoted as proof that *Salammbô* is a work of escapism, a retreat into a distant world that had no connection with his own.[36] When Flaubert said that he wanted to write a novel set in the third century B. C. because he wanted to escape from the modern world, and that he found it as wearisome to write about contemporary society as to live in it, he was telling only part of the truth. After all, the letter was written at the very beginning of his preparations for the novel, and even if he did feel at the time that he needed to escape into the past, the creative process was soon underway and the need to "get away from the modern world" was not mentioned again. Moreover, if he was prompted, at the outset, to choose the Carthaginian subject because of his revulsion for contemporary society, the choice must be seen as a reflection on his own period. It is a natural extension of his distaste for and bewilderment at the present rather than a complete withdrawal from it.

Notes

1. György Lukács, *The Historical Novel*, translated by H. and S. Mitchell (Harmondsworth, England: Penguin, 1969), p. 220; Victor Brombert, *Flaubert par lui-même* (Paris: Seuil, 1971), p. 76; Dennis Porter, "Aestheticism versus the Novel: The Example of *Salammbô*," *Novel*, 4 (1971): 101–106; Albert Thibaudet, *Gustave Flaubert* (Paris: Gallimard, 1935), p. 135; Jean-Paul Sartre, *L'Idiot de la famille: Gustave Flaubert de 1821 à 1857*, 3 vols. (Paris: Gallimard, 1971–72), III, 450.

2. Lukács, pp. 223–28.

3. "Du Progrès dans les siècles de décadence," *Correspondant*, 30 (1852): 257. Quoted in Koenraad W. Swart, *The Sense of Decadence in Nineteenth-Century France* (The Hague: M. Nijhoff, 1964), p. 86. Cf. Homais, who, on seeing the blind beggar, comments: "Progress, on my word of honor, is advancing at a snail's pace! We're floundering around in the midst of barbarism!"

4. Flaubert, "Dictionnaire des idées reçues," in *Bouvard et Pécuchet*, edited by René Dumesnil. 2 vols. (Paris: Les Belles Lettres, 1945), II, 308.

5. Pierre Citron, *La Poésie de Paris dans la littérature française de Rousseau à Baudelaire*, 2 vols. (Paris: Editions de Minuit, 1961), I, 11, 122, 125, 332; II, 28, 29, 31.

6. Pierre-Henri Leroux, *La France sous Louis-Philippe (1842)*, in his *Oeuvres*, 2 vols. (Paris: Lesourd, 1850 [vol. I]; L. Nétré, 1851 [vol. II]). I. 414–15.

7. Jules Michelet, *Histoire de la révolution française*, 7 vols. (Paris: Chamerot, 1847–53), I, vi. Compare the orgies and atrocities of *Salammbô* with the imagery of these nineteenth-century views of Paris: "The great city runs through the streams of an orgy, / Exhaling only fire from its burning lungs, / Hair plastered down with wine, shreds of flesh in its teeth." J.-F. Destigny, "Mascarade politique," quoted by Citron, I, 359. And

> I did not see you, frivolous Babylon . . .
> I did not see you, in the mire and blood,
> Driving a white-hot populace from crime to crime,
> The beacon of the nations, giving more heat than light,
> Inflaming and betraying the people's rage,
> And giving to your vassal cities as examples
> The horrible scenes of your atrocities.

Louise Colet, "Paris," in her *Poésies complètes*, 2 vols. (Paris: C. Gosselin, 1844–54), I, 32.

8. Jules Michelet, "A. M. Edgar Quinet" (1846), in *Le Peuple*, edited by R. Casanova (Paris: Julliard, 1965), pp. 70–71. Cf. François Pierre Guillaume Guizot, *Histoire de la civilisation en France depuis la chute de l'Empire romain*, 4 vols. (Paris: Didier, 1846), I, 25: "They say . . . that . . . dedication and energy, man's two great strengths as they are his two great virtues, and which shone forth in ages we call barbaric, are lacking and will be lacking more and more in the ages that we call civilized, and especially in our own." While believing that there is some truth in this, Guizot had faith in man's ability to find other sources of energy.

9. Dossier of *L' Éducation sentimentale*, Rouen MSS 138 and 139, quoted by Alberto Cento, *Il realismo documentario nell' "Éducation sentimentale"* (Naples: Liguori, 1967), p. 273.

10. Flaubert, Letter to Louise Colet, September 1, 1852, in his *Correspondance*, 9 vols., from the *Oeuvres complètes*, 21 vols. (Paris: Conard, 1923–54). Further references to Flaubert's letters are from this edition.

11. Maxime Du Camp, *Souvenirs littéraires*, 2 vols. (Paris: Hachette, 1882–83), I, appendix, "Pièces justificatives no. 1."

12. NAF, 23659, folio 31 verso (Bibliothèque Nationale, Paris. Manuscripts. "Nouvelles Acquisitions Françaises").

13. NAF 23659, folio 74 verso.

14. NAF 23659, folio 73: "as in times of plague, the houses were shut up."

15. Théophile Gautier, "Premières poésies," in his *Poésies complètes*, 2 vols. (Paris: Charpentier, 1884), I, 109 ("Paris" was written in 1831).

16. See Citron, II, 443.

17. Jules Sénard, *Banquet réformiste de Rouen, 25 décembre 1847: Discours de M. Sénard, président du banquet* (extrait du Journal de Rouen) (Rouen: D. Brière, 1848); Prosper

Léon Duvergier de Hauranne, *Discours prononcé à Rouen par M. Duvergier de Hauranne au banquet de la réforme électorale et parlementaire* (Paris: Claye et Taillefer, 1847) (December 25, 1847).

18. III, 40. Letter to Louise Colet, October 8, 1852.

19. Alexandre Moreau de Jonnès, *Éléments de statistique* (Paris: Guillaumin, 1856 [1847]), p. 300.

20. 1857, the year in which Flaubert began to write *Salammbô*, was one of extreme draught in Paris. The water in the Seine dropped to the lowest level since records of river stages were first kept in 1719, and caused a severe water shortage in the city. See David Henry Pinkney, *Napoleon III and the Rebuilding of Paris* (Princeton, N. J.: Princeton University Press, 1958), p. 112, and chapter 5, "A Battle for Water," passim.

21. V, 70. Letter to Charles Augustin Sainte-Beuve, December 23–24, 1862 [Flaubert's major defense of *Salammbô*, and the best source of information regarding his views on that novel — Editor].

22. Is there not an analogy here with the superficial, physical order which Haussmann and his colleagues imposed on Paris, a replanning which many claimed was motivated by strategic considerations? [Broad straight avenues facilitated troop movements and artillery fire on rebellious Paris mobs — Editor.] Haussmann himself said quite openly that "razing the old neighborhoods would deprive rioters of a gathering place." See Joan Margaret Chapman and Brian Chapman, *The Life and Times of Baron Haussmann: Paris in the Second Empire* (London: Weidenfeld and Nicolson, 1957), p. 184.

23. Saint-Marc Girardin, "De la Domination des Carthaginois et des Romains en Afrique comparée avec la domination française," *Revue des Deux Mondes* (May 1, 1841), pp. 413–14.

24. IV, 302. Letter to Eugène Delattre, January 10, 1859. Cf. similar comments in two letters to Louise Colet: II, 414 (May 15–16, 1852), and II, 58 (December 9, 1852).

25. NAF 23659, folio 217.

26. See Edmond and Jules de Goncourt, *Journal* (Monaco: Éditions de l'Imprimerie Nationale de Monaco, 1956–58), 22 vols., V, 228 (December 14, 1862): "Flaubert misses high barbarism, an era of brute strength, of displays of nakedness, a primitive and sadistic age, the full-blooded period of world history: battles, great exploits; heroic, savage times, tatooed with raw colors, laden with glass baubles."

27. Charles Leconte de Lisle, *Poèmes barbares* (Paris: Lemerre, 1947), p. 356. See also Bénédict Auguste Morel, *Traité des dégénéréscences physiques, intellectuelles et morales de l'espèce humaine* (Paris: J.-B. Baillière, 1857).

28. III, 150. Letter to Louise Colet, March 31, 1853.

29. Alphonse Esquiros, "Des études contemporaines sur l'histoire des races," *Revue des Deux Mondes*, new series, 21 (1848): 982–1003. See also a lecture on race by Serres in Esquiros, editor, *Paris ou les sciences, les institutions et les moeurs au XIXe siècle* (Paris: Comon, 1847); and Michel Lémonon, "L' Idée de race et les écrivains français de la première moitié du XIXe siècle," *Die neueren Sprachen*, 69 (June, 1970): 283–92.

30. See for example Guizot, I, 32–33, where he describes how a combination of Roman and Germanic elements have produced "the character of French civilization," and Michelet, *Le Peuple*, pp. 251–58.

31. Augustin Thierry, *Dix ans d'études historiques*, in his *Oeuvres complètes*, 5 vols. (Paris: Furne, 1851–53), III, 292. See also Anne Green, *Flaubert and the Historical Novel* (Cambridge, England: Cambridge University Press, 1982), pp. 25–26.

32. Arthur de Gobineau, *Essai sur l'inégalité des races humaines*, 4 vols. (Paris: Firmin-Didot, 1853–55), I, v.

33. Gobineau, I, 50 and 56. Other commentators held similar ideas. Cf. Auguste Romieu, *Le Spectre rouge de 1852*, 3rd edition (Paris: Ledoyen, 1851): "The French nation

exists no more. There are, on the ancient soil of Gaul, anxious rich people and the greedy poor; that's all there is." And Flaubert himself lamented that in France "aristocratic blood is depleted." III, 129. Letter to Louise Colet, March 25–26, 1853.

34. Hippolyte Taine, introduction to his *Histoire de la littérature anglaise*, 5 vols. (Paris: Hachette, 1863), I.

35. III, 129. Letter to Louise Colet, March 25–26, 1853.

36. IV, 164. Letter to Mlle Leroyer de Chantepie, March 18, 1857.

L' ÉDUCATION
SENTIMENTALE

L' *Éducation sentimentale:*
Profanation and the Permanence
of Dreams
Victor Brombert*

THE BORDELLO: IN THE END IS THE BEGINNING

Ten years after the publication of *L' Éducation sentimentale*, Flaubert
was still pained by the critics' hostile reaction. To his friend Turgenev, he
wrote in 1879: "Without being a monster of pride, I consider that this
book has been unfairly judged, especially the end. On this score I feel
bitter toward the public."[1] Few endings of novels have indeed baffled, even
outraged more readers. The hero's flat assertion that an adolescent
excursion to a brothel has been the most precious experience of a lifetime
confirmed suspicions that Flaubert was an incurable cynic. It was bad
enough that the "hero," Frédéric Moreau, after a life distinguished by
failure, returns to the somnolence of a provincial existence, a death-in-life
which corresponds to a total abdication and to a permanent vocation for
nothing. But did the author have to bring Frédéric and Deslauriers
together in this scene, pointing up the weakness and bad faith inherent in
their reconciliation? Did he have to indulge in an inventory of decay? And
does the exalted expedition to the provincial bawdyhouse not cheapen
whatever might have been salvaged (the very memory of Mme Arnoux!) by
stressing venal love and by linking almost perversely the prurient excitement of early adolescence with the impotence of precocious senility?

Yet Flaubert felt surer of the validity of this scene than of almost any
other scene in the novel. Endings were for him a matter of utmost concern
even when, as in *Madame Bovary* or *L' Éducation sentimentale*, they may
at first appear like an unfunctional appendix. But the anticlimactic last
three chapters in *Madame Bovary* are far from gratuitous. In *L' Éducation
sentimentale*, the ending is even more intimately bound up with the very
structure and meaning of the book. Paradoxically, it almost engenders the

*From *The Novels of Flaubert: A Study of Themes and Techniques* (Princeton, N.J.:
Princeton University Press, 1966), 125–38. Reprinted by permission of Princeton University Press.

very beginning. It is an epilogue, no doubt: but this epilogue echoes and parallels one of the earliest passages in the book. I refer to the second chapter, which is partly a flashback to Frédéric's and Deslauriers' childhood, and partly an early conversation between the two friends as they look forward to the future, but already have a past to talk about. Thus the book can be said to begin and to close with a conversation between Frédéric and Deslauriers in which projects or reminiscences take priority over action. The immediate effect of this extension in time (the prologue carries us back to 1833, the epilogue forward to the winter of 1868) is a feeling of temporal circularity and erosion. All the dreams have come to nought. And already during the first conversation, the light the two friends can see shining from the small window of the *maison basse*, the house of ill repute, seems like a shimmering symbol of unattainable desire. "I am of the race of the disinherited," says Frédéric, convinced before the event that no worthwhile woman will ever love him. In the meantime, they do not have enough money to respond to the blinking light. But they do remember a common adventure of some years back, the same adventure that, twenty-seven years later, they will tell each other, agreeing that it had been the best moment of their lives. "C'est là ce que nous avons eu de meilleur."

If, however, we look at this last scene more closely, we must notice that the bordello motif is not exploited for its sheer anecdotal value, nor even primarily to allow for the devastating final comment. The episode, as remembered by the two friends — though it occurred some time before the events of the novel itself — does in fact sum up, in miniature fashion, a whole pattern of events and meanings. What happened is banal enough: on a late Sunday afternoon, the two boys plucked some flowers, gathered them into bouquets and proceeded furtively to the house of "La Turque." "Frédéric presented his bouquet, like a boyfriend to his fiancée. But the heat of the day, the fear of the unknown, a kind of remorse, and even the excitement of seeing at a glance so many women at his disposal, affected him so much that he grew very pale and could neither move nor speak. They all laughed, amused at his embarrassment. Thinking that he was being made fun of, he ran away; and since he had the money, Deslauriers was forced to follow him."[2] Several aspects of this passage deserve analysis. To begin with, the author provides here a subtly nuanced sketch of Frédéric's character. The naïve gesture of appearing with flowers at a brothel points up a latent and ineffectual idealism. The comparison with the boyfriend and his fiancée is touching enough, but suggests a tendency to see reality through a deforming imagination. The heat which paralyzes him reminds us of many other states of dreamy indolence in Frédéric's life. The vague sense of guilt, which, one must assume, is here related to a mother-image, is elsewhere associated with the pure and "maternal" image of Marie Arnoux. The multiplicity of women making the choice impossible corresponds not only to the constant and inconclusive wavering, within the novel, from one woman to another, but to Frédéric's basic inability to focus on anything and impose a single direction on his life. The immobility, the speechlessness and the ultimate flight underline a chronic timidity, the fear of judgment and humiliation. Thus he also tears up his first letter to Mme Arnoux: ". . . he did nothing, attempted nothing — paralyzed by the fear of failure" (I.3). And the flight itself corresponds, of course, to a flight from the realities of the capital and a return to the sheltered life of the province.

But there is more to this passage. The naïve arrival in the whorehouse, the flustered departure, the very *fiasco* of the expedition symbolize the poetic illusion that clings tenaciously to unfulfilled love. It symbolizes the orgyless orgy, the love-dream remaining pure because it was unrealized. After all, Frédéric leaves "La Turque" chaste! The debauches have been of the imagination: mere velleities. So that the final comment ("C'est là ce que nous avons eu de meilleur"), far from being exclusively a cynical remark, or a symptom of arrested development, must also be interpreted as a lasting nostalgia for innocence.[3] This preference for the past conceals another form of idealism. Memory illumines. And although both friends seem to have lost everything, this final dialogue between the man who sought Love and the man who sought Power reveals that it is the search for Love (no matter how clumsy and frustrating) which retrospectively bestows the only meaning. The episode thus combines, in the most ambiguous manner, touching illusion and adult disillusionment, flights of fancy and retreat into the self, attraction to the multiform manifestations of life and paralysis caused by the very proliferation of forms and possibilities, eternally youthful memories and the pathos of aging. In other words, it is a retrospective prolepsis of the very essence of the novel. Even the relationship of Frédéric and his friend is prefigured in the terse remark that since the one had the money, the other was obliged to follow him!

The bordello motif, or in a more general sense the image of the Prostitute and the theme of Prostitution, is at the core of *L' Éducation sentimentale*. Frédéric's erotic sensibility and erotic dreams as a boy crystallize around visions of satin-covered boudoirs where he and his friend will experience "fulgurant orgies with illustrious courtesans" (I.2). Such exotic passions are inevitably linked to dreams of success. He and Deslauriers spend so many hours constructing and peopling their harems that they are as exhausted as though they had indulged in real debauches. Later, when Frédéric actually penetrates into the world of Parisian women, he is almost overcome by the luxurious *odor di femmina*. There is, to be sure, a certain literary tradition behind this particular mystique of the senses. Romanticism had cast the eternal hetaera, whether simple *fille de joie* or high-class courtesan, in the role of initiator into the deep mysteries of life. Even social, artistic and political success — in nineteenth-century literature — is often related to one form or another of prostitution. Such literary expressions no doubt correspond to certain social and psychological patterns: the bourgeois adolescent looked at the prostitute with mixed feelings of admiration, contempt, desire to redeem and even a yearning for profanation. There is for instance a curious letter from Alfred Le Poittevin to Flaubert which tells of the young man's desire to desecrate in the company of a whore places where he has been "young and credulous."[4] As for Flaubert himself, it is clear that he is haunted by the image of the prostitute, whom he associates, in an almost Baudelairean manner, with equally complex monastic and ascetic urges.

In the novel, the bordello motif and the theme of prostitution assume in part a satiric function. The world of the *lorettes* into which Frédéric is ironically introduced by Mme Arnoux's husband, appears to him at first in the guise of a masked ball, where the most tempting display of flesh, costumes and poses inevitably brings to mind the variegated offerings of an elegant house of prostitution providing "specialties" for every whim. Frédéric is so dazzled that, during the first moments, he can distinguish only silk, velvet and naked shoulders. Then, gradually, he takes stock of the contents of this Parisian seraglio: the languorous Polish beauty, the placid and falsely modest Swiss siren, the provocative Fishwife, the Primitive with peacock feathers, the avid Bacchante, the carnival Work-woman — all the "refinements of modern love" dance before him, and the beads of perspiration on their foreheads further suggest a hothouse atmosphere (II.1). This scene, ending in a collective hangover the following morning, recalls the famous Taillefer orgy in Balzac's *La Peau de chagrin*: the same display of available carnality, the same specter of disease and death, the same garish coupling of the lascivious and the macabre. Only Flaubert is not concerned with sheer pyrotechnics. He is not out to rival Petronius' description of decadence in the *Satyricon*. His aim is neither sensational nor allegorical. He works and weaves his images patiently and deliberately into the general pattern of the novel. But there are some immediate effects, and the most noteworthy is a vertiginous proliferation of forms and gestures which ultimately transforms human beings into mechanized objects. In her drunken stupor, one of the women imitates "the oscillation of a launch."

The easy-virtued world of Rosanette is not the only one to be described in terms of lupanar images. Frédéric's suggestive vision imposes these very same images onto the assembly of elegant feminine guests in the salon of Mme Dambreuse (II.2). The upper-class ladies all sit in a row, "offering" their bosoms to the eye, the rustling of their gowns suggests that dresses are about to slip down. The lack of expression on their faces is in perverse contrast to their "provocative garments." The animal-like placid-ity of these ladies in décolleté evokes the "interior of a harem." Flaubert's intention becomes quite explicit, for he adds: "A more vulgar comparison came to the young man's mind." Here too, the salon provides a sampling of physical and regional types to satisfy every possible taste: English beauties with keepsake profiles, Italians with ardent eyes, three Norman sisters "fresh as apple trees in April"—an alluring and appetizing display of sophisticated impudicity. The total effect is once again dehumanization: the crescendo of feminine chatter sounds like the cackle of birds.

Even public locales (cafés, restaurants, *bals publics*) are seen as places of prostitution, for instance the Alhambra, where, according to Deslauriers, one can easily get to know "women." The exotic name corresponds to fake exotic architecture, or rather to jarring elements of architecture: Moorish galleries, the restaurant side in the form of a Gothic cloister, Venetian lanterns, a Chinese roofing over the orchestra, neoclassical painted cupids (I.5). This shocking combination is not merely a sign of vulgarity. It represents the particular attempt at facile poetry, or rather at facile estrangement, which is the special function of all purveyors of bought pleasures. In this light, the bordello becomes the convenient metaphor for any catering to the thirst for illusion. The Alhambra provides sensual pleasures for the public. The reader witnesses a collective debauchery: the last firecracker of the evening provokes an orgastic sigh. But in reality, nothing really happens. The policemen who wake up Frédéric on the boulevard bench where he has fallen asleep, and who are convinced that he has "fait la noce," are as wrong as his own mother concerning his visit to "La Turque." For Frédéric, it has been an innocent orgy, combining in characteristic fashion exposure to depravity with an exacerbated yearning for ideal love. Frédéric's only activity right after the Alhambra is to stare at Mme Arnoux's window.

This aspect of the metaphorical unity of *L' Éducation sentimentale* is further strengthened by the presence of key characters who, in one form or another, are for sale. The most important of these is Rosanette Bron, "La Maréchale." That Rosanette is a kept woman, and most often kept by several men at the same time, is of course no secret. Her true calling is perhaps never more graphically suggested than by her portrait, commissioned by M. Arnoux, eventually purchased by Frédéric, but which in the meantime stands exposed in the window of a gallery with the following words written in black letters underneath: "Mme Rose-Annette Bron, appartenant à M. Frédéric Moreau, de Nogent" (II.4). True to her vocation, she specializes, one might say, in sexual provocation. Innumerable passages in the novel stress this talent. Her laughter has a whiplike effect on Frédéric's nerves. At times, she assumes the poses of a "provocative slave." Most often, her sex appeal is less indolent: her way of pulling up her stockings, her movements, her very chignon are "like a challenge" (II.2). When she eats, and the redness of the fruit mixes with the purple of her lips, the insolence of her look fills Frédéric with mad desires. As for her innumerable caprices, her disconnected cravings, they correspond to the usual versatility associated with the prostitution metaphor; only here the multiplicity of forms and possibilities is internalized. The capricious, unpredictable nature of Rosanette also corresponds to her treachery—and in a broader sense, to the theme of treason so important in this novel. Hers is partially an irresponsible type of cruelty best exemplified by her coldly abandoning Frédéric at the Café Anglais after accepting from de Cisy a bracelet with three opals.

A far more cold-blooded selfishness is the main feature of the "grande dame," the regal prostitute Mme Dambreuse. Frédéric finds that she has something "languorous" and "dry" (II.4). Her sterile cupidity appears in full light when, after the death of her husband, and in the presence of her lover, she stares, disconsolate, into the empty strong box! As for the perfidious Vatnaz, the eternal procuress, she provokes only disgust. The mere touch of her "thin, soft hand" sends shivers down Frédéric's spine. The world of Paris thus insistently proposes to Frédéric images of prostitution: *lorettes* at the hippodrome; streetwalkers under the gaslight; scenes of slave markets with lewd sultans and cheap puns in boulevard plays. At the horse races, he glimpses an obscenely made-up queen of the burlesque theater known as the "Louis XI of prostitution." Everywhere he turns, it would seem that, as in Baudelaire's *Tableaux parisiens*, "La Prostitution s'allume dans les rues." ["Prostitution is kindling itself in the streets"].

But actual prostitution is of course not the only form of prostitution. There are less literal manifestations, all pointing to some manner of depravity. For the bordello motif is closely bound up with Frédéric's apprenticeship of life. His "education" in Paris—the subject as well as the title of the novel place it squarely in the tradition of the *Bildungsroman*— is to begin with the discovery of one type or another of pandering, cheapening or desecration. One could almost take one by one every character and every activity. The very name of Arnoux's hybrid establishment, *L'Art industriel*, is like a profanation of art. And his career sadly illustrates this profanation: an amateur painter, he is in turn director of an art magazine, an art dealer, the owner of a pottery factory manufacturing "artistic" soup plates and mythological decorations for bathrooms. With every chapter he takes a step down. After designing letters for signboards and wine labels, and going bankrupt through shady deals, he has the idea of a *café chantant* and of a military hat-making business, and he finally winds up dealing in beads and cheap "religious art." The very word "décadence" (III.4) aptly sums up his career. There is the same brutal deflation in the life of Pellerin, the painter who wanted to rival Veronese, then places his art in the service of politics, and ends up being a professional photographer. The actor Delmar, a coarse histrion, similarly illustrates the prostitution of art: he sells out his vulgar talent to political parties, and gives public recitals of humanitarian poetry on . . . prostitution (III.3). This propensity for selling out is most strikingly symbolized by the epitaph-like résumé of the life of the financier Dambreuse, who "had acclaimed Napoleon, the Cossacks, Louis XVIII, 1830, the working-man, every régime, adoring Power with such intensity that he would have paid in order to have the opportunity of selling himself" (III.4).

As for Frédéric himself, much could be said. In a letter to Amélie

Bosquet, written some ten years before the publication of *L' Éducation sentimentale*, Flaubert makes this revealing confession: "One has spoken endlessly about the prostitution of women, but not a word has been said about that of men. I have known the tortures of prostitutes, and any man who has loved for a long time and who desired no longer to love has experienced them."[5] Unquestionably Frédéric's ambiguous situation vis-à-vis the Arnoux household, combining the duplicity of an adulterer, the frustrations of an unsuccessful suitor and the embarrassment of being Arnoux's rival not only with his wife, but with his mistress, exposes him to complex compromises and turpitudes. His dilettantish vacillations and reliance on others are almost those of a "kept" person. Frédéric is not only weak (Flaubert often depicts strong women and weak, virginal men), but passive and "feminine." He holds, for his friend Deslauriers, "un charme presque féminin" ["an almost feminine charm"] (II.5). The projected marriage to Mme Dambreuse, for money and social prestige, shows us Frédéric morally at his most depraved.

Finally, the prostitution motif provides a link between individual and collective attitudes. Society itself, as represented by various groups, corporations or institutions, is the great whore who always embraces the winner. Like Rosanette, who after despising the revolutionaries now declares herself in favor of the Republic, so do all the representative authorities — "as his lordship the Archbishop had already done, and as the magistracy, the Conseil d'État, the Institut, the marshals of France, Changarnier, M. de Falloux, all the Bonapartists, all the Legitimists, and a considerable number of Orleanists were about to do with a swiftness displaying marvelous zeal" (III.1). Politics in particular, which held a somewhat perverse fascination for the apolitical Flaubert, is viewed as a slattern. During the obscenely violent and profanatory sack of the Tuileries palace, a slut is seen, on a heap of garments, assuming the motionless, allegorical pose of the Statue of Liberty.

The bitterness of an image such as this stresses the coarseness and the fickleness of political allegiances. But it is part of a more general theme of betrayed ideals. *L' Éducation sentimentale* is a novel of bankruptcy and of pathological erosion. Certain chapters accumulate one form of betrayal on top of another, until the feeling is that of an immense desertion. Friendship, ambition, politics, love — nothing seems immune from this chronic deterioration and devaluation.[6] The most brutal manifestation of this aspect of the novel is the double betrayal of the political turncoat Sénécal, the former Socialist now turned police agent who during the coup d'état of 1851 coldbloodedly kills the sentimental revolutionary Dussardier. This stunning act, which leaves Frédéric agape, is like an allegory of treason destroying idealism.

And it is no gratuitous coincidence that makes Frédéric the witness to this despicable deed. The images of prostitution and degradation exist primarily in relation to Frédéric's personal vision, to his longings, his sadness, his disappointments and his defeats. The bordello motif may permeate the novel as a whole and may have a universal significance within its context. It represents ersatz on all levels, transmuting almost every gesture into parody: the duel with de Cisy is no real duel; the props Pellerin uses for his "Venetian" portrait are fake props; all creative efforts are derivative. But it is in relation to Frédéric's "sentimental education" that all this counterfeit acquires dramatic meaning. No matter how obviously depraved the objective world may be, it is his sentimental life which, subjectively, is most affected by the principle of degrading vicariousness. Thus Frédéric bounces from one woman to another, permanently oscillating between contradictory desires and contradictory experiences, always driven to seek a poor substitute for the *authentic* experience he dreams of, and which, in the process, he steadily defiles. One desire awakens a contradictory desire, suggesting a repetitive discontinuity. "The frequentation of the two women provided, as it were, two strains of music in his life, the one playful, passionate, amusing; and the other almost religious . . ." (II.2). And there are not two women in his life, but four — if one includes the young girl, Louise Roque. This oscillation at times obliges Flaubert to resort to devices which appear extraneous: chance encounters, unexpected letters, coincidences which further underline the passivity of the hero and his easy surrender to the easiest path. Almost symbolically, at one point, the "strumpet" Rosanette (Flaubert actually uses the word "catin") interrupts a love scene in progress, thus making the ideal "irrevocably impossible" (III.3).

What is worse, Frédéric *uses* the image of one woman in his relationship with another. It is bad enough that he has learned to make one sentiment serve multiple purposes: in his courtship of Mme Dambreuse, he "makes use of his old passion" for Mme Arnoux (III.3); he repeats to Mme Dambreuse the very oath he just uttered to Rosanette, sends them both identical bouquets and writes them love letters simultaneously (III.4). Even more sadly, he has to rely on substitute images to stimulate himself sexually. "He found it necessary to evoke the image of Rosanette or of Mme Arnoux." (Thus Flaubert himself once told the Goncourts that "all the women he ever possessed were no more than the mattresses for another woman he dreamed of.")[7] In the novel, this sexual substitution takes place quite literally when Frédéric, desperate because Mme Arnoux failed to show up at their rendezvous, makes love to Rosanette on the very bed he had so devoutly prepared for Mme Arnoux.

Such a pattern of substitution and profanation — underlined by the permanent prostitution motif — leads to contradictory results. On the one hand, we witness a strange paralysis, reminiscent of the scene in the brothel when Frédéric could not make his "choice." Life is a planned orgy which never quite amounts to one. As boys, Frédéric and Deslauriers had such extravagant dreams that they were "sad as after a great debauch" (I.2). Frédéric feels destined to accept defeat before even attempting a victory. He has a keen sense of loss before even having possessed. His imagination builds and furnishes Moorish palaces (always the exotic yearning!); he sees himself lounging on cashmere divans listening to the murmur of fountains — and these sensuous dreams become so precise "that they saddened him as though he had lost them" (I.5). Make-belief and mental aphrodiasics turn out to be manifestations of impotence.

The other result appears as a complete contrast to this atony: a vertiginous proliferation. But this proliferation, much like the dizzying display of women at "La Turque," only leads to another form of futility. Innumerable examples in *L'Éducation sentimentale* illustrate this coupling of diversity with sterility: the different esthetic "theories," the contradictory literary projects, the cacophony of political ideas, the jarring clash of opinions and inept clichés. Polymorphism, in the Flaubertian context, is nearly always a sure sign of an almost hypnotic attraction to nothingness, a suicidal yearning for annihilation. "Exhausted, filled with contradictory desires, no longer even conscious of what he wanted, he felt an extraordinary sadness, the desire to die" (II.4).

It is significant that this allurement to nothingness, so explicitly stated, should be experienced by Frédéric while in the company of a high-class prostitute. For somehow, in Flaubert's own imagination, prostitution and an almost ascetic staring into the emptiness of existence are closely related. To Louise Colet he writes that the sight of streetwalkers and of monks "tickles" his soul in its deepest recesses, that prostitution evokes simultaneously "lewdness, bitterness, the nothingness of human relations . . ."[8] The theme of sterility and even abortion in *L'Éducation sentimentale* is illumined by a comment such as this. Flaubert's admiration for the marquis de Sade, which he shares with Baudelaire, makes him suspect Nature and explains in part why he views the Prostitute both as an antiphysis and the very incarnation of sterility. With bitter irony, Flaubert describes the "maison de santé et d'accouchement" where Rosanette gives birth to a sickly offspring in terms that are most equivocal: the chambermaid looks like a "soubrette," the director of the establishment is called "Madame," the establishment itself (with its closed shutters and continuous sounds of piano playing) is called a "maison discrète" (III.4) — leaving little doubt as to the analogy the author had in mind. Originally, Flaubert had even planned to have the "Madame" explain to Frédéric how to dispose of the newborn baby! And when the sickly child soon after dies, Rosanette's grief coincides with the grief of Mme Dambreuse as she realizes that her husband has left all his wealth to someone else. "A mother grieving beside an empty cradle was not more pitiful than Mme Dambreuse at the sight of the open strong-boxes" (III.4). The theme of sterility could not possibly be pushed much further.

Profanation, betrayal, sterility . . . and yet. And yet the reader is never permitted to forget the ideally pure figure of Mme Arnoux. Frédéric may use other women, and forget himself with them; they are nothing but substitutes for an ideal. One might even say, paradoxically, that profanation is here in the service of purity. . . .

Notes

1. Flaubert, *Lettres inédites à Tourgueneff* (Monaco: Editions du Rocher, 1946), p. 206.

2. Flaubert, *L' Éducation sentimentale*, from the *Oeuvres complètes* (Paris: Conard, 1910), 18 vols., III, 7. Here and from henceforth, references to this work are given in the form of a Roman numeral to indicate the part and an Arabic numeral to indicate the chapter.

3. A nostalgia for innocence which, as Harry Levin suggests, goes hand in hand with the need to be "sheltered from the contingencies of adult existence" (*The Gates of Horn: A Study of Five French Realists* [New York: Oxford University Press, 1963], p. 229).

4. Alfred Le Poittevin, *Une Promenade de Bélial et oeuvres inédites* (Paris: Les Presses Françaises, 1924), pp. 194–95.

5. Flaubert, *Correspondance* (Paris: Conard, 1926–33), 9 vols. Letter to Mlle Amélie Bosquet, November–December 1859, IV, 352.

6. For instance, in chapter 2, Part II, Rosanette betrays both Arnoux and Frédéric, Arnoux betrays his wife, and Frédéric betrays the confidence of Arnoux.

7. Edmond and Jules de Goncourt, *Journal* (Monaco: Éditions de l'Imprimerie Nationale de Monaco, 1956–58), 22 vols., VI, 172.

8. *Correspondance*, III, 216 (June 1, 1853).

The Art of Decharacterization in *L' Éducation sentimentale*
A. W. Raitt*

In his fine "essay on literary onomastics," "Noms et prénoms dans *Madame Bovary*," Jean Pommier writes, "In addition to being appropriate to the individuals, it is good for names to be distinct enough among themselves to reinforce the particular idea that the reader is to form about each character. An author should not violate this rule, even when seeking subtle effects. In this respect, as in several others — with apologies to supporters of the 1870 novel[1] — *L' Éducation sentimentale* seems inferior to *Madame Bovary*."[2]

At first glance the facts seem to justify the severity of this judgment. Names such as Moreau or Arnoux are hardly as picturesque or rich in resonances as the names Bovary, Homais, Bournisien, or Lestiboudois. When Flaubert names one of his secondary characters Compain and another Comaing, it is obviously very easy to confuse them. Pommier himself notes the existence of a list of first and last names that Flaubert

*From *Flaubert: La Dimension du texte*, edited by P. M. Wetherill (Manchester; Manchester University Press, 1982), 157–74. Translated for this volume by Robert Magnan. Reprinted by permission of Manchester University Press, Manchester, England.

drew up for *L' Éducation sentimentale*, entitled "bourgeois names,"[3] which seems to suggest an intention not to differentiate too clearly among them. Furthermore, we know that the name given to Frédéric, Moreau, was originally meant for the character who became Mme Arnoux.[4]

Upon closer consideration, however, this lack of distinction among the names seems to be only part of a system that extends far into the conception and the presentation of the characters in *L' Éducation sentimentale*. After all, it is not merely a question of names not being very expressive: in many cases the name of the character actually remains undetermined, in doubt. The most notable case is certainly that of Delmar, the actor, who called himself Auguste Delamare, Anténor Dellamarre (with a change in spelling), Delmas, and Belmar, before finally deciding on Delmar. M. Dambreuse was originally the comte d'Ambreuse, before dropping the apostrophe and combining the particle and the surname as one word. Officially Rosanette is Rose-Annette Bron, but she is also the Maréchale, and the baron even calls her "that good Rose." Moreover, she does not hesitate to rename Frédéric the first time he comes to visit her alone. "What is your first name?" "Frédéric." "Ah! Federico! It doesn't bother you if I call you that?" The baby born to Frédéric and Rosanette never receives a name, although he lives at least six months. Flaubert even on occasion forgets that Mme Arnoux's daughter is named Marthe and he calls her Berthe, the name of Mme Bovary's daughter.[5] It may also be noted that it is only at the last moment that he decides on the spelling of the name Vatnaz, which is still written with an 's' as late as in the copyist's manuscript.[6] As for Mme Dambreuse, we never know her first name, although she becomes Frédéric's mistress. Even Mme Arnoux, whose first name, Marie, seems so appropriate to her role and her character, is not free of such uncertainty. When Cisy calls her Sophie Arnoux, we may well believe that this is a mistake or a bad joke. The confusion is later aggravated, however: when Hussonnet comes to invite Frédéric to the Arnoux home in Saint-Cloud, he says, "It is next Saturday, the 24th, Mme Arnoux's name-day." Frédéric is surprised: "What? But her name is Marie!" Hussonnet answers, "It is also Angèle, no matter!" And yet it is apparently June,[7] and the feast of Saint Angela is 22 December. The information provided by the journalist is false, then, so that in the end we do not truly know Mme Arnoux's first name, any more than we know her maiden name.

So many converging facts leave no room for doubt: Flaubert deliberately deprived his characters of the identification that we normally expect from a name. This process is carried to extremes in the remarkable scene at the masquerade ball given by Rosanette, where the guests, costumed, made up and masked, do not appear under their own names, but rather under the names of what they represent — the Sphinx, the Fishwife, the Altar Boy, the Medieval Baron, the Angel, the Bacchant, and so forth. This crowd of characters assuming all these fictitious identities produces an effect that is unreal, inauthentic, at times almost nightmarish. So many people, we might say, in search of an identity.

But names are not the only aspect of the characters of *L'Éducation sentimentale* to be treated in a way quite different from those in *Madame Bovary* — and, one might add, from those in most novels of the nineteenth century. If we consider what constituted the character and even the identity of an individual for people of that period, we shall see that Flaubert systematically removed or reduced the features that would be normally the most striking.

Think of their homes, for example. It is difficult to visualize Emma Bovary without seeing the Bertaux farm, the house in Tostes, and especially the house in Yonville. But the figures of Frédéric and Mme Arnoux are not attached to any particular residence. We see them for the first time on a moving boat, and this instability, this lack of ties, sets the tone for the entire novel. Tossed about between a house, hardly described at all, on the place d'Armes in Nogent and a string of addresses in Paris — rue Saint-Hyacinthe, quai Napoléon, rue Rumfort, rue Tronchet — Frédéric never remains in one place long enough to permit any symbiosis between residence and personality. At the end of the novel, "he traveled" for an indefinite length of time, before returning to France to end up in a place that is not even identified. As for Mme Arnoux, born in Chartres, she lives at address after address with her husband — rue de Choiseul, Saint-Cloud, rue Paradis-Poissonnière, Creil, Auteuil, and rue de Fleurus, before retiring to a remote corner of Brittany; finally, after her husband dies, she moves off to Rome to live with her son.

This feeling of rootlessness is even more striking in the secondary characters. We know that Rosanette has at least six different addresses in Paris, not to mention the slum where she was born in Lyons. Nobody knows where Hussonnet lives: "Where might such a man be found?" exclaims Frédéric. Apart from a brief stay in a sixth-floor apartment on rue des Trois-Maries, Deslauriers never has a place of his own: he lives either with Frédéric or else in rooms that are never seen. As for Regimbart, his case is extraordinary: Flaubert lists at least twenty-five cafés that he visits frequently, only to reveal, ironically, in one of the final chapters, that he owns a little house on the rue de l'Empereur in Montmartre. Furthermore, the last time that he is mentioned, he is not even seated inside a tavern: "he is loitering in front of the cafés." Obviously, the image of the oyster and the rock used by Balzac in *Le Père Goriot*[8] is not applicable to the world of *L'Éducation sentimentale*.

Characters are no better defined by occupation than by residence. Here again Flaubert seems to take a position opposite that held by Balzac, for whom the "Social Species" were strictly defined categories. Arnoux provides the most characteristic example of this. Painter, editor of an art journal, property owner, speculator, soldier in the national guard, pottery manufacturer, military hatter, dealer in religious items — one after the other or at the same time, he has dabbled in all trades and been involved in the shadiest and most diverse businesses, without ever settling on any. Deslauriers ends up with a string of occupations almost as impressive: law student, lawyer's clerk, tutor, journalist, lawyer, commisssary of the Republic, assistant to M. Dambreuse, police commissioner, colonial administrator, secretary to a pasha, manager of a newspaper, advertising canvasser, member of the legal department of a manufacturing company. Likewise Sénécal, who is first a mathematics tutor, then works for a machine manufacturer, then as a foreman in a pottery factory, then as secretary to Deslauriers, then as business manager, and finally as a police officer.

Sometimes the occupation of a character is shrouded in mystery. Regimbart appears to have none, and only toward the end of the novel do we learn that his wife supports him with her sewing shop. As for la Vatnaz, we suspect that she is a pimp, but we know that she has also earned a living as a governess, a cashier, a director of a hotel dining establishment, a fashion journalist, a piano teacher, a lace merchant. And Frédéric himself, although he toys with being a painter, or a novelist, or a historian, or an industrialist, or a deputy, has actually no trade at all, except for that of lawyer's clerk, at which he is totally incompetent.

Occupation contributes little, then, to defining the identity of the characters; does social class provide them with greater substance? Certainly, their social origins are sometimes quite clear. In particular, we may mention Dussardier, the archetype of the honest and conscientious blue-collar worker, or Rosanette, the daughter of Lyons silk workers, or else the comte d'Ambreuse. But in the world of *L' Éducation sentimentale* the lines of class distinction are extraordinarily vague. In the case of the comte d'Ambreuse, "from 1825 on, leaving behind his nobility and his party little by little, he had turned toward industry." As for Rosanette, Frédéric knows nothing about her rise in society: "By what steps had she been able to escape from poverty? To what lover did she owe her education? What had happened in her life before the day when he visited her for the first time?" — questions never to be answered. Even Dussardier, who may seem to be acting according to his class, ends up not knowing what he is, and, after his injury in June 1848, wonders in agony if it was right for him to fight against his former companions: "Maybe he should have joined the other side, with the blue collars." Frédéric himself is from a mixed background: his mother, born De Fouvens, "came from an ancient family of gentlemen, whose name had died out," while his father, "a plebeian that her parents had made her marry, had died of a sword wound during her pregnancy, leaving her a compromised fortune." Martinon, son of a wealthy farmer, ends up a senator in the Second Empire. Mme Arnoux, whose parents were of the lower middle class in Chartres, gains access through marriage to all social circles — and they are indeed numerous — open to her husband. People such as Hussonnet, Pellerin, Regimbart, even

Sénécal, belong to no clearly defined class. Even if we admit that the mixing of social classes around 1848 is a historical fact, it must be agreed that the absence of obvious class characteristics is an important factor in blurring the outlines of the characters in this novel.

Race plays an even more subtle role than physical or social environment. Several of the characters—Frédéric, Deslauriers, Martinon, Roque and his daughter Louise—are originally from Nogent or the surrounding region; but as Flaubert provides very few details about this province, the inhabitants of which show no particular character traits, we are no better off in understanding their personalities. Cisy is from lower Brittany, but we learn this only in one of the final chapters, and we would have been hard pressed to guess it earlier. And what about Arnoux, one might ask, this type of man who, according to Albert Thibaudet, "is found throughout the Midi, handling soap, proof spirits, and wine"?[9] Yes, but admitting him to be typically meridional (and even if we disregard the fact that this character closely resembles Moritz Schlesinger, a Prussian Jew),[10] Flaubert reveals his origins to us only after a long while, almost by chance, casually, when he mentions that Arnoux, in playing with his son, "lisped affectionately in the patois of Marseilles, his native tongue." As for his wife, although she was born in Chartres, she is so unlike the physical stereotype of this region (to the extent that there is one) that Frédéric "believed her to be Andalusian, perhaps Creole." What a difference from *Madame Bovary*, where a character such as Lheureux is depicted entirely in terms of his origins ("born Gascon but now Norman, he added the cunning of the Caux region to the fluency of the Midi") and where Flaubert, with regard to Emma, speaks of "her peasant blood impelling her to profit"!

It would be inaccurate, then, to claim that the characters of *L' Éducation sentimentale* are formed by race or environment. But at first one might be tempted to believe that the third element of the deterministic equation proposed by Hippolyte Taine—the historical moment—assumes a fundamental importance. After all, the Revolution of 1848, with its early rumblings and its aftermath, has a very significant presence throughout the novel, and Flaubert gathered facts with such scrupulous care that *L' Éducation sentimentale* remains a historical document of unquestionable value.[11] It is also obvious that, in certain respects at the very least, some of the characters represent attitudes and tendencies typical of society during that era: Dambreuse, "cherishing Power with such love that he would have paid to sell out," is a perfect portrait of the corrupt, egoistic, fickle politician who served in all the administrations of that period, just as Sénécal is first and foremost the representative of narrow, fanatical, authoritarian socialism as Flaubert saw it. And yet, although the characters pass through the political events of 1848, these events generally touch only the edges of their world, at least insofar as Frédéric and Mme Arnoux are concerned—it is significant that it is not the riot that prevents Mme

Arnoux from keeping her appointment on rue Tronchet, but rather her son's illness. In his fine article "Structure et sens de *L' Éducation sentimentale*,"[12] Jacques Proust admirably demonstrated to what extent the "foregrounds" and the "backgrounds" of this novel can be considered independent of each other: between them there is a relationship that could be termed contrapuntal, rather than a relationship of necessity and determinism.

In fact, even on the psychological level, it would be difficult to speak of determinism in the evolution of the characters. In *Madame Bovary* Flaubert took great pains to suggest causes and motives for the actions and feelings of his characters and, although he may not have tried to construct a strictly deterministic psychological system, at least he strongly emphasized the role of an obvious causality in human nature.[13] In *L' Éducation sentimentale*, on the other hand, it is chance, above all, that dominates in the behavior of his characters.[14] It would be superfluous to underscore the degree to which Frédéric is inconsistent, impulsive, fickle, a character in which the "lack of a straight line" that he acknowledges at the end of the novel is quite evident throughout: this is one of the major themes of the work. Frédéric allows himself to be distracted from his intentions, from his ambitions, even from his loves, by minor incidents, trifles, gestures or words often misunderstood. We can regard this, obviously, as the essence of his character, in which case Flaubert did nothing other than depict, through traditional methods, a young man who is weak, passive, and thoughtless. In reality, however, we have here a sort of deconstruction of the character, evident as well in the presentation of the other characters, even if the means are not always exactly the same. Flaubert took care not to provide plausible explanations for all the actions of his characters and not to show these actions developing much in advance. On the contrary, he very often makes his characters act unpredictably, to the point that their actions seem gratuitous.

Of all the characters in this novel, Martinon is perhaps the one who seems most consistent. Calculating, egoistic, and coldly ambitious, he means to achieve his ends at any cost, and he succeeds in full: he acquires wealth by marrying Cécile Dambreuse and the respect of society by becoming a senator. However, his success depends on an action that nothing in his nature would suggest. M. Dambreuse, wishing to find out if Martinon has ulterior motives in seeking to marry Cécile, makes it clear to him that, as the daughter of poor parents, she will have no dowry. If Martinon were consistent in his thinking, he would try to find an excuse to withdraw. But he does nothing of the sort. "Martinon, not believing this to be true, or too involved to withdraw, or in one of those moments of insane obstinacy that are acts of genius, answered that his patrimony, 1500 pounds annual income, would be enough for them." This response, so inconsistent with his usual character that Flaubert accompanies it with three possible explanations that are not only different but contradictory, ensures his fortune and his future, an ironic paradox that sheds light on the originality of the psychology that emerges in this episode.

Another example will show the curious discontinuity of cause and effect to be found in the behavior of the characters in *L' Éducation sentimentale*. In *Madame Bovary* the reader well understands why a certain character experiences a certain feeling; here, however, Flaubert often gives no explanation. At the height of Emma's affair with Rodolphe the repugnance that Charles inspires in her is expressed by, among other things, an irritation with his hands: "never did Charles seem so unpleasant, with such thick fingers, so dull-witted, with such inelegant manners as when they were together after these rendezvous with Rodolphe." Dullness of wit, plebian behavior, coarse body: everything is of a piece, and the aversion that Emma feels toward these thick fingers is perfectly understandable. Now here is Arnoux in the offices of *L' Art industriel*: "he handled the spread out samples, discussed their shapes, colors, borders; and Frédéric grew more and more irritated by his air of meditation, and particularly by his hands running over the posters, big hands, somewhat flabby, with flat nails." Nothing is more natural than for Frédéric to dislike Arnoux personally. But Flaubert does not tell us why the young man's irritation is focused on his hands, and if we try to construct explanations for this fact, we run the risk of soliciting the text. This refusal to show the logical sequence of cause and effect is characteristic of the lacunary presentation of psychology in *L' Éducation sentimentale*. Whereas the characters in *Madame Bovary* appear as homogeneous units, in the 1869 novel they create the effect of being rather bundles of impulses and feelings that are scarcely interconnected.

It is true that this discontinuity results in part from the viewpoint adopted by Flaubert in this work, which is usually that of Frédéric, not a very perspicacious or curious observer.[15] Frédéric has many friends, whom he meets only occasionally; he often knows very little about their pasts and their private lives; he is not much interested in divining their true feelings — or, when he does so, as with Mme Arnoux, it is with such naïveté and blindness that the results are miserable. At times Flaubert compensates for these deficiencies in observation by allowing us to be present at scenes from which Frédéric is absent, as when Mme Arnoux's son is ill or when Deslauriers attempts to seduce her. At times, too, the reader can easily penetrate secrets that elude Frédéric, such as the plotting by Mme Dambreuse when her husband is on his deathbed, which is eminently transparent. But very often the reader is hardly in a better position than Frédéric to fill in gaps in the text. What brings Arnoux and Regimbart together? Just what lies behind the quarrels and the reconciliations between Rosanette and La Vatnaz? What sort of feelings did Mme Arnoux have for her husband at the time that they married? It would be useless to try to answer these questions, since we do not have the evidence to allow a complete reconstruction of reality.

Moreover, even when there is a possible explanation, the fact that it is suppressed or that it appears late entirely changes the perspective of the reader toward the characters. If, by any remote chance, we could picture the incident at the house of La Turque in its proper chronological setting, that is, at the beginning of the story, we would have a completely different view of Frédéric's character: we would feel tempted to explain it in terms of timidity originating in this youthful failure and we would probably speak about traumas and complexes. Obviously, extrapolations of this sort find no justification at all in the novel as we have it, and to attempt any would be to distort the text. In this respect it is significant that there are so few flashbacks in *L'Éducation sentimentale*. Normally flashbacks serve to provide us with information necessary to our understanding of the actions and emotions of the characters—that is why Balzac fills his novels with them. The fact that they are rare in *L'Éducation sentimentale*, particularly in view of the great number of characters, indicates that Flaubert intended to provide minimal explanatory facts in this manner.

All of these particular features are concordant. In *L'Éducation sentimentale* Flaubert is no longer using the techniques of character construction that had served him in *Madame Bovary* and perhaps even in *Salammbô*, and that his contemporaries in general were using. Name, place of residence, occupation, social class, origins, moment in time, determinism of behavior—all of these are systematically blurred or substantially reduced. There is an abyss between this technique and that used by Zola, for example, who would declare only a few years later, "we hold that a human cannot be separated from his *milieu*, that he forms a whole with his clothing, his house, his town, his province."[16] Does this mean that Flaubert had abandoned the principles of psychological determinism which had guided him in the preparation of his first great novel? It does not seem so. In his letters as well as in *Bouvard et Pécuchet*, Flaubert seems to have kept intact his belief in the influence of these factors, especially that of race in the development of personality; there is no question of his repudiating, on a philosophical level, convictions that seem to be as solidly rooted in 1869 as in 1856. To what, then, are we to attribute such a radical and dramatic reversal? And more important, is this novel so obviously marked by this reversal the better for it or not?

If it is not on the philosophical level that the reason for this change is to be discovered, then it is doubtless on the aesthetic level, which is always primordial in the Flaubert novel. Flaubert once wrote, "everything must come from the subject—ideas, comparisons, metaphors,"[17] and he never stopped repeating that in a novel "everything is of a piece."[18] Let us see, then, if the famous Carnet 19 contains anything instructive in this respect. We note immediately that the author, from the very beginning of his meditations, had the idea of this sort of gratuitousness that we have just examined: "by chance," "the feeling ends by itself," "chance also is involved in this," "intermittences," "a fortuitous circumstance," "no consistency in his ideas" — these are some of the expressions to be found there. And when we observe, among the first ideas that Flaubert notes for this novel still in embryo, the words "boat trip to Montereau," we begin to sense that what are conventionally termed "the characters" are in reality only one aspect of the universe of the novel, conceived by the author as an indivisible whole. Good critics, particularly Bernard Masson,[19] have already analyzed the importance of images of water, liquidity, flowing, and instability in L' Éducation sentimentale. The world of L'Éducation sentimentale is essentially elusive, and Flaubert strove to blur, one might even say vaporize, anything that could make it too solid, too tangible. This process extends even into stylistic revision of the manuscript, which has been the subject of a masterly study by Michael Wetherill.[20] It is obvious that the characters had to be treated in the same manner, or else they would have been incongruous with the novel.

As for deciding if this technique, so individual and so new, makes the work better or not, the question is probably inappropriate. Pommier cites and concurs with the opinion expressed by Emile Faguet: "In short, the astonishing sharpness with which even secondary characters, and even minor characters, are presented in Madame Bovary, is a secret that Flaubert seems to have lost in L' Éducation sentimentale."[21] Yes, if we hold that the characters of a novel must always be vividly established, well sketched, and brilliantly illuminated. No, if we consider that the characters are only one element of a text which has its own particular aesthetic, which forms a coherent and unified whole, and which obeys laws of its own nature.

Be that as it may, it seems undeniable that in L' Éducation sentimentale Flaubert found a way of understanding and presenting characters which is profoundly original and which would later have incalculable reverberations in the French novel. The names Proust, Gide, Robbe-Grillet, Nathalie Sarraute, Claude Simon, and Georges Perec immediately come to mind. This is no small claim to fame. Yet the finest of all is doubtless to have been able to change so completely from one novel to the next that each one forms a separate and distinct world.

Notes

1. I take no responsibility for this date given by Pommier.

2. Jean Pommier, Dialogues avec le passé: études et portraits littéraires (Paris: Nizet, 1967), p. 156. This article first appeared in 1949.

3. Ibid., p. 157, n. 1.

4. Marie-Jeanne Durry, Flaubert et ses projets inédits (Paris: Nizet, 1950). "Madame Moreau" was the working title for the early outlines.

5. Flaubert made this mistake two or three times in the original edition. He corrected it in the 1880 edition, except in one passage where he left it, correcting it only in one of his personal copies (Lucien Andrieu, "Les dernières corrections de *L' Éducation sentimentale*," *Bulletin des amis de Flaubert*, 27 [1965]).

6. See my edition of *L' Éducation sentimentale* (Paris: Imprimerie Nationale, 1979), vol. I, p. 77. The reasons for this change remain unknown.

7. Pierre Cogny places this episode in May of 1843 and accuses Flaubert of having erred, as 24 May that year was a Wednesday (*L' Éducation sentimentale de Flaubert: le monde en creux* [Paris: Larousse, 1975], p. 255). But according to the text of the novel it could equally well be June, and 24 June 1843 was indeed a Saturday.

8. These words are found in the introductory description of the Vauquer house: "The old people . . . never left the neighborhood, and they lived in the boarding-house like oysters on a rock." [Translator]

9. Albert Thibaudet, *Gustave Flaubert* (Paris: Gallimard, 1935; revised edition, 1973), p. 169.

10. Gérard-Gailly, *Le Grand Amour de Flaubert* (Paris: Aubier, 1944), particularly p. 149, n. 1, where he discusses the statement made by Thibaudet; Helmut Steinhart-Leins, *Flauberts grosse Liebe: Elisa Foucault, das Urbild der Madame Arnoux* (Baden-Baden: Kairos Verlag, 1951).

11. Consult, in particular, Alberto Cento, *Il Realismo documentario nell' 'Éducation sentimentale'* (Naples: Liguori, 1967).

12. *Revue des Sciences Humaines* 32:125 (January–March 1967), 67–100.

13. In this regard should be mentioned the splendid study by D. A. Williams, *Psychological Determinism in "Madame Bovary"* (Hull: University of Hull Publications, 1973).

14. Jean Bruneau made this point in his article, "Le Rôle du hasard dans *L' Éducation sentimentale*," *Europe*, September-October-November 1969, pp. 101–107.

15. The study by R. J. Sherrington, in *Three Novels by Flaubert: A Study of Techniques* (Oxford: Clarendon Press, 1970), is fundamental.

16. "De la description," in *Le Roman expérimental* (Paris: Charpentier, 1894), p. 228.

17. In a letter to Louise Colet (June 12, 1852), *Oeuvres complètes de Gustave Flaubert* (Paris: Club de l'Honnête Homme, 1971–76), 16 vols. XIII, 202.

18. This is one aspect of his well-known insistence on form and substance being one.

19. "L'Eau et les rêves dans *L' Éducation sentimentale*," *Europe*, September-October-November 1969, pp. 82–100.

20. "Le Style des thèmes: Étude sur le dernier manuscrit autographe de *L' Éducation sentimentale*," *Zeitschrift für französische Sprache und Literatur*, 81 (1971): 308–51, and 82 (1972): 1–52.

21. Op. cit., p. 156.

La Tentation de saint Antoine

Flaubert's *Temptation of St. Anthony*

Saint Anthony, as most readers know, was an Egyptian monk who, toward the end of the third century, hid himself in the desert to pray, and was visited by a series of hallucinations painfully irrelevant to this occupation. His visions and his stout resistance to them have long been famous — so famous that here is M. Gustave Flaubert, fifteen hundred years afterwards, publishing a large octavo about them, and undertaking to describe them in every particular. This volume, we confess, has been a surprise to us. Announced for publication three or four years ago, it seemed likely to be a novel of that realistic type which the author had already vigorously cultivated, with Saint Anthony and his temptation standing simply as a symbol of the argument. We opened it with the belief that we were to find, not a ragged old cenobite struggling to preserve his virtue amid Egyptian sands, but a portrait of one of the author's own contemporaries and fellow-citizens engaged in this enterprise in the heart of the French capital. M. Flaubert's strong side has not been hitherto the portrayal of resistance to temptation, and we were much in doubt as to whether the dénouement of the novel was to correspond to that of the legend; but it was very certain that, whatever the upshot, the temptation itself would be elaborately represented. So, in fact, it has been; but it is that of the dim-featured founder of monasticism, and not of a gentleman beset by our modern opportunities. The work has the form of a long monologue by the distracted saint, interrupted by voluminous pictorial representations of his visions and by his imagined colloquies with the creatures who people them. We may frankly say that it strikes us as a ponderous failure; but it is an interesting failure as well, and it suggests a number of profitable reflections.

In so far as these concern M. Gustave Flaubert himself, they are decidedly melancholy. Many American readers probably have followed his career, and will readily recall it as an extraordinary example of a writer outliving his genius. There have been poets and novelists in abundance

*Reprinted from *Literary Reviews and Essays* (New Haven, Conn.: New College and University Press, 1957), 145–50. Originally published in 1874.

who are people of a single work, who have had their one hour of inspiration, and gracefully accept the certainty that it would never strike again. There are other careers in which a great success has been followed by a period of inoffensive mediocrity, and, if not confirmed, at least not flagrantly discredited. But we imagine there are few writers who have been at such extraordinary pains as M. Flaubert to undermine an apparently substantial triumph. Some fifteen years ago he published *Madame Bovary*, a novel which, if it cannot be said exactly to have taken its place in the "standard literature" of his country, must yet have fixed itself in the memory of most readers as a revelation of what the imagination may accomplish under a powerful impulse to mirror the unmitigated realities of life. *Madame Bovary*, we confess, has always seemed to us a great work, and capable really of being applied to educational purposes. It is an elaborate picture of vice, but it represents it as so indefeasibly commingled with misery that in a really enlightened system of education it would form exactly the volume to put into the hands of young persons in whom vicious tendencies had been distinctly perceived, and who were wavering as to which way they should let the balance fall.

The facts in *Madame Bovary* were elaborate marvels of description, but they were also, by good luck, extremely interesting in themselves, whereas the facts in *Salammbô*, in *L' Éducation sentimentale*, and in the performance before us, appeal so very meagrely to our sympathy that they completely fail in their appeal to our credulity. And yet we would not for the world have had M. Flaubert's novels unwritten. Lying there before us so unmistakably still-born, they are a capital refutation of the very dogma in defence of which they appeared. The fatal charmlessness of each and all of them is an eloquent plea for the ideal. M. Flaubert's peculiar talent is the description — minute, incisive, exhaustive — of material objects, and it must be admitted that he has carried it very far. He succeeds wonderfully well in making an image, in finding and combining just the words in which the *look* of his object resides. The scenery and properties in his dramas are made for the occasion; they have not served in other pieces. "The sky [in St. Anthony's landscape] is red, the earth completely black; under the gusts of wind the sand-drifts rise up like shrouds and then fall down. In a gap, suddenly, pass a flight of birds in a triangular battalion, like a piece of metal, trembling only on the edges." This is a specimen, taken at random, of the author's constant appeal to observation; he would claim, doubtless, for his works that they are an unbroken tissue of observations, that this is their chief merit, and that nothing is further from his pretension than to conclude to philosophize or to moralize. He proceeds upon the assumption that these innumerable marvels of observation will hold together without the underlying moral unity of what is called a "purpose," and that the reader will proceed eagerly from point to point, stopping just sufficiently short of complete hallucination to remember the author's cleverness.

The reader has, at least, in *La Tentation de Saint Antoine*, the satisfaction of expecting a subject combining with a good deal of chance for color a high moral interest. M. Flaubert describes, from beginning to end, the whole series of the poor hermit's visions; the undertaking implies no small imaginative energy. In one sense, it has been bravely carried out; it swarms with ingenious, audacious, and erudite detail, and leaves nothing to be desired in the way of completeness. There is generally supposed to be a certain vagueness about visions; they are things of ambiguous shapes and misty edges. But vagueness of portrayal has never been our author's failing, and St. Anthony's hallucinations under his hands become a gallery of photographs, executed with the aid of the latest improvements in the art. He is visited successively by all the religions, idolatries, superstitions, rites and ceremonies, priests and potentates, of the early world—by Nebuchadnezzar and the Queen of Sheba, the Emperor Constantine and the Pope Calixtus, the swarm of the early Christian fanatics, martyrs, and philosophers—Origen, Tertullian, Arius, Hermogenes, Ebionites and Encratites, Theodotians and Marcosians, by Helen of Troy and Appollonius of Rhodes, by the Buddha in person, by the Devil in person, by Ormuzd and Ahriman, by Diana of the Ephesians, by Cybele, Atys, Isis, by the whole company of the gods of Greece and by Venus in particular, by certain unnamable Latin deities, whom M. Flaubert not only names but dramatizes, by the figures of Luxury and Death, by the Sphinx and the Chimæra, by the Pigmies and the Cyno-cephali, by the "Sadhuzag" and the unicorn, by all the beasts of the sea, and finally by Jesus Christ. We are not precisely given to understand how much time is supposed to roll over the head of the distracted anchorite while these heterogeneous images are passing before him, but, in spite of the fact that he generally swoons away in the *entr-acte*, as it were, we receive an impression that he is getting a good deal at one sitting, and that the toughest part of his famous struggle came off on a single night. To the reader who is denied the occasional refreshment of a swoon, we recommend taking up the book at considerable intervals. Some of the figures in our list are minutely described, others are briefly sketched, but all have something to say. We fancy that both as a piece of description and a piece of dramatization M. Flaubert is especially satisfied with his Queen of Sheba:

> Her dress, in golden brocade, divided regularly by fur-belows of pearls, of jet, and of sapphire, compresses her waist into a narrow bodice, ornamented with applied pieces in color representing the twelve signs of the zodiac. She wears high skates, of which one is black and spangled with silver stars, with the crescent of the moon, while the other is white, and covered with little drops in gold, with the sun in the middle. Her wide sleeves, covered with emeralds and with feathers of birds, expose the nakedness of her little round arm, ornamented at the wrist by a bracelet of ebony; and her hands, laden with rings, terminate in nails so

pointed that the ends of her fingers look almost like needles. A flat gold
chain, passing under her chin, ascends beside her cheeks, rolls in a spiral
around her hair, which is powdered with blue powder, then, falling,
grazes her shoulder and comes and fastens itself on her bosom in a
scorpion in diamonds which thrusts out its tongue between her breasts.
Two great blood pearls drag down her ears. The edges of her eyelids are
painted black. She has on her left cheek-bone a natural brown mole,
and she breathes, opening her mouth, as if her bodice hurt her. She
shakes as she walks, a green parasol surrounded with gilt bells, and
twelve little woolly-headed negroes carry the long train of her dress,
held at the end by a monkey, who occasionally lifts it up. She says: *"Ah,
bel ermite! bel ermite! mon cœur défaille!"* ["Oh, handsome hermit!
handsome hermit! My heart is swooning!"]

This is certainly a "realistic" Queen of Sheba, and Nebuchadnezzar is
almost equally so. Going on from figure to figure and scene to scene in this
bewildering panorama, we ask ourselves exactly what it is that M.
Flaubert has proposed to accomplish. Not a prose-poem from the saint's
own moral point of view, with his spiritual sufferings and vagaries for its
episode, and his ultimate expulsion of all profane emotions for its
dénouement; for St. Anthony throughout remains the dimmest of
shadows, and his commentary upon his hallucination is meagre and
desultory. Not, on the other hand, a properly historical presentment of the
various types he evokes, for fancy is called in at every turn to supplement
the scanty testimony of history. What is M. Flaubert's historic evidence for
the mole on the Queen of Sheba's cheek and the blue powder in her hair?
He has simply wished to be tremendously pictorial, and the opportunity
for spiritual analysis has been the last thing in his thoughts. It is matter of
regret that a writer with the pluck and energy to grapple with so pregnant
a theme should have been so indifferent to its most characteristic side. It is
probable that, after M. Flaubert's big volume, we shall not have, in
literature, for a long time, any more 'Temptations of St. Anthony'; and yet
there is obviously a virtue in the subject which has by no means been
exhausted. Tremendously pictorial M. Flaubert has certainly succeeded in
being, and we stand amazed at his indefatigable ingenuity. He has
accumulated a mass of curious learning; he has interfused it with a mass of
still more curious conjecture; and he has resolved the whole into a series of
pictures which, considering the want of models and precedents, may be
said to be very handsomely executed. But what, the reader wonders, has
been his inspiration, his motive, his *souffle*, as the French say? Of any
abundant degree of imagination we perceive little in the work. Here and
there we find a touch of something like poetry, as in the scene of the
Christian martyrs huddled in one of the vaults of the circus, and watching
through the bars of the opposite vault the lions and tigers to whom they
are about to be introduced. Here and there is a happy dramatic turn in the
talk of the hermit's visionary interlocutor or a vague approach to a

"situation" in the attitude of the saint. But for the most part M. Flaubert's picturesque is a strangely artificial and cold-blooded picturesque — abounding in the grotesque and the repulsive, the abnormal and the barely conceivable, but seeming to have attained to it all by infinite labor, ingenuity, and research — never by one of the fine intuitions of a joyous and generous invention. It is all hard, inanimate, superficial, and inexpressibly disagreeable. When the author has a really beautiful point to treat — as the assembly of the Greek deities fading and paling away in the light of Christianity — he becomes singularly commonplace and ineffective.

His book being, with its great effort and its strangely absent charm, the really painful failure it seems to us, it would not have been worth while to call attention to it if it were not that it pointed to more things than the author's own deficiencies. It seems to us to throw a tolerably vivid light on the present condition of the French literary intellect. M. Flaubert and his contemporaries have pushed so far the education of the senses and the cultivation of the grotesque in literature and the arts that it has left them morally stranded and helpless. In the perception of the materially curious, in fantastic refinement of taste and marked ingenuity of expression, they seem to us now to have reached the limits of the possible. Behind M. Flaubert stands a whole society of æsthetic *raffinés*, demanding stronger and stronger spices in its intellectual diet. But we doubt whether he or any of his companions can permanently satisfy their public, for the simple reason that the human mind, even in indifferent health, does after all need to be *nourished*, and thrives but scantily on a regimen of pigments and sauces. It needs sooner or later — to prolong our metaphor — to detect a body-flavor, and we shall be very much surprised if it ever detects one in *La Tentation de Saint Antoine*.

[Flaubert and His *Temptation of Saint Anthony*]
Theodor Reik*

. . . It is no accident that we have emphasized Flaubert's sexual behavior and psycho-sexual constitution to such a prominent degree. This is exactly the source from which the artist draws his greatest energies. We have seen how the seeds of Flaubert's entire development already existed in his youth. Like every child, he was polymorphously perverse. His first libido was directed toward the mother, his first hate toward the father. The deep impressions of these affects persist in his later life: he bears their marks as galley slaves used to bear the sign of the punishment they had to endure. Both affects — love and hatred — are repressed, but the repression is

*From *Flaubert and seine "Versuchung des heiligen Antonius"* (Minden: J. C. C. Bruns, 1912), 176–85. Translated for this volume by Tina M. Gikas, Michigan State University. Reprinted by permission of Slatkine Reprints, Geneva, Switzerland.

not completely successful. All his libidinous fantasies are debarred from the domain of consciousness as being frivolous and laughable. Combinations of physiological and self-generated alterations result from sexual abstinence. The repressed desires emerge in dream and poetry. The ego refuses them. A split of the personality results, which is the second state of the hysteric. In addition seizures occur, whose mechanism resembles that of the dream: they are wish fulfillments of repressed complexes. Flaubert is — to use Otto Gross' expression[1] — a psychopath with a restricted consciousness. In his case, the concentration of affect is related to his fanatically loved art. The total affect is diverted from all other areas and occupies this one. It leads to intellectual hyperactivity, a heightened ability for creative work. Every sublimation, however, has its limits. The countless perversions, which inhabited the child and affected him, are too strong to be abreacted in sado-masochistic descriptions. First, the neurosis shapes the obverse of the perversions. The inability to cope with one's own affects impels one toward melancholy, makes it difficult to endure the world. Sensitivity to the highest degree, addiction to doubt and brooding are quite typical of the restricted consciousness. Here, however, in the inability to become free of affects, lies the source of our author's productivity (talent was naturally a prerequisite). His tendency toward isolation has its basis in masturbation and in the imaginative processes which result from Flaubert's secret wishes. The "obsessive idea" of art destroys all relationships with normal life and finds pleasure only in itself. "A person who has trained himself to be an artist no longer has the right to live as other people do." He suffers under the burden of his art as only a martyr does, but in it he also enjoys delights which only God bestows. We had a certain right, therefore, to relate the author's psychosexual phenomena to his creative activity. We know that the major portion of energy for creative activity flows from sexuality (taken in the broadest sense), with all of its predispositions toward perversion. We will not permit ourselves to question the right to associate sexuality with intellectual creation, all the more so since the author himself emphatically admitted:

> . . . but in the end mustn't one become acquainted with all the apartments of the heart and the social body, from the cellar to the attic — and not overlook even the toilets, and above all not the toilets! A marvellous chemistry unfolds there, decomposition that produces fertility takes place. Who knows to which excremental juices we owe the scent of roses and the delicious taste of melons? Have we taken into account all of the deliberate baseness that is required in order to constitute greatness of soul? All of the sickening miasmas one must swallow, all the grief one must experience, all the torture one must endure, in order to write one decent page? That's what we are, we artists — vintagers and gardeners. From the decay of humanity we extract delights for it. We make basketfuls of flowers grow upon its displays of wretchedness.[2]

We know that Flaubert identifies himself with St. Anthony in his letters. He himself was the saint in the work. At that time, he wrote his whole self. He loved to sign his letters with "old hermit." He characterized himself as "another saint." In his circle of friends he liked to be called St. Polycarp, and he himself would say: "I am the last of the church fathers." We are already familiar with his predilection for ascetics, for the secret thrill which the light touch of a monk's cowl stimulated in him, and at the same time the feelings which the sight of prostitutes aroused in him. We have explained this relationship to the point that we hit upon a link between incestuous infantile fantasies and the masochistic ascetic idea. Here lies also the deepest foundation for creativity and for the author's method of working, as I hope to have demonstrated.

There remains only to show in detail the connection between the figure of St. Anthony and the author. Flaubert also withdraws into solitude, immerses himself in work with fanatic love, tortures himself and is conscious of all the temptations of life. When Anthony speaks of his longing for distant places, we remember the artist's wish to travel. It is above all the desire to change his entire way of living; at the deepest level, however, it is the transformation of sexual deprivation. Anthony compares his life with the other monks' more comfortable ones. Flaubert draws comparisons with other writers and buries himself likewise in his sorrow. Just as the saint's thoughts turn toward the satisfaction of desire inspite of — or rather, because of his Bible readings, so Flaubert, too, was tortured during his work by sexual thoughts. Anthony compares his travail with that of other martyrs and finds that he endures more than all of them. Flaubert, too, thinks of his contemporaries in this way. And he also seeks to denigrate other writers, to insult them as the hermit insults the church fathers. In the author's attacks of hysteria, the visions he describes are strikingly similar to those of the saint, and similar complexes have emerged: desire for fame and the love of women, raging ambition, the wish to take revenge on others for his own suffering. (Vision of the Nicene fathers in the "Temptation.") Sadistic instincts awaken and sexual desire breaks through. He, Flaubert, would also like to lead a purely animalistic life, a life of the gratification of desire. (Anthony's metamorphosis into Nebuchadnezzar.) He rejects these images and wishes, however, and punishes himself for it, frees himself through unrelenting work (Anthony flagellating himself). Yet work cannot bring him the yearned-for freedom; seductive fantasy images hover around the author and call forth desires. (Anthony feels the sexually stimulating effect of the whip lashes. Fantasy of a lover's death with Ammonaria.)

Just as the Queen of Sheba appeared before Anthony, so did the image of his distant love float before the author during his work. Doubts arise about the sublimity of art, about its exclusivity, about its higher worth with respect to life. A part of his being revolts against it. (Hilarion appears to the hermit.) He begins to doubt his art because of the call of life.

Perhaps his troubles and work are in vain and the right thing would be to enjoy life to the fullest. A thousand doubts torture him. (Hilarion puts insidious questions to Anthony and shakes his belief.) The fantasy leads him to Paris. (Anthony is transferred to the large basilica.) A thousand ways of looking at life, particularly from a sexual perspective, confront him and seek to draw him to their side. He sees unscrupulous self-indulgence and self-abnegation, joy of life and repression and the emergence of all perversions. Which is the proper path? (The heretics surrounding Anthony, his doubts about religion. Thus, a relationship is revealed: religion has also taken over the duty of keeping watch over the sexual life of the individual.) The author imagines all of the possibilities of his life: he will be destroyed by the conflict between desire and obligation; he will sacrifice his life to his art, which to him is the highest religion. (Scene of martyrdom in the arena. Killing of the Christians by wild animals.) But this sacrifice is foolishness. Life still celebrates its triumph on his grave; the others will only enjoy themselves and forget him. (Cemetery scene: the mourners' sexual intercourse on the graves.) The best thing is probably to be alone, to worry about nothing, to look down on everything with inner peace, undisturbed by all desires. Who could do that! (Vision of the Gymnosophist.) Or is it not better after all to pleasure oneself with females, to have prostitutes? (Ennoia appears, the essential female, the unchangeable in all forms. The prostitute figure.[3] She is Minerva. She knows all secrets of the world as a seer of all heights and depths.) Or should the man stand higher? Homosexual tendencies rise from below, almost stronger than all others. (Apollonius appears, from whom the strongest enchantment emanates.) How insane to torture oneself so for an ideal, to spend one's life so. All ideals disappear, even yours. (Religions come, pass by, and fall to ruins.) How stupid is your sexual abstinence, the author says to himself. There is no escape from the laws of nature. Even art cannot shelter you from the rush of feelings, because it itself has its ultimate roots in these desires. (Emphasis on the sexual customs and conceptions in religion, all perversions occur in the cults.) Lust hides behind even the most sublime desire. What remains then, what is certain? The mother and the beloved. Here, the love object that is hotly desired and unattainable, whose possession would bring punishment and death. There, the prostitute, for she only can provide sexual gratification. (The Mother and Ammonaria change into Death and Lust.) You, however waste your life, torturing yourself with martyr-like work. Look, there lust tempts you and already death awaits you!

The author would like to experience the secret of the world, to perceive the inmost essence of each thing. The infantile sexual curiosity has been sublimated. He would like to know the "Becoming" of things. He would like to know everything about the nature of God (= Father). Would like to see what the nature of matter (= the body) is. How the world order (= sexual intercourse) is organized. He finds it completely different than he imagined; everything is empty, there is nothing lofty, holy in the world and in love. The first experience with love destroyed his illusion. (The explanations of the devil, who symbolizes desire, about the nature of the world. The saint's emotions.) It is no coincidence that the mother fantasy now appears again in the "Temptation." During her intercourse with the father, which the child overheard, he received those disillusioning impressions. Since then his libido has become fixated on the prostitute figure. Earlier, the Mother of God had already climbed down to the saint and had tempted him. The mother also has something of the prostitute about her — we now understand why Flaubert suppressed this scene, how great inner inhibitions conflicted with its becoming conscious and its objectivization. This conflict corresponds to the other one for the historical Flaubert, who vacillates between fantasy and reality, the realms of art and life, sublimation and sexual enjoyment. (Chimera and Sphinx.) Mother or prostitute?

All sorts of passions and desires rise up around him. (Animals surround him.) On the other side the Philistines, the limited ones, those who have achieved harmony by sacrificing part of their personality. (Half-humans, Pygmies.) He stands in the middle, however, observes everyone, sees everything as an artist, their desires and their fortunes, and feels himself blessed in the sight. This last scene is, of course, overdetermined by the wish — already disclosed in the *Temptation* — to see that which is secret, hidden, sexual (the secret instinctual life is related to the appearance of the animals). This wish originates from the infantile emotional life and has been repressed. Anthony's famous exclamation "To be matter!" is explained by the desire to be free from all of the tortures of conventionally bound sexuality, to be a creature of nature. This interpretation is confirmed by the following comment by Flaubert; "I see the heavens, the trees, with a joy that I have never felt before; I would like to be a grazing animal so that I could eat grass." We recall the same wish in the Nebuchadnezzar scene of the *Temptation*. We are at the end of our psychoanalysis. It has demonstrated the closest relationship between art and sexual life. I am unable to determine to what extent this is generally the case.[4] But with this literary work I was able to prove it, I believe, with logical certainty. I am personally of the opinion that every literary work draws strong energies from the psychosexual sphere. To prove this, however, we needed a psychology of literature. For the most part academicians have been occupied to a greater extent with literary-historical tendencies and philological textual criticism than with emotional impulses.

I believe that much in this method, which attempts to trace the work back to sexual crises of the author, can be offensive to the reader. Yet I cannot understand why research on the human nature of great personalities should be demeaning. Their memory is in no way diminished by this. Yes, I even believe I revere Flaubert the more since I have known the torments he suffered; since I have known that this eccentric man sacrificed his life's happiness to his higher striving. I admire his accomplishments even more since I have known the history of how they came into being and their motives. Does the rose smell less beautiful because it has sprung from a dunghill? . . .

Notes

1. *Über psychopathische Minderwertigkeit* (On psychopathic inferiority), Vienna, 1909.

2. Flaubert, *Correspondance*, II, edited by Jean Bruneau. (Paris: Gallimard, 1980), p. 485. Letter to Louise Colet, December 23, 1853.

3. Regarding Zola's *Nana*, the author said, the title figure "evolves toward myth without ceasing to be a woman" (Letter to Caroline, 15 February 1880. *Correspondance*, VIII, 391 (Paris: Conard, 1930)).

4. Nietzsche may have been the first to have specifically referred to this relationship. *Genealogy of Morals* 1887, p. 105ff and *Twilight of the Gods*, Leipzig 1889, p. 76ff. Compare further Gustav Neumann, *Geschlecht und Kunst* (Sex and art), pp. 3, 119f, 188, who claims that "the oldest and most powerful root of creative activity is the sex life." Compare further Dr. Reibmayer, *Entwicklungsgeschichte des Genies und des Talentes* (The developmental history of genius and talent), Munich 1908. Paul Möbius, *Über Kunst und Künstler* (On art and artists), Leipzig 1901, pp. 44ff, 120ff. Max Dessoir, *Archiv für systematische Philosophie* (Archive for systematic philosophy), vol. 5, p. 73. M. Guyau, *Les problemes de l'esthétique contemporaine*, 4th edition, Paris 1897, p. 22ff, and the book by the Munich neurologist, Dr. L. Löwenfeld, *Die sexuelle Konstitution* (The sexual constitution), predominantly in the chapter "Die Libido als geistige Triebkraft" (The libido as an intellectual driving force), Wiesbaden 1911. Lately, Professor S. Freud and his school (Otto Rank, Sadger, Steckel, etc.) have shown this relationship in a new light.

Projection as Ego Defense in Flaubert's *Tentation de saint Antoine*

Laurence M. Porter[*]

Flaubert's *Tentation de saint Antoine* is foreshadowed in his earlier writings.[1] He completely redid the work at least three times between 1848 and 1872. The saint was an alter ego of the author. Both men withdrew from society in response to an overwhelming vocation; both struggled to control an exuberant fantasy life with austere self-discipline. Flaubert too had ascetic tendencies. He claimed that he wanted to castrate himself when he was nineteen, and that he didn't touch a woman for two years around that time. "There comes a moment when you need to make yourself suffer," he wrote, "to loathe your flesh, to hurl mud in its face

[*]From *The Literary Dream in French Romanticism: A Psychoanalytic Interpretation* (Detroit: Wayne State University Press, 1979), 47–67, 191–93. Revised and abridged by the author. Reprinted by permission of Wayne State University Press.

because it seems so frightful. Were it not for my love of form, I might have been a great mystic."[2] In later life, Flaubert so often styled himself as a spiritual descendent of Saint Polycarp—a bishop of Smyrna who inveighed against his age—that from 1877 on his friends honored him and this patron with a series of annual banquets.

In their solitude, both Flaubert and the desert monk Saint Anthony were assailed with a riot of tempting visions. On first consideration, one would expect the writer to welcome such visions as sources of inspiration, while the saint would reject them as unwelcome distractions from the thought of God. But Flaubert embraced a cult of art that saw beauty and truth as identical. The reactions of his friends and of society toward the *Tentation*, plus his extreme self-critical tendencies, inclined him to the belief that much of the work had resulted from his indulging personal weaknesses or needs and that it did not therefore reflect a transcendent esthetic truth. After his closest associates, Louis Bouilhet and Maxime Du Camp, heard the 1848–49 version read outloud for four days, they urged Flaubert to burn it rather than endanger his career as a writer by continuing such incoherent fantasizing. The public received episodes from the second version with indifference when they were published in *L'Artiste* in 1856 and 1857—but the government prosecuting attorney used them as supporting evidence at Flaubert's trial for corrupting public morals by publishing *Madame Bovary*.

Flaubert took these criticisms to heart. To avoid merely wallowing in the slough of his own fantasies, he subjected himself to a threefold discipline as he revised the *Tentation*: a faithful description of real places; serious historical documentation; and the careful notation of plausible sources for Anthony's wild imaginings—physical stimuli during sleep, the day residue, personal memories, and the return of the repressed. From late 1849 to 1851, Flaubert journeyed to the Middle East, visited the region where Anthony had lived, discussed the saint with local scholars, and kept a travel journal. When he returned, he did extensive research on church history, which led him to remove many of the apocryphal and anachronistic elements of the first version: the cult of the Virgin, the rosary, the crucifix, and the pet pig. Documentation allowed Flaubert to indulge himself in another way, however; he increased descriptions of weird pagan gods and heresies from one-quarter of the 1849 version to over half of the 1874 version of the *Tentation*. His choice of the Alexandrian period of the early Christian church history, when it had just been sanctioned by the Roman Empire only to fragment into competing cults, let him describe the extravagant aberrations of the latter under the pretext of faithful historical reporting.

But Flaubert found that neither research nor observation could ensure the coherence of his work. He repeatedly expressed dissatisfaction with the 1849 and 1856 versions for lacking two essential elements: an overall organization and a unifying impression of Anthony's personality.[3]

Stimulated by his long journey from home, however, in 1850 he stated the decisive insight that was to govern his definitive revision of the *Tentation* twenty years later, and which anticipates psychoanalysis: "You know that the earliest childhood impressions never fade. Throughout our life we carry our past along with us; we feel the influence of the woman who nursed us. When I analyze myself, I rediscover, still fresh and with undiminished power . . . my childhood daydreams."[4]

From one version of the *Tentation* to the next, Flaubert gradually moved from a conventionally Christian-medieval, comic-epic depiction of the struggle between good and evil to an inner, psychological portrait of the saint, by presenting Anthony's memories of the past as the sources of his visions. Near the beginning of the second of three parts in the 1856 version, Anthony recalls his parents' house and his old mother weeping at his departure. And in 1856 Flaubert also added a passage (later suppressed) which proves he understood the psychic mechanism of projection, the ego defense that gives rise to the hallucinations composing the *Tentation*. The saint exclaims: "It seems to me that outside objects are penetrating my person, or rather that my thoughts are escaping from it like lightning bolts from a cloud, and assuming corporeal form by themselves, there . . . in front of me! Perhaps that's how God conceived Creation."[5] But it was Taine's queries concerning the artistic imagination that incited Flaubert to link hallucinations explicitly with memory in 1866. He says his own epileptic visions occurred "suddenly, like lightning, in an invasion or rather an instantaneous bursting in *of memory*, for the true hallucination is nothing other than that—for me, at least. It's a sickness of the memory, an unloosing of its hidden contents. You feel images escaping from you like spurts of blood."[6]

So as Flaubert began composing the final version of the *Tentation* late in July 1869, he sought a logical connection between the saint's diverse hallucinations that would preserve the dramatic interest of his story by preventing it from seeming fragmented.[7] He described Anthony's past experiences in much greater detail than before. He expanded the cursory mentions of Anthony's mother and of his childhood playmate Ammonaria into detailed scenes that provided quasi-explicit indications of the sources of the fantasies of lust and death in Part VII, the last section of the final version. Anthony's fantasies of power and revenge in Part II are now motivated by three letters received from the Emperor Constantine, and by the saint's humiliation in theological debate at the Nicene Council. The Bible reading introduced in 1856 was shifted to the beginning of the work to provide a "day residue" (experience remembered from the previous waking period, and incorporated into a dream) that explained the origin of Anthony's visions of Nebuchadnezzar and the Queen of Sheba. That he misses his favorite former disciple, Hilarion, prepares the events of Part III. His memories of heretics preaching in Alexandria anticipate the dream of the assembly of heretics in Part IV. Wall paintings seen in the temple of

Heliopolis, and ranks of idols carried by the barbarians who were concluding a treaty with the Emperor in Anthony's presence, announce the procession of the gods in the dream of Part V. In Part VI, the Devil's supreme attempt to destroy Anthony's belief in a personal god employs — as the saint later realizes — the arguments he had heard from the pre-Socratic philosophers concerning the infinite, the Creation, and the impossibility of attaining certitude. Preconscious impressions from the monstrous mural paintings seen at Belus, and from a mosaic in Carthage, lead to the fantasies of the Sphinx, Chimera, and monsters in Part VII. In short, Anthony's lived experience provides a source from almost every major vision in the 1874 version of the *Tentation*.

Physical stimuli provide a constant source of visions throughout the three versions. The sleeping Anthony's hunger and thirst stimulate dreams of gluttony; the final assault of the allegorical figure of Lust is caused by an early morning erection.[8] Flaubert added the moonlit Nile gleaming far below as the catalyst for the saint's vision of the Ophite heretics' serpent god, and the fire that singed his beard as the source of his dream of the Gymnosophist's funeral pyre (pp. 106, 120). For all his belief in the Devil, Saint Anthony acknowledges at least once in the final version that his temptations derive from his own body: "Why these things? They come from restless stirrings of the flesh."[9] Flaubert progressively eliminated from the work allegorical figures representing Anthony's strengths and weakness of character — the pig, the Virtues, the Seven Deadly Sins, the Devil. He sacrificed the pungent comedy of their grotesque appearance and their quarrels (in the 1849 version, see pp. 212–22, 318ff, 357–58, e. g.). As he multiplied indications that preconscious memories were the sources of the content of Anthony's visions, he decreased other sorts of suggestions that Anthony's was an internal, mental drama. In 1874, only half as many of the metaphors explicitly evoke the saint's inner world as in 1849.[10] But he also carefully eliminated many expressions that betrayed the structuring hand of an omniscient narrator. The margins of the final manuscript are covered with reminders to avoid using too many "then's, suddenly's, but's."[11] And the preparation for the onset of Anthony's visions becomes much more elaborate. In 1849 we hear hallucinatory voices on page two, and the pet pig talks on page four. In the shorter 1856 version wind noises become voices only of page twenty-three, and the first apparitions are postponed till page forty-three.

Flaubert retained those historical inaccuracies which enrich the psychological implications of the *Tentation*. That his Anthony can read, although the historical saint could not, creates a secondary source of fantasies through Constantine's letters and the Bible. The exaggeration of the heretics' repellent behavior dramatizes Anthony's resistance to his own heretical thoughts. For him to live in a cave on a high cliff above the Nile — not his actual residence — brings home the alluring terror of the idea of self-destruction. The poignant scene of family rupture when the young

Anthony departs with an old hermit (a weeping mother, reproachful sister, and desperate playmate whom some sentimental critics inaccurately identify as Anthony's fiancée) emphasizes the stress of self-definition and of the quest for independence in Flaubert's version of the saint's life. In reality, Anthony's parents had died before he left his native village; he stayed there for some years after their death. He had arranged for his sister to be lodged in a religious establishment, and he had neither a known romantic attachment nor a surrogate father to lead him away.[12]

Literal-minded critics have accused Flaubert's Saint Anthony of being a weak, uninteresting character, disconcertingly passive.[13] This false problem is resolved once one realizes that the saint's passivity results from his being torn between two painful choices — asceticism or sin — and that the Devil functions as the repressed part of his personality, embodying his unadmitted doubts and resistance to the will of God.[14] The Devil incarnates Anthony's obvious lust for knowledge and his rebellious mental surge toward self-sufficiency which would demand from God a full explanation of the universe. In the guise of Anthony's disciple Hilarion, returned for a visit, the Devil grows in physical stature and in rhetorical impressiveness throughout the work. At the same time, the setting for Anthony's visions expands steadily from local to cosmic, from historic to mythic, and from personal to universal, reflecting the human intellect's hubristic efforts to subject the external world to a system of thought. Having renounced active involvement with the material world, the saint unconsciously craves a compensatory mastery of the world of ideas. Having served his function of crystallizing Anthony's self-dissatisfaction, issuing an imperative call to self-examination, and provoking a constructive personality change, the Devil becomes expendable and disappears, like the other nineteenth-century devils who appear to Goethe's Faust and Dostoevsky's Ivan Karamazov. The saint ends his temptation by accepting his mental limitations and seeing himself as in rather than above Creation.

Flaubert's initial description suggests a polarity between Anthony's ascetic ambition and his weakness. The saint is undergoing a crisis typical of old age: looking back over his life, he must convince himself that his sacrifice of comfort and company has been worthwhile. Despite his isolation, self-imposed, he needs to believe that he exists in meaningful solidarity with others, and that his own life, ending as he gives way to the generations to come, still contributes something irreplaceable to them.[15] Formerly his least actions seemed meaningful; now he feels a chronic disgust with everything (pp. 3, 252). Such displeasure masks self-contempt.

To escape the present, he reminisces. He longs to join the passing birds or sail on the boats he used to watch. His fantasies become increasingly secular as his desire for companionship grows. First he wishes he had joined the monastic community at Nitria instead of becoming a hermit; then he thinks of being a priest among lay persons; finally he dreams of worldly occupations. His desire for physical affection becomes so strong that he feels an impulse to caress one of the jackals in a passing troop. During this first phase of temptation, Anthony remains sufficiently self-aware to recognize his own weakness as the source of his unworthy thoughts (p. 10). He reads the Bible in an attempt to redirect them. But his repressed stirrings of gluttony, anger, pride, and avarice return via the very instrument of their repression: Anthony notices biblical passages that seem to justify such feelings. So a new flood of fantasies overwhelms him. They culminate in a series of lustful memories of the wealthy female penitents who used to visit him.

During the second phase of his temptation Saint Anthony's thoughts become less controllable because he unwittingly exteriorizes them and disclaims responsibility. The sound of the wind seems to turn into the tinkling of harness bells in a procession bringing a female penitent to him. Momentarily ashamed when he calls out only to realize the procession was imaginary, he quickly lapses again: the wind noise becomes hallucinatory voices cajoling him. Sharply defined visual hallucinations follow, bright, isolated against the night sky, sharply defined like the epileptoid visions that Flaubert himself experienced and described. Anthony collapses into helpless passivity.

The third phase of the temptation coincides with the beginning of the second section of the dream narrative that fills nearly the entire work. While Anthony's eyes remain closed, the appearance of the Devil as "a vast shadow, more insubstantial than a natural shadow" signals a modulation of the saint's perceptions from the natural-external to the supernatural-internal. No longer do the visions have an ostensible cause in the real world, yet their origin has now been personified as Satan, an externalized figure with whose activities the saint can deny any voluntary connection. At the same time he attempts to deny his real situation by dreaming that he is an Egyptian hermit—as he is in fact. The resultant doubling of Anthony into a real and a fantasy self becomes progressively more marked. His desires take external, concrete form as rich food, then a pile of coins and gems. Intoxicated with this false wealth, the saint throws himself on it, coming to his senses when he lands on the bare ground. He has passed from the first stage of temptation—suggestion—through the second (taking pleasure in contemplating a sinful potential act) to the third, the consent of the will. And lusting for money instead of food cannot be excused by physical need.

Saint Anthony's self-contempt becomes unendurable when he realizes what he has done. He must project the feeling outward, in the form of hostility against others richer and more comfortable than he. "You can't be more stupid and vile. I'd like to strike myself, or better yet, tear myself out of my body! I've been holding myself in too long. I need to avenge myself, to lash out, to kill! It's as if I had a pack of wild beasts in my soul" (p. 29). He seizes his knife to stab at an imagined crowd, but then collapses in a trance. The previous movement through greed to vengeful repression recurs in another form. Anthony dreams he is enjoying the rich novelty of city life in Alexandria. Then an army of desert monks invades the city and massacres the inhabitants. Anthony becomes one of them. He meets all his enemies and slaughters them, wading in blood.

But repression, however violent, creates frustration. Reaction against his self-denial leads to fantasies of power in which the saint is the emperor Constantine's chief confidant. His rivals are humiliated. Self-aggrandizement intensifies: Anthony becomes the heathen king Nebuchadnezzar, planning to rebuild the Tower of Babel and dethrone God. Waking abruptly, the saint realizes he has sinned in thought. He flagellates himself, but the return of the repressed transforms pain into voluptuous delight.

When Anthony left home many years before, he suppressed all desire for women. In consequence, his attraction to the three women — mother, sister, and childhood playmate Ammonaria — who loved him assumes great importance in his psychic life. He now imagines himself being beaten next to a naked woman; he associates her with Ammonaria; and then the apparition of an amorous Queen of Sheba transposes the chain of visions from history to legend. She functions simultaneously as an archetypal *anima*-figure (the unconscious feminine side of the male personality) and as the first incarnation of the Devil directly visible to Anthony. The Devil himself is for Anthony the archetype of the entire unconscious, combining sinful desire and forbidden object in the form of a demonic temptress.

The saint drives her away with the sign of the cross, but a dwarfish *puer senex* (aged boy) from her train remains behind. He symbolizes the emerging contents of the unconscious. As Part III begins, he identifies himself as Anthony's former disciple Hilarion. That he has emerged from the saint's unconscious through psychic projection is underlined by Flaubert, who has him say: "Know that I have never left you. But you spend long periods without noticing me" (p. 55). Hilarion encourages a debauchery of the mind. With specious humility, he points to internal contradictions in Christian dogma and revelation. Anthony admits that he has long been struggling with the problems Hilarion raises; they perplex him so often that he fears he is damned. Hilarion reassures Anthony by promising that once he uses his reason rather than trusting in revealed religion, the face of the unknown shall be revealed. He claims that the mortification of the flesh is a spiritual discipline inferior to efforts to understand the nature of God: the believer's only merit is a thirst for truth, and there are no restrictions on intellectual speculation outside the purview of dogma. Anthony responds eagerly. He thinks his straining mind may burst free of the prison of the body. He does not yet realize the danger, which will emerge only slowly, of the Gnostic temptation of knowledge. Reason can lead him into the sin of demanding that the transcendent God reveal himself and justify his ways to man, under penalty of ceasing to exist if he does not.

In Part IV Hilarion leads the saint to an immense basilica (a metaphor for Saint Anthony's head) to confront him with a crowd of heretics from the early Christian era. Hilarion uses the multiplicity of their beliefs, and the intensity of their conviction, to assail tradition as a basis for faith. They illustrate the excesses of opposing reactions to the frustrating fact of our physical existence: debauchery and asceticism. Finally Tertullian appears, harshly insisting on subduing both the body and the mind: "Pray, fast, weep, mortify yourselves! No philosophy! No books! After Jesus, knowledge is useless!" (p. 84).[16] The scene culminates in the Circoncellions' frenzy of universal destruction. The heretics join in a howling chorus. Challenged by Anthony, they brandish their apocryphal gospels to refute the claim that they possess no revelation. They surround him and close in, turning into the swelling, tightening coils of the Ophite heretics' serpent god. This motif of the protagonist surrounded by a ring of animals is common in Flaubert (see Bart, *infra*). It represents the demands of our animal self to be acknowledged.

To escape it, Anthony "faints," replacing the heretic dream with a defensive countervision of Christian self-sacrifice. He finds himself among Christian martyrs at the Roman coliseum. But the lurking animal menace remains in the form of the big cats in the arena. At first Anthony, transported with love, is eager to face them and to die for the Lord. But soon his resolve weakens until he feels he would prefer any other death (pp. 108–11). The lion, which in conventional Christian iconography can represent either Christ or Satan, here stands for the indeterminate, morally ambiguous nature of one's own, unrecognized unconscious. The following scene, a late addition, shows a visit of surviving relatives to the martyrs' graves, degenerating into a sexual orgy. The event suggests that exemplary self-sacrifice does not ensure that one's followers will be worthy and persevere in the faith. This is precisely what Anthony, who has withdrawn from society in order to help regenerate it by his example, has been worrying about. He evades his dilemma with a new fantasy of the self-sufficient gymnosophist (naked sage), whose voluntary self-immolation does not depend on the behavior of followers to preserve its full meaning (pp. 117–19).

Yet Anthony's encounter with his heretical unconscious has made him calmer, more enlightened. He now recognizes the quest for God as a unity underlying all the heretics' extravagances, rather than rejecting them with horror as he did at first (p. 121). The temptation of doubt gives way to that of pride. Apparitions of the supreme heretics Simon the Magician (rival to Saint Peter) and Apollonius of Tyana (rival to Christ) embody Anthony's ambition to become a miracle worker and to possess ultimate truth. Apollonius boasts of knowing all gods, all rites, all prophecies (p. 154).[17]

His claims provoke Anthony's curiosity concerning the pagan gods, preparing the parade of these described in Part V.

By moving the procession of the gods from the end of earlier versions of the *Tentation* to the middle of the 1874 version, Flaubert freed Anthony's personal drama from its subordination to the sweep of religious history. The saint thus comes to represent human religious experience in general rather than just one phase of it. He reflects the interest of Flaubert and his contemporaries in the relativity of religious beliefs and their underlying resemblances. Non-Christian religions are now seen not as impostures, but as provisional forms of an eternal ideal. The evolution of the *Tentation* reflects the ever-increasing influence of the nascent discipline of comparative religion: in 1849 the saint's only reaction to the spectacle of the dying gods was to say "so mine will pass also"; in 1856 he makes comparisons among them; and in 1874 Hilarion offers a virtual course in comparative mythology.[18] From Flaubert's perspective, then, any particular image of God is an illusion—like Félicité's parrot in *A Simple Heart*—created by "our soul projected onto objects."[19] Flaubert's own *Correspondance* proves how completely he had freed himself from projected images of God, by "demythologizing" his religious attitudes.[20]

The grotesque forms of the first, primitive gods in the procession reflect Anthony's initial shock and fear at encountering these unconscious products—personified pride, lust, rapacity, and rage. His resultant repression culminates in a polarization of good and evil (a way of saying "all good is within me; all evil, outside"): Ormuz, the Persian god of light, battles Ahriman, god of darkness. But this dichotomy proves too artificial to be maintained. "The distance between the two of us is disappearing," says Ormuz in despair (pp. 182–84). Anthony intuitively realizes that what he has repressed may have been good. This insight clears the way for a series of *anima*-figures to appear. They manifest the unconscious in its positive guise, as Great Mother-Goddesses: Diana of Ephesus, Isis, and Cybele. Besides bringing potential enlightenment, however, they also stimulate Anthony's desire to regress to a childlike closeness to his mother, symbolized by the good earth: "How good it is, the scent of the palm trees, the trembling green leaves, the limpid springs! I'd like to lie flat on the earth, feel it next to my heart; and my being would once again be immersed in the earth's eternal youth!" (p. 185). The danger of this impulse to fuse with the *anima* appears when Atys emasculates himself in order sexually to resemble the goddess who loves him. He vanishes, and a coffin appears with a veiled figure which Anthony fears to recognize. The body could be himself, but it turns out to be made of wax—only the image of a tendency in his personality.

Next the Roman gods, the greatest rivals to Anthony's Christianity, march by to fall into the void. But Anthony feels no joy at their passing. As Hilarion points out, their manifold, pervasive association with human life had imbued it with a sacred character. For them to fade and die implies the desacralization of the human world. And to provide a derisive commentary by juxtaposition, the ahistorical Crepitus, god of flatulence, brings up the rear immediately after Jehovah. So the God of Moses' appearances of might and virtue are reduced to a mere evil-smelling void.

Generally speaking, the despair of the dying gods reflects Anthony's own despair at being unable to impose an imaginative or rational structure on the universe. The saint's supreme temptation, then, will be to fill the empty cosmos with his own personality. So he accepts a ride through space on Hilarion's back. His disciple, at last openly revealed as the Devil, comes from within himself, Anthony now realizes. He acknowledges the familiar demonic voice as an echo of his thoughts, a response from his memory (p. 232).

Anthony still seeks to anchor himself to a higher being. But as he ascends, the comforting structures and personalities projected onto the universe by the cosmologies of the ancients all disappear — the harmony of the spheres, the crystalline roof of the heavens, the spirits of the dead inhabiting the moon, the angels holding up the stars (pp. 232–35). At first the saint feels great joy at being enlightened. Scornfully he recalls his former ignorance and mediocre dreams (p. 234). But then the Devil dismays him by preaching a compound of Spinozistic doctrine and Kantian exposition of the limits of empirical knowledge. The universe has no purpose. God is not a person. He is indivisible, contained in all things. Therefore the transcendent cannot be apprehended. Anthony must renounce hope for union with a personal God. He feels the meaning of his entire existence threatened:

> "What? My prayers, my sobs, the sufferings of my flesh, my transports of zeal, has that taken wing toward a lie? . . . in the void . . . uselessly — like a bird's cry, like a whirlwind of dead leaves!"
>
> He weeps:
>
> "Oh! no! higher than all, there is someone, a great soul, a Lord, a father, whom my heart adores and who must love me!" (pp. 239–43).

"Perhaps there is nothing," the Devil replies. "So worship me! And curse that phantom you call God!"

In the earlier versions Anthony was saved by accident: his hand brushed against his rosary and reminded him to pray as the Devil was about to devour him. In the final version, Flaubert consistently reorients the work by giving the saint a more active role: an impulse of hope saves him when he raises his eyes for help. Once the Devil has departed, Anthony recognizes his captious words as insidious restatements of the pagan doctrines he had once studied with the sage Didymus.[21]

Restored to himself, in Part VII Anthony once more attempts to reestablish contact with the *anima*-principle of tenderness within himself. He deplores his spiritual dryness. He no longer can pray. He tries to defend himself against the feeling of having lost God as a personal object of love by recalling past moments of cameraderie with other religious men. But these emotionally charged memories evoke the still stronger ones of his family and Ammonaria, whom he abandoned to follow his own destiny. His adult sexuality, combining with his memories of childhood dependency and physical closeness, subverts the latter and makes them sources of guilt. First, in a disguised fantasy of sexual violation of his mother's body, he imagines a hyena poking its muzzle through a hole in the wall to sniff at her corpse before devouring it (a few pages earlier, a metaphor in the Chimera's speech explicitly associates the hyena with lust: "Like a hyena in heat, I circle around you, begging for the impregnation I desperately desire," p. 262). Here, eating the desired object reflects regression to the earliest, oral stage of infantile sexual development.

Sobbing, overcome with horror, the saint wards off his incest fantasy by transferring cathexis to Ammonaria. He lets himself imagine her undressing until he gets an erection, when he reacts with disgust and contemplates suicide. He flees his unacceptable sexual impulses with intellectualization that modulates thoughts of his mother and Ammonaria into a stylized twofold vision of Death and Lust, whom at their first appearance he takes for his mother and Ammonaria respectively (pp. 248, 250) before recognizing them as "the Devil in his twofold aspect." The transition is strongly motivated. Anthony's longing to return close to his mother transforms death into something desirable because it is where she can now be found. And Anthony's impulse to liberate himself from inadmissible needs also generates the death instinct as he strives toward a biological equilibrium that can end libidinal tension.

By directly confronting the death instinct, Anthony transcends it to reach theological illumination. He now recognizes that the destiny of the body and of the soul without God — Eros and Thanatos — are both illusions masking the continuity of life, the immortal soul, and tempting him to despair (p. 257). Here is the dramatic climax of the *Tentation*. It was critical to Flaubert: in the final manuscript version (NAF 23667) he first crossed out the entire page and then restored it as if he could find nothing better.[22] Nowhere else in this manuscript did he change, even provisionally, more than a few lines. He extricates Anthony from the impasse of pathological psychic regression by shifting from an individual perspective to an abstract philosophical one. Thus he can win through to a conclusion.

No longer fearing the Devil, convinced at last of his immortality, Anthony now diverts his attention from the question of good and evil to speculation concerning why Forms are many when Substance is one (p. 257). This new preoccupation reflects long-standing concerns of Flaubert the artist, who for the last thirty years has been trying "to calm the irritability of the Idea which seeks to assume a form and which shifts about restlessly in us until we have found an exact, precise, self-sufficient one for her."[23] In order to unite himself with a transcendent God, conceived as pure Idea, Anthony had pridefully attempted to suppress the body so as to become pure Idea himself. He has not renounced this ambition; but at this stage of his meditation, he still commits the error of trying to make matter subservient to thought. He aspires to glimpse primordial figures whose bodies are only images of some quasi-Platonic Essence. But the allegorical vision of the unsuccessful mating attempt of the Sphinx (matter) and the Chimera (thought) then appears to show him that one cannot subordinate the material and encompass it with the intellect. "All those tormented by the desire for God, I have devoured," the Sphinx declares (p. 261). This remnant of unvarnished allegory, a mode far more prevalent in the earlier versions, betrays that Flaubert has momentarily lost control of the dramatic progression of his subject.

A pulsating mass of monstrous forms then seethes forth from the earth to confront Anthony — as Job was confronted with Behemoth and Leviathan — with a Creation that the intellect cannot grasp.[24] At length the animals in the heap blend with plants, and plants with stones. Overcoming his initial fear of these apparitions, Anthony lies down flat on the ground to contemplate the basic unit of life, the biological cell (pp. 274–75. This anachronism again reveals Flaubert's difficulty in coming to a conclusion.). In earlier versions, Anthony's fascinated desire "to be matter itself, to know its thoughts" was followed by Satan's exclamation "You'll know them!" as he seized Anthony and carried him off. Thus matter was identified, if not with evil, at least with imperfection, since Anthony's desire for communion with it was what gave the Devil power over him. But Satan has vanished for good at this point in the 1874 version. Anthony feels elation: "I should like to huddle within all forms, penetrate each atom, descend to the depths of matter — be matter!" (p. 276). He does not condemn himself for these words, as he had earlier condemned himself for having had tempting visions. For pantheistic ecstasy is not a sin. It reveals God's presence in the physical world: for Flaubert, the Deity and matter are not incompatible as they were for the visionary romantics like Hugo. As he put it in 1857, "I don't know (and nobody knows) what these two words mean: soul and body; where the one begins and where the other ends." And again in 1853: "Are we not composed of the emanations of the Universe? . . . And if atoms are infinite in number and pass into Forms like an eternal river flowing between its banks, then what holds back thoughts or connects them? Sometimes, by dint of contemplating a pebble, an animal, a picture, I have felt myself enter into it. No communication between human beings is more intense than that."[25]

Saint Anthony's final cry, "être la matière!", could be considered a defeat for an orthodox Catholic, subjugated by an overwhelming experience of hylozoism. But from Flaubert's viewpoint this experience implicitly grants the saint a final wisdom shared with Spinoza, whom Flaubert called the most religious of men because he saw God everywhere.[26] Once Anthony abandons his arrogant attempt to comprehend the transcendent God, the immanent God is restored to him.

Critics who interpret the ending of the 1874 version as a defeat for Anthony (relying on a casual remark that the saint was overcome by the biological cell) forget that Flaubert's manuscript notes show he always intended to have the saint win, exhausting, by his resistance, all the Devil's stratagems.[27] Flaubert knew full well that the historical Anthony—as Harry Levin points out—"emerged from his trials in the desert to strengthen the faithful and confound the heretics of Alexandria. In the monastery he had organized, among those who were attracted to the stringencies of his rule, he died a serene and natural death at the age of a hundred and five."[28] In the final draft, Flaubert clarified his intentions by removing the adversative "mais" (but) which had set the concluding apparition of Christ's face in the sun against the apparition of the monsters. He also removed the last phrase, "the temptation has ended," which suggested that the saint's final pantheistic effusion was part of the temptation. And by shifting the appearance of Christ, that "classical symbol for the unity and divinity of the self,"[29] from the procession of the dying gods to the end, where He replaces the three Theological Virtues, Flaubert showed that he meant the *Tentation* to be a drama of personality.

For Christ to appear in the sun, of course, meant no apotheosis for the heterodox Flaubert. Other gods, he knew, had appeared there too, only to fade. In the 1849 *Tentation* Uranus had complained: "Saturn has mutilated me, and God's face no longer appears in the disk of the sun."[30] Until the very last draft, indeed, Tertullian's description of the soul suggested a physiological explanation for such visions: "It has a human face, and is transparent like those aerial disks that sometimes float between your eyelids and the sun."[31] What really matters to Flaubert is not what one sees, but how. So long as Anthony insists on trying to impose his own intellectual structures on the universe, he generates the Devil, vainglorious self-sufficiency writ large. Once Anthony renounces his secret desire for rational explanations, the entire cosmos becomes for him a mediator through which God is mystically knowable. For Flaubert's spirituality is not what is left over once the material has been taken away, by means of rationality or asceticism: the spiritual is anything in a right relationship to God.

Notes

1. See Alfred Lombard, *Flaubert et saint Antoine* (Paris: Victor Attinger, 1934), pp. 17–18 (a fine study); and René Dumesnil and Don-L. Demorest, "Bibliographie de Gustave Flaubert," *Bulletin du bibliophile et du bibliothécaire*, 1938, pp. 27–29, 135–38, 315–17, and 408–13. For a recent overview of the evolution of the work and the significance of its variants see Laurence M. Porter, "A Fourth Version of Flaubert's *Tentation de saint Antoine* (1869),"

Nineteenth-Century French Studies, 4 (Fall 1975–Winter 1976, Festschrift for Jean Seznec): 53–66.

2. Gustave Flaubert, letter to Louise Colet, December 27, 1852, in his *Oeuvres*, 18 vols., edited by Maurice Nadeau (Lausanne: Editions Rencontre, 1964–67), VI, 392. Henceforth abbreviated *O*. Jean Bruneau's magisterial edition of the *Correspondance* (Paris: Gallimard, in progress) will supersede earlier editions.

3. Letter to Jules Duplan, May 1857 (*O*, IX, 76); see also *O*, VI, 225–26, 210, 315; and VII, 470–71, 489, 493, and 498.

4. Letter to his mother, November 14, 1850 (*O*, IV, 496).

5. Flaubert, *Oeuvres complètes* (Paris: Louis Conard, 1910–54), XVII, 589. This volume contains the 1849 and 1856 versions of the *Tentation* as appendices to the 1874. Future references to the 1849 and 1856 versions come from this edition.

6. *O*, XII, 159.

7. Letter to George Sand, *O*, XII, 405.

8. Bibliothèque Nationale, Paris: Nouvelles Acquisitions Françaises, MS 23671, fol. 107. Henceforth abbreviated NAF.

9. *La Tentation de saint Antoine*, edited by Edouard Maynial (Paris: Garnier, 1968), pp. 38–39. Future references to the definitive 1874 edition, given in parentheses in the text, are taken from this accessible source. All translations mine.

10. See Don-L. Demorest, *L' Expression figurée et symbolique dans l'oeuvre de Gustave Flaubert* (Geneva: Slatkine Reprints, 1967), pp. 323–24.

11. NAF, 23667, fols. 19, 44, 59.

12. For an excellent evaluation of the historical accuracy of Flaubert's *Tentation*, see the *Oeuvres complètes* [note 6 above], XVII, 655–65. Accounts of the saint's life can be found in the *Catholic Encyclopedia* and in Hastings' *Encyclopedia of Religion and Ethics* (Protestant). The primary source is the biography of Anthony by his disciple Athanasius.

13. Paul Valéry, "La Tentation de (saint) Flaubert," *Variété V* (Paris: Gallimard, 1944), pp. 204–05. And Jonathan Culler, *Flaubert: The Uses of Uncertainty* (Ithaca, N.Y.: Cornell University Press, 1974), who claims "The Saint has no psychology" (p. 181; see also pp. 136–37).

14. See Carl Gustav Jung, *Psychological Types or the Psychology of Individuation* (London: Kegan Paul, 1946), p. 441, henceforth abbreviated *PT*; Jung, *Aion: Researches into the Phenomenology of the Self* (Princeton, N.J.: Princeton University Press, 1968), p. 42; Sigmund Freud, "Negation," *The Standard Edition of the Complete Psychological Works of Sigmund Freud*, edited by Lytton Strachey. 24 vols. (London: Hogarth, 1953–74), XIX, 235, 239, henceforth abbreviated *SE*. "The devil is certainly nothing else than the personification of the repressed unconscious instinctual life," Freud claimed in "Character and Anal Eroticism," *SE*, IX, 174, and in XII, 188.

15. See Erik H. Erikson, *Identity and the Life Cycle: Selected Papers* (New York: International Universities Press, 1959), pp. 99–100.

16. See Jung, *PT*, pp. 18–33, 70–75, for an overview of the Gnostic heresies which dominated the Alexandrian period; for a discussion of Tertullian and Origen; for speculations concerning how the Gnosis—like alchemy after it—anticipated depth psychology; and for comments on how Anthony's battles against demons, as reported by Athanasius, constituted an attempted repression of the personal unconscious.

17. In the psychosexual sphere, Anthony's recurrent visions of prostitutes like the Ennoia who accompanies Simon, and the latent homosexuality manifest in his effusions concerning Damis and Apollonius (Anthony says Apollonius charmed him more profoundly than the Queen of Sheba, and represented a stronger temptation than all Hell put together) derive from a fixation of libido on the mother, and its consequent diversion from ordinary heterosexual outlets. See Reik, *supra*.

18. See Jean Seznec's definitive *Les Sources de l'épisode des dieux dans "La Tentation de saint Antoine"* (Paris: Vrin, 1940), pp. 10–31.

19. Flaubert, letter to Mlle Leroyer de Chantepie, February 18, 1857, in *O*, IX, 203.

20. Letter to Mme Roger des Genettes, 1860, *O*, IX, 246.

21. The historical Didymus was sixty years younger than Anthony, but Flaubert probably knew that "Didyme" was an appropriate name for Anthony's teacher because it was also a name for the apostle "Doubting Thomas."

22. NAF, 23667, fol. 125; the deletion runs from the stichomythic exchange between Lust and Death to the apparition of the Sphinx.

23. Letter to Louise Colet, December 13, 1846, *O*, IV, 229. Mallarmé expressed similar concerns.

24. "The 'monster' is indeed a symbol of totality, of the complete inventory of what is possible in nature," claims Gilbert Durand, *Les Structures anthropologiques de l'imaginaire: Introduction à l'archéotypologie générale* (Paris: Bordas, 1969), p. 360.

25. Letter to Mlle Leroyer de Chantepie, February 18, 1857, *O*, IX, 203; and to Louise Colet, May 27, 1853, *O*, VI, 146. For a collection of similar statements with a lucid commentary, see Alison Fairlie, "Flaubert et la conscience du réel," *Essays in French Literature*, 4 (1967): 1–12, esp. pp. 2–3.

26. Literally, "because he acknowledged only God," as Flaubert said in November 1879 after having read Spinoza's *Ethics* for the third time (*O*, XVIII, 515).

27. See NAF, 23669, fol. 290 / 432; and NAF, 23671, fol. 107.

28. Levin, "Flaubert: Portrait of the Artist as a Saint," *Kenyon Review*, 10 (1948): 43.

29. Carl Gustav Jung, "Individual Dream Symbolism in Relation to Alchemy: A Study of the Unconscious Processes at Work in Dreams," *Psychology and Alchemy*, XII, 83–84 in *Collected Works*, 2nd. ed. (Princeton, N.J.: Princeton University Press, 1960–   ). The early Christians sometimes identified the rising sun with Christ.

30. NAF, 23664, fol. 461.

31. NAF, 23667, fol. 46.

Trois Contes

Narrative Figures of Speech in
A Simple Heart

Raymonde Debray-Genette*

We would like to make a systematic comparison of the syntax and the rhetoric of a narrative. To use the term "syntax" about a narrative text, in this case *A Simple Heart* by Flaubert, is not equivalent to substituting it for the word "construction." It is, in fact, to work from a postulate the merits of which can only be established by the efficacy of its application: "The homological relation between sentence and discourse . . . Discourse would be a long 'sentence' (the units of which would not necessarily have to be sentences), just as the sentence, according to certain specifications, is a short discourse."[1] To recall this postulate and apply it to the term syntax is to provide a reason for not giving an exhaustive account of the construction of *A Simple Heart* in its linear and syntagmatic character (in particular it is not a question of organizing true discursive sequences, nor of examining the formal organization of the chapters). It also provides a reason for not giving an account of a true discursive structure, one of a more distinctly paradigmatic character, even though the question of the relation of signs between themselves is more important than that of their relation to what they designate. On the other hand, if the narrative is treated as a long sentence there is no doubt but that, classical in its appearance, narrative invokes rhetoric, that one finds on a larger scale some of the great figures of speech which nourish classical discourse. This treatment amounts to bringing together the problem of narrative generators, which are distributed throughout the text, and that of figures of speech, which organize the text's vertical space, so to speak.[2] We would like the technique and aesthetics of narrative each to involve the other.

All the items of information given in a narrative are in principle generators, but only to the extent that they will be taken up again and exploited. One can say as much of indices in the sense in which Roland Barthes defines them, as involving "a decoding activity" whereas items of information "deliver a readymade knowledge."[3] If, for example, it is said in Chapter 1, where, as one might expect, a great number of items and

---

*From *Poétique* 3 (1970):348–64. Translated for this volume by Mark W. Andrews, Vassar College. Reprinted by permission of Éditions du Seuil, Paris, France.

indices are assembled, "under a barometer an old piano supported the weight of a pyramidal heap of boxes and cartons,"[4] then neither the barometer nor the boxes nor the cartons will be taken up again in the rest of the text. No box is opened when the clothes of Virginia, who has been dead for some time, are inspected: they are laid out on the shelves of the wardrobe; Felicity never consults the barometer; indeed the piano itself is never heard, Virginia only seems to play at boarding school. In order to comment upon such passages one must adopt a different point of view from our own. One must speak of "realistic effects," as Barthes has done, or else decode the words "old," "pyramidal" in such a way as to constitute thematic elements. One might also introduce sociocriticism or psychoanalysis here.[5] If the narration was trying to be enigmatic these pieces of information could constitute decoys. On the other hand, the first paragraph is nothing but a series of items of information, as is frequently the case at the beginning of classical novels. "For half a century the bourgeois of Pont-l'Eveque envied Madame Aubain her servant Felicity" (p. 3). There are at least eight items here. Let us note in passing that of all these items, the main verb is the one that will be least exploited in the text which follows, so that the essential items are given in an oblique way with respect to it. Extended to the entire work this observation on the oblique character of items which are indispensable to it remains valid: this device even constitutes one of its original aspects. For reasons which remain to be shown, it is not a simple means of advancing the action and, as the phrase so aptly goes, *knotting*[6] it. The device responds to difficulties in writing which are frequent in Flaubert, acute in *A Simple Heart*, "the malady of the interval,"[7] the essential discontinuity.

If we have said that every item of information, every index, taken up in the rest of the text can in a broad sense of the term be called generators, it was only to distinguish them from that which does not have as its principal function to inform, to alert, to mark out the text, so to speak. Moreover, in the dense space of a short story (this term still remains to be justified), it is quite foreseeable that it will be necessary to propagate items of information, to put them in close proximity one to the other, especially at the story's beginning. Like the inaugural sentence quoted above. But true generators are phenomena of anticipation: the item of information is given well before it is necessary for comprehension; it appears at the moment when it is read as a sort of padding which "rings true" and gives flesh to the narrative. At the beginning of Chapter II it is said: "her father, a mason, had killed himself by falling from a scaffolding; then her mother died, her sisters moved away . . ." (p. 5). The general idea is to strip Felicity of all her immediate family (and particularly of her father), so as to deliver her up, alone and bereft, to vicarious elements which are in turn stripped of their power of affective substitution. A good number of these items of information have immediate consequences. But much later a sister will reappear, and nephews, one of whom will play an important role. The converse of a generator should have as its function a retrospective explanation (whether contained in a flashback or not), it would be a motivation proposed after the fact. So it is with this group of wooden figures Felicity looks at in church as she listens to the catechism lessons destined for Virginia, a group which "represented Saint Michael smiting down the dragon." Several pages earlier, while out walking, Felicity had confronted a bull alone and saved three people "not even suspecting that she had done anything heroic" (p. 12). Many years later people still speak of it. Her act becomes legendary. It is recounted: in this way the legend of Felicity could be born.

If it is true that a generator is an anticipatory item of information, Chapter I must nevertheless be set aside momentarily to the extent that it relates the story as having ended; it is itself an enormous anticipation; it destroys all interest based on waiting and holding in suspense, constructing a narrative which has drawn to a close even before it has opened: in it items of information and indices are given once and for all; the narrative which follows will consist only in their revival and their unfolding. The narrative must be taken up at the moment when it is reborn from its ashes in Chapter II. The anticipations of Chapter I are not in fact such, since time has already elapsed and has come to a halt, so that linked to what follows, this chapter, curiously enough, is a rare example of an anticipation which functions as a flashback; the items of information which it contains are not so much anticipatory as perhaps incomplete, and on the contrary, deferred. Thus the entire house of Madame Aubain is described, according to a Balzacian method, from the semibasement to Felicity's room on the third floor; now the description of this room remains in suspense until page 39 (the narrative in Dumesnil's edition takes up 45 pages); so for the present a window is missing; the contents especially are missing: all the alluvium which the narrative will deposit in successive waves to make this a strange place, half bazaar, half chapel.

More than others, this narrative plays on the displacement of items of information, the manner in which they migrate. Deferred or anticipatory elements and those justified after the event shape the flow of the text. Their dispersal upstream or downstream testifies to a hiatus, to a problematic contiguity (the control experiment will be the episode of the love affair with Theodore where the items of information are all in the order dictated by the logic of the narrative and are all more or less exhausted by the narration). Their repetition, their revival affirms a need for expressivity, for redundancy, a surplus of meaning born of the hyperfunctioning of the device. They say more than themselves, something other than themselves. They figure something else, they are themselves figures of speech.

Their chains form series of *metonymies* or *repetitions*, nesting effected by *synecdoches* (we refer consistently to Fontanier's definitions).[8] They organize the space of the text, elicit an effect of meaning and contribute to the realistic illusion. As soon as they touch on *metaphor* they deconstruct this space, pile up the meanings, forming, in their term, a "pyramidal heap." As our topic remains on the order of novelistic technique, we will halt at the approaches to metaphor.

Before going into the detail of these figures, it must be specified that they are, in fact, only the cogs of a general figure according to which the text functions. Here we come back to the sources of Russian formalism. Under Chklovsky's pen for example,[9] novellas and novels trace metaphorical loops, platforms, parallels, particular sorts of "images in the fabric." Another trait is that Chklovsky, always attentive to linguistic associations, is struck by the fact that a given motif, a given general construction, is often based on some kind of trope: for example, Chekhov "carries out a semantic displacement, he takes a notion from the semantic series where it was to be found and with the aid of other words (of a trope) he places it in another semantic series.[10] The Russian formalists seemed to be more interested in the problems of the spatiality of narrative than in those of its temporality. As we will see it is very evident that the spatial construction of a narrative has close links with its temporality. A study of the general figure of a narrative invokes or completes that of its temporality.

Flaubert summarized A Simple Heart in the following way: "She, Felicity, loves in turn a man, the children of her mistress, a nephew, an old man she cares for, then her parrot; when the parrot is dead she has it stuffed, and, dying in her turn, she confuses the parrot with the Holy Ghost."[11] In Chapter I, which includes everything up to her death, to be surmised from expressions indicating finite duration: "for half a century . . . ," Flaubert gives both the "fable" (the events recounted according to the natural chronological order) and the "subject" (the events recounted according to the order of their appearance in the text), these terms being employed in the sense which the Russian formalists gave to them.[12] Two expressions in this text hold our attention: "in turn," on the one hand, and "confusion," on the other. They literally describe the cloth of the narrative, interlaced with parallel threads, its quasi-geometrical horizontality: the story of Felicity's love for Theodore is followed by that of her love for Virginia, daughter of Madame Aubain, her mistress; her love for Paul, Virginia's brother, is a broken, stippled parallel line. Paul is not to be confused with Virginia, he exists aside from her (they do not join in each other's games) not at her side. All that remains of Bernardin of Saint Pierre's melon is its divisibility, no longer is there the harmonious roundness that joins the family together. The episode of Felicity's nephew Victor takes place in parallel to that of Virginia: perhaps Virginia has never spoken to Victor, who, on the contrary, dared to use the familiar form of address with Paul. Victor does not move in until Virginia's departure to the boarding school. Moreover, he moves into the kitchen. Victor and Virginia die "in turn." Other affections form more or less well-developed parallel lines underneath the preceding ones: Felicity becomes attached to some soldiers, some cholera patients, some Poles, to old Colmiche. The device of derivation is obvious: all these affections are only more and more degraded, more and more remote substitutes for what are called "natural" affections — those of the father, of the mother, of which her childhood has been deprived, those of a young man of her own age, of a husband. Felicity, stubborn as she is ("no one showed more stubbornness in bargaining," p. 4), as little inventive and given to compulsive repetition as she is, never tried the amorous experience again; also, and as a consequence, she misses the experience of a mother's affection for her child. Freud says of the neurotic, in whom a compulsion for repetition is manifested: "that which remained misunderstood comes back; like a suffering soul, it can find no rest, it has no rest until resolution and deliverance have been found."[13] Now here are the last parallel lines, the longest, the story of Lulu. Here the model is modified at the conclusion of the parallel (it is important that the parrot has died: "*when the parrot dies* she has it stuffed and *dying in her turn* she confuses the parrot with the Holy Ghost"; emphasis added). There are two lives it seems for Lulu: a life and an afterlife. Her life obeys the same rules as the preceding ones: substitution of one being for another, heterogeneity, absence of communication between these beings (Lulu could, after all, have belonged to Virginia or Victor), hiatus. Her afterlife as an object, and that alone, leads the narrative to its point of conclusion where, because of the comparison with the Holy Ghost, and then of the metaphorical fusion, a meaning, a possible interpretation, is founded, and perhaps, as stated above, "resolution and deliverance."

This "perhaps" stems from the fact that until the end of the text a *metonymical relation* is maintained aside from the metaphorical relation which the parrot entertains with the Holy Ghost. They are juxtaposed, contiguous, side by side in the room, on the altar constructed for the Corpus Christi. We must speak here in rhetorical terms, for to say that the cloth of the narrative traces parallel lines is only an imaginary spatialization (which, moreover, is not contrary to the temporal linearity of the narrative, as we have remarked concerning the identity of the "fable" and of the "subject"). In rhetorical terms Fontanier classes this device with the figures of elocution by deduction[14] and according to him, it includes *repetition, metabole,* and *gradation*. We will have cause to come back later to the variants of repetition (and particularly to *anadiplosis*: beneath this "diplodocus-word" is concealed a familiar characteristic of the narrative). The advantage of rhetoric over the geometry which served us as a point of departure is that of presenting linked form and meaning: all repetition, all gradation (ascending or descending) makes us reflect upon degrees of synonymy, of homology, upon the relations of the same to the other. None of these devices is pure form, each founds a meaning, each is meaning. Demorest expressed himself from a purely stylistic point of view in 1931, and in quite different language: "Felicity indeed represents all humanity with its cosmic confusions at the surface, tragic at the bottom, confusions due to the imperious need which men feel to find relations in everything, which leads them to see an *identity* there where finally there is *not the shadow of a resemblance*."[15] What parallel repetition describes is the illusion of identity where, certainly, there is not the shadow of a resemblance, but where there are metonymical relations. Metonymy supposes a break in continuity, one which we have tried to show in regard to the parallel episodes which never meet; it also gives importance to a relation of contiguity, whether it be founded on chance, cause or effect, or more generally, on the sign for the thing signified.

Metonymies will thus constitute the vertical weave of a cloth made of horizontal parallels. The true generators of the narrative are *metonymical*. They link vertically what in fact has no link, jumping from page to page, transgressing the space of parallelism. They serve to braid the narrative. Felicity is in a similar situation to the aphasic who could only say fork for knife. She says Victor for Theodore, Virginia for Victor (here there is a curious element of "vi(e)"[16] in common). Lulu for God, God for ? (Felicity?) (we would not dare play on the fact that Theodore is a gift of the gods, which would close the circle of the narrative). It is, in fact, a matter of looking at this phenomenon from the angle of narrative syntax. The phenomenon has been studied at the detailed level of sentences, paragraphs, and their linkage by a Danish stylistician. Flaubert's writing in *A Simple Heart* proceeds from a flat and horizontal linearity which moves forward by a series of small jerks, maintaining at times a precarious equilibrium between a "dissolve" and a jerk (this is the role of the personal pronouns), most often causing the disappearance of linking terms and logical relations. "It is a sort of system where there is at once too much and too little linkage, hence a pronounced state of imbalance."[17] Flaubert was always aware of this difficulty. He said of *Madame Bovary* "each paragraph is good in itself and there are pages, I am sure, which are perfect. But precisely because of this it doesn't work, it is a series of well-turned, self-sufficient paragraphs, which do not flow into one another, they will have to be slackened off, the joints loosened."[18] While correcting a re-edition of *A Sentimental Education* he attributes the partial failure of this novel to the fact that it lacks "the falseness of perspective." "Every work of art must have a pivot, a summit, make a pyramid, or else light must strike one point on the ball."[19] This idea proceeds from a classic conception of the novel, quite close to that of drama. Now when Flaubert writes this phrase he has already produced almost all of his work and has on several occasions contravened his aesthetic principles. There is neither summit, nor pivot, nor point of reflection in *A Sentimental Education*. In *A Simple Heart* the infringement is more subtle: it is not the story of crisis with its "acme" and its denouement: nor is it a series of crises which move the action forward (the moments of crisis are scattered at the heart of the chapters, which finish in anticlimax). The construction is not that of a novella. Neither could one talk of a novel even though this is the story of a life. It is from the short story that Flaubert seems to borrow a device which is common in this genre: the repetition of more or less identical actions with ascending or descending gradation (one can take as a model: *What the Old Man Does Is Always Right* by Andersen) and an unexpected conclusion which overturns the perspective from which we were reading the adventures. But this device is transformed under Flaubert's pen: the link between episodes is erased, the meaning escapes not only the hero but the reader; time seems to produce nothing, not to "cause to move forward" (either the hero or the narrative) but to toss the character from chance event to chance event. "To live from now on will be to pass from metamorphosis to metamorphosis, to live through a monotonous succession of experiences, each of which will close in upon itself without communicating with any of its neighbors, unless by its most negative part, its formless foundation."[20] The narrative tends to cancel itself out, to immobilize itself, yet it is neither the work of Beckett nor of Robbe-Grillet: Flaubert works hard to give a dramatic illusion, and this is the role of the metonymic, anaphoric, and synecdochic elements of organization.

A *Simple Heart* is demarcated by generators, the function of which is essentially narrative. They establish a *metonymical* relation between the different episodes. An element named for the first time in an episode, as if in passing and without particular importance, will be revived in another episode and will serve as a link between matters which have no relation but that of textual contiguity. This device is systematic in the text. The element may be an object or a character. Let us mention just the most striking examples. On page 10 there appears for the first time, in regard to the education of the Aubain children, a "geography composed of prints": "to instruct the children in an agreeable way, he (M. Bourais) made them a present of a geography composed of prints. They depicted different scenes of the world, cannibals with feather headdresses, a monkey abducting a young lady, Bedouins in the desert, a whale being harpooned, etc." These prints evoke either the sea or exotic countries. They are given by Bourais, an anecdotal character, an assiduous visitor of Madame Aubain, and who seems destined to have no role to play other than that of a friend of the family. This geography, commentated by little Paul in front of Felicity, constitutes "her entire literary education." It reappears on page 23: her nephew Victor has left on an ocean voyage. Felicity, in anguish, fears for his life and as often happens with Flaubert's characters, terrifying visions are summoned by her imagination, yet these are, of course, hackneyed visions, ones already recorded, drawn, taken from books: "Or else— memories of the geography of prints—he was eaten by savages, caught in a wood by monkeys, was dying on a deserted beach." Curiously enough, Bedouins and whale have been *condensed* into a deserted beach. *Condensation*, which we know to be one of the fundamental mechanisms by which the work of dreaming is carried out, seems to be one of the essential steps of Felicity's unconscious thought: it is this which will facilitate the identification of the parrot with the Holy Ghost. It is linked to *displacement*, on which the construction of this narrative could be based. It was only a dream, half-premonitory in nature: Victor will die of yellow fever. The geography has established a link, without causality, between Virginia and Victor; from this point on it will establish one between Victor and the parrot: "It (the parrot) had been occupying Felicity's imagination for a long time, for it came from America: and this word reminded her of Victor" (p. 33). If one reflects that this geography has been given by the satanic Bourais (the revelation of his black deeds will cause the death of Madame Aubain), the ways of God, or of the novelist, trace a novelistic geography which goes from Satan to the Holy Ghost: by degrees a life is constituted, the life of one who is only an instrument, a place of welcome and of passage.

In the same way Flaubert takes care to present in advance, in the form of generators, characters as important as Victor, the Holy Ghost, and the Virgin, the parrot, or even simple "utilities" like Mother Simon. Here is to be found, doubling metonymy, at the level of a long text, the amplification of a figure which is called *anadiplosis* and which is a form of concatenation or chain.[21] This consists in repeating at the beginning of a segment of verse, one or two words from the preceding verse segment:

> He espies from afar the young *Teligny*
> *Teligny*, whose love has deserved his daughter . . . (Voltaire)

In the first segment of verse, the function of the word is often secondary. It becomes of prime importance in the second segment. So it is with Victor: we are at the seaside; we are being entertained watching the return of the fishing boats "and women in cotton bonnets rushed to take the baskets and to embrace their men" (p. 15). First generator. "One of them, one day, accosted Felicity who a little later came into the room full of joy. She had found a sister; and Nastasie Barette the Leroux wife appeared holding an infant to her breast, in her right hand another child, and on her left a small ship's boy, his fists on his hips and his beret over his ear" (p. 16). Here we find generators but also possible decoys. Who will emerge from this picture to come to the foreground? The sister, the infant, the other child, the little ship's boy? One might lean towards the one who is named, the first sign of novelistic density: Nastasie Barette, the Leroux wife, (she even receives two names, this is more than we have for Madame Aubain; Felicity herself has only a first name). This family takes over the holiday-makers somewhat: "they exploited them. This weakness annoyed Madame Aubain who, moreover, did not like the familiar manners of the nephew" (p. 16). Of the three children only one remains, yet he is without a name. The naming of the nephew is deferred, he is just a simple presence, just a voice (he uses the familiar form of address with Paul); he has not yet entered into Felicity's heart; another is occupying it, Virginia. The naming of the parrot will be similarly deferred. When Virginia leaves for boarding school Felicity will become bored. "To 'dissipate herself' she asked for permission to receive her nephew Victor" (p. 20). This time he is named, he becomes a subject, the subject of the new episode. The anadiplosis is not coyness on the narrator's part, it is the only way to write in an elegant, economical manner, and without commentary by the narrator, about Felicity's narrow mental and affective life, quite taken up as she is by one sole object at a time, an object to which she devotes herself, and with which she identifies; if *by chance* it should happen to fail her, another will come to occupy its place, it too encountered by chance. Felicity who, sharing a trait of the common people, employs words in a somewhat slanted and inaccurate way, calls this "to dissipate herself." Without Virginia "she was awkward with everything, had lost sleep, according to her own word was 'mined out' " (p. 20).[22] If every figure "manifests presence and absence" Felicity is a figure, the supreme figure: every being that she loves is a presence which substitutes itself for her absence of being (a very Flaubertian theme), a plenitude which fills her essential void; if this presence disappears Felicity excavates herself, hollows herself out, her being is mined out; she needs a new presence. So it is with the parrot: it is substituted for old Colmiche. He also comes from far away, not so much from America as from a Revolution. Chapter III, the July revolution, brings a new subprefect, his wife, his sister-in-law with three young ladies: "They possessed a Negro and a parrot" (p. 31). Then Felicity devoted herself to soldiers, to the cholera patients, to the Poles, to old Colmiche. "He (old Colmiche) died. She had a mass said for the peace of his soul.

On that day great good fortune came to her . . ." (p. 33). The subprefect offers the parrot to Madame Aubain. The Negro, a superabundance of exoticism, disappears with the subprefect. Flaubert never indicates a causal link in the text: is she rewarded for having cared for old Colmiche's cancer, for having had a mass said for the peace of his soul, or is it chance (and it is important that a new paragraph is started) which causes a gift to follow a death? The asyndeton functions according to the two usual meanings of this figure: it underlines the absence of a link, it connotes the normal expectation of a link which is denied us and which we tend to reestablish.

Sometimes the concern for a linkage between episodes is so great that it enters into the least details. Felicity goes into a decline in the empty house after the death of Madame Aubain: "Since her dizzy spell she dragged one leg; as her strength diminished, Mother Simon, her grocery business ruined, came every morning to chop her wood and pump water" (p. 43). A modest labor compared to that awaiting this minor character: to help Felicity in her last agony, but, much more significantly, to serve as an intermediary between the space outside and that inside, at the moment of the final procession of the Corpus Christi. Felicity follows the procession in her thoughts as far as the first station at the bottom of the slope. She makes out the second station by the noise of a salute which pierces through her deafness. At the third station, "the clergy appeared in the courtyard, Mother Simon climbed onto a chair to reach the deadlight and in this way looked out on the temporary altar" (p. 46). From then on everything is described through the eyes of Mother Simon. At last "an azure vapor rose up into Felicity's room." We will no longer need Mother Simon, everything will take place in Felicity's mind.

It seems that some importance must be attached to the distance which separates the first mention of a character, who is at that point very secondary, and the moment of his principal reappearance. The greater it is, the more substantial the effect: surprise, questioning, interpretation. There is in *A Simple Heart* a page of an extreme density, the one where Felicity accompanies Virginia to the catechism. It is rich from every point of view: by the mixture of devices (the unprecedented mixture of the iterative and the singulative, internal focalization,[23] represented discourse, interior monologue), by the presentation of characters "in high places": "on a stained glass window of the apse the Holy Ghost looked down on the Virgin; another showed her on her knees before the Child Jesus, and behind the tabernacle, a group in wood depicted Saint Michael smiting down the dragon" (p. 17). (The *Three Tales* are each based on the narration of a stained glass window or a sculpture. They are the narration of a narration in another pictorial or sculptural language; it is a narration in the second degree.) This page is rich with semantic units, again scattered around one character-object, the Holy Ghost, at once bird, fire, breath, light, and voice. The Virgin will reappear indirectly (without counting the name of Virginia) in the striking of poses. Felicity prays for Victor at the foot of the calvary, "and she prayed for a long time, standing, her face bathed with tears, her eyes turned towards the clouds" (p. 22. Flaubert added in the margin "as the holy women are depicted at the foot of the cross." Amongst the few words pronounced by the parrot are "I greet you, Marie!" Felicity dedicates a particular cult to the Virgin, to which attest amongst others "a number of good Virgins" in her room. The representation of the Virgin oscillates, in a sort of displacement, a sort of confusion, between image, statue, and personal identification, but it never quite achieves the stature of a character. The Holy Ghost on the contrary reappears on page 40: "In church she always contemplated the Holy Ghost and observed that it had something of the parrot about it. Its resemblance appears even more striking to her in a likeness by Epinal, representing the baptism of Our Lord." Stained glass window, likeness, print, nothing is recorded in Felicity's life which is not first recorded in the book of simple folk, the book of the unlettered, a quasimediaeval book (illuminations and book of engravings): far from being a contemporary slice of life, *A Simple Heart*, like *Saint-Julien* and *Herodias* is a short story of former times.

Drawn in this manner the Holy Ghost can be incarnated, at the moment of Felicity's death, in the form of an essential character which we shall examine further. "A gigantic parrot soaring over her head." Of all the anadiploses of the text this is the most subtle, first by the distance placed between its two positions in the narrative, next because it is very rigorously an *inverse concatenation*, of the type proposed by Fontanier: *"emulation* created a taste for it, the *rewards* increased the *emulation"* (p. 331). The Holy Ghost suscitates the parrot; the parrot resuscitates the Holy Ghost.

Certain generators of a metonymical nature involve a notion of causality in a more banal sense. It is a matter of expressing the cause by the effect, or the converse. To say that this displays less originality is to remind ourselves that the classical narrative does tend to order itself according to a logic of events, a psychological, indeed a philosophical logic. It is evident that the generators constitute an original quality which Flaubert gives to the narrative. They are inserted into the text as kinds of cells, which are independent, closed, mobile, migrant but impermeable, impervious to all acts of aggression by the surrounding meaning insofar as that is possible in the conjunctive tissue of a text. They are not there to produce meaning, but in their way, to authenticate a manner of non-meaning.[24] On the contrary, in the classical narrative, juxtaposed events must form a comprehensible explanatory chain. Yet there are degrees of this: chance, for example, offers a causality which is not very satisfying to the mind. Now in this short story, as in Flaubert's novels, chance presides over the essential events: Felicity began to find comfort beside Madame Aubain and her children: "When the weather was fine they went off early to the Geffosses' farm" (p. 10). It is while returning from one of these walks that a bull attacks the women and children. A qualifying test but one of no consequence to Felicity. On the contrary Virginia "had a nervous indisposition as a result of her fright and M. Poupart, the doctor, prescribed Trouville's sea-bathing" (p. 12). Only there does a true causality begin, since the illness will lead Virginia to her death. On the other hand chance again grafts itself onto this complaint of Virginia's: it brings about the encounter in Trouville with the little ship's boy who will become Victor, who will occupy such an important place in Felicity's heart, and who will precede Virginia into death. Again the chance encounter is not sufficient: as we have seen it is because she regrets Virginia's departure for boarding school that Felicity again thinks of Victor and asks to receive him regularly. There is a kinship in construction between *A Sentimental Education* and *A Simple Heart:* great loves are born, grow, and perish by chance. On several occasions Frederick has forgotten Madame Arnoux: "A little higher up than the Rue Montmartre a traffic jam made him turn his head and on the other side of the street, just opposite, he read on a marble plaque the words: *Jacques Arnoux.* How was it that he had not thought of her earlier?"[25] If Felicity's swollen clumsy fingers had not prevented her from making lace she would not have thought of her nephew. Forgetfulness, especially after *Madame Bovary*, is the form adopted by Flaubert's inability to bring dramatic forms to life on the level of character. No more progressive forms: the narrative meanders and most frequently comes back to its own beginning as in *A Sentimental Education*, as in *Bouvard and Pécuchet*.

The impression of a chain is born from a walk in the country. But it is more often a question of consecution then of consequence: the temporal order tends to give the illusion of causality. We must again remind ourselves of what Forster said in *Aspects of the Novel:* "the king died and then the queen died" is a narrative;[26] "the king died and then the queen died of sorrow" is a plot. *A Simple Heart* is a narrative which tends to get rid of the plot. The sure sign of this absence is Chapter I, which is much more conclusive than it is introductory. The rest of the narrative confirms this will to divestiture: to divest a narrative of its plot is also to divest it of traditional psychology. We will not say that it is because he wanted to paint a character with an impoverished psychology, incapable of comprehending or of analyzing herself, as she is of inventing an inner life for herself, that Flaubert constructed his narrative according to a disjointed temporal order, what one might call a "decausated" order. It seems to us that the converse is true: a given form of construction, especially when it is confirmed on each line, each paragraph, so to speak, produces a certain effect of reading, an effect of meaning, for a discontinuous form, a psychology of discontinuity: for an iterative form, a psychology of iteration. Yet Flaubert maintains the feeling of an "afterwards," of a "then" (an ambiguous word, both temporal and causal). Madame Aubain dies: one might imagine that Felicity is going to die of sorrow. She certainly wept for her "as one does not weep for masters." But what literally kills her is the pillage of the house by the heirs. The material decay of a house for sale which no one is maintaining any longer: "the slats of the roof were rotting: her bolster was damp for a whole winter. After Easter she began spitting blood." She will not die of sorrow, an overly psychological causality, but of humidity, a causality entirely of events.

Two episodes seem, however, to be deliberately linked, showing solidarity in an obvious way. When Madame Aubain was in torment about her daughter, of whom she has received no news for four days, Felicity, for her part, is in silent torment about her nephew, who has not written for six months. The mistress understands nothing about the servant's torment, but the servant, on her side, understands her mistress: "the two children had an equal importance, a link of her heart united them, their destiny was to be the same" (p. 24). For the first time the narrator intervenes to link what he had previously juxtaposed.

We must, however, note the ambiguity of the verb "was to", an ambiguity in meaning, an ambiguity as to the subject of the enunciation, the narrator and / or Felicity. One may think that this most recent sentence segment is in free indirect speech, thus confirming the accord between the

narrator and his character. Now as we have seen, Virginia's life is not
mingled with that of Victor; the nephew only assumes a name and a
presence in the absence of Virginia. When both are absent, one in
boarding school, the other at sea, they begin to coexist, to exist by virtue of
each other in Felicity's mind, by an effect of metonymy. But in this
narrative, for there to be a true link, the living beings must disappear.
That is why the link will be total when they are both dead, to the point
where a fusion is almost established. At Virginia's burial "she thought
about her nephew, and not having been able to render him these honors,
was overcome by sadness, as if he had been buried with the other" (p. 29).
It is no accident that Flaubert employed the term "destiny." It is not yet
Felicity's destiny which is being woven before our eyes, but that of the
other beings that she loves. Flaubert heavily underscores the use of ruse in
narrative: this consists in relating first one story then another, and
suddenly joining them up, as in the cinema a splice gives us the illusion
that the man on this side of the door has indeed crossed the threshold,
since his hand is now on the other side. To portray a magical and naive
thought, to create fantasy one only has to affirm in two phases that all
consecution will become consequence; still more that two elements at first
autonomous, then metonymical, can be united by an "as". Fate will befall
Virginia *as* it does Victor; she will die. The story of Virginia and Victor
merely prefigures that of the Holy Ghost and the parrot: at first totally
isolated in their presentation, one on page 17 for the first time, the other
on page 31, they are brought together in the same room on page 40,
juxtaposed, then compared, and finally in extremis identified (which is
not quite the case for Virginia and Victor). Every metaphor in this text
passes through a metonymy. Depending on whether one goes from
asyndeton to metonymy or from metonymy to metaphor in the construction of the narrative one can produce an absence of meaning (which, of
course, creates meaning by a system of opposition), an undecided meaning, or a more well-defined meaning. The reader is thus led from the idea
of consecution to that of consequence, or from the idea of consequence to
that of Destiny.

If the general figure of this text is that of successive parallel lines, on
which are recorded isolated yet in part identical episodes, a figure of detail
commands attention, that of *repetition* (the variants of which are called
anaphora, epiphora, reduplication, synonymy, gradation). Such a figure
has the characteristics of metonymy by combination on the syntagmatic
axis, and metaphor by combination on the paradigmatic axis. Its use
interests us in two ways: it confirms the idea that a general construction
calls for its equivalent at the level of detailed organization. Repetition aids
in understanding from a kind of perspective which is at once horizontal
and vertical, how a narrator produces an effect of meaning without
making it explicit. Each one of these repetitions constitutes a generator for

the following one: an attentive reader projects the ones onto the others without ceasing until the narrative has been exhausted, and it is quite obvious that between the first and the last occurrence there is much more at stake than a supplement of meaning: the first and the last term of the series are privileged; one is the matrix, the other the complete product in which all the others are to be read as nestings and interior reduplication, as being no more than abortive forms of what was seeking to be born, if only to die.

For the finest example of anaphoric generators (anaphoras and epiphoras differ only by their place at the beginning or the end of the sentence, but the term anaphora is better known) is the series of deaths which demarcate the different parts of the narrative. Ten deaths in a narrative of 45 pages makes for a remarkable "decuplication."[27] Now the first terms of this are the fathers: M. Aubain, father of Paul and Virginia (Chapter I); Felicity's father, then her mother (Chapter II). The only two fathers in the narrative are thus removed at the beginning. One, M. Aubain, in a partial way since he is still present in the form of a portrait, or a frock coat kept in Felicity's room; the other, Felicity's father, like her mother, disappears totally, an absolute loss, a void that will have to be filled with borrowed beings, who will themselves die: her nephew Victor, followed by Virginia; Lulu the parrot; Madame Aubain (a death brought about by that of Bourais); old Colmiche, the object of Felicity's care, and, to finish, Felicity herself. Not all these deaths have the same narrative value; certain of them are grouped in twos, as if out of a need for redundancy and echo, for complementarity (masculine and feminine): that of Felicity's father and mother (as in *Saint-Julien*), that of Paul and Virginia, that of Bourais and Madame Aubain. But the moment of death is never described, it is always in ellipsis, the narrative always arrives too late, so to speak, except for Felicity's death which occupies the entire ending. What the narrative usually dwells on are the corpses, present ones like that of Virginia (the only complete description that we have of Virginia's face, which is in the process of decomposing), and of the stuffed but rotting Lulu; or absent corpses evoked, as we will see, metaphorically, like that of Victor, or metonymically like that of M. Aubain. This is not a "realistic" narrative: the corpse does not denote a scientistic frequenting of death; it connotes on the one hand the successive loss of living beings who elude Felicity, on the other hand what one might call Felicity's necrophilia; she can only possess what is well and truly dead. Felicity's life is no more than a succession of partial deaths which little by little reduce her to her own self, to her own final agony. Metonymically, death migrates throughout the narrative; metaphorically, it becomes a model of life; in a paradoxical way these deaths permit survival of the narrative until they refer it to the being who will receive them all in an exemplary death. This effect is reinforced by other anaphoric generators on the level of detail, which also concern this theme and redouble the effect of identity. If

Chapter I, in portraying Felicity, indicates to us that she wore "a bibbed apron over her morning jacket, as hospital nurses do," this is neither a picturesque nor a pictorial detail (in this respect Flaubert's portraits, unlike those of Balzac, do not refer us to a pictorial code. One could not *paint* Felicity). It's that Felicity is dedicated to caring for all those beings whom she meets, all except Madame Aubain, her mistress; and more especially her vocation is to care for more and more repugnant beings. We see her dressing old Colmiche's tumor, then with her nails ripping out that which is lodged under the parrot's tongue and curing it (Saint-Julien for his part stretches himself out upon a leper). An effect which is even more peculiar is that four of these deaths are due to a pulmonary ailment and present more or less the same symptoms: that of Virginia, of Lulu, of Madame Aubain, of Felicity. Flaubert certainly read a treatise on pneumonia, however, elsewhere he described other maladies and other types of death. He is not, therefore, looking for diversity but indeed for the monotony of repetition. Chance (the narrator) would have it that the death of Felicity be identical to those of the beings that she has loved. Language speaks well that lends a will to chance and makes it divine; the narrator does well who scatters identical elements which the reader must assemble. Each one, as Barthes says, "hangs like the momentarily inactive spindle which waits while its neighbor works then, when its turn comes, the hand takes up the thread, brings it over the drum; and as the design is progressively filled in, each thread marks its advance by a pin which retains it and which one moves up little by little."[28]

A well-woven narrative will necessarily offer forms of repetition of a spatial and temporal order. These repetitions are not in contradiction to the temporal linearity of the narrative, they do not prevent it (not yet, we will say, thinking of the modern novel); nevertheless it is certain that reading them muddles the temporal indications which serve as landmarks and allow us to follow the hero in his evolution (here from birth to death). Some constitute a narrative with an evolutive perspective; others a static narrative where every recurrence is perceived as a relapse. Some seem to open, others to close the narrative. This contradictory movement is very frequent in Flaubert's works and its ultimate form is that of a narrative which finishes as it has begun. This device of spatiotemporal multiplication can take on very simple, almost coarse, aspects; such as the succession of the seasons and of certain privileged seasons. It is very normal that Virginia and Lulu should both die of cold in winter, but it is in summer that Felicity will experience her two greatest despairs: her first (and only) broken heart when Theodore leaves her; her final and anguished farewell to Victor in the port of Honfleur, when he embarks for America. Finally it is in the hot season (at the Corpus Christi, "the pastures gave off the odor of summer") that Felicity will undergo her final agony and will die. This effect is reinforced and specified by several points of detail which scarcely strike us at first reading, but which lead to a point of convergence: page

18, Virginia as a child and Felicity her nanny pursue their religious education: "from then on she (Felicity) imitated all Virginia's practices, fasted when she did, went to confession with her. At the Corpus Christi they constructed a temporary altar together." Corpus Christi and altar disappear until page 40; Felicity is already weakened, Lulu already dead and stuffed: "communicating with no one, she lived in a somnabulistic torpor, the processions of the Corpus Christi brought her back to life. She went to the neighbors to collect torches and matting to embellish the temporary altar that was put up in the street." That many generators of a grand final phase demarcated by: "after Easter she spat blood . . . The moment of the temporary altars was drawing near . . . From Tuesday to Saturday, on the eve of the Corpus Christi she coughed more frequently." Lulu occupies a fine position on the temporary altar, "hidden under roses, [it] showed only its blue forehead, like a plaque of lapis lazuli." She enters her final agony. To describe a banal and exemplary life, to produce it, is to create the meeting on an altar table, by the will or by the error of a poor servant, of a parrot and a Holy Ghost. It is to create a meeting between elements which are heteroclitic, scattered, teeming in the body of the text then reduced in number at its end. The narrative proceeds by sprouting, then pruning.

Repetition of a temporal order is the most obvious. That of a spatial order is more diffuse: this is because we are dealing with a unity of place. Practically the entire narrative is located in Madame Aubain's house in Pont-l'Evêque "between a passage and a narrow street ending at the river." A single space, a closed space which one cannot really leave. Felicity has only been torn from a place on one occasion, when she left the farm and the memory of Theodore, her cruel sweetheart; henceforth she cannot leave. It is the others who will go away. To take to the road, to take the road from Pont-l'Evêque to Honfleur, either to say farewell to Victor or to carry Lulu to be stuffed, is never a free act, a liberating act: it is often an abortive act (Felicity decides not to remain in the gig which would take her to Lisieux in time to see Virginia while she is still alive); it is a useless act (she runs around like a madwoman looking for the lost Lulu which will come back of its own accord, no one knows how); it is a failed act (she loses her way just outside Honfleur: "when she came to the calvary, instead of taking the left turn she took the right"; Victor's boat is about to leave: "she was rushing forward when the ladder was suddenly removed"). But the repetition of identical material elements: ascents, descents, stops before a calvary, prayers, meditation "at the summit of Ecquemanville," a series of painful stages, marked on one occasion by a flagellation ("with his long whip, using all his force, [the postillion] dealt her such a blow from her stomach to her chignon that she fell on her back"), all these elements end up by sketching a sort of road to the cross; a stump drawing which suddenly takes precise shape yet again, at the moment of her final agony; the stages of the procession towards the altar are so many stages of the journey towards death; but here there is identity and inversion. The procession comes to Felicity, the mind of Felicity goes out, so to speak, of its own accord, advances to meet the procession, rises up to meet the heavens and on this occasion the ascent is liberating, the heavens are "half open." There will be no return to earth. Thus the repetition of spatial elements can be taken to form a series of setbacks and something like inclusion in a more and more narrow space (the very space of her room), but here again the final term of the series certainly includes the others, but equally differs from them. Everything happens as though the quantitative accumulation was producing an abrupt qualitative evolution.

Amongst the figures of repetition Fontanier names metabole (or synonymy): "Muse lend to my mouth a more savage voice / To sing of *scorn*, of *anger*, of *rage* . . ." (Boileau). Here a slight displacement of meaning intervenes. To substitute, then, is to seek for an identity, but to warp the meaning a little, to deviate toward some "analogon." Fontanier quite correctly rejects the term of synonymy in favor of that of metabole which implies change, transfer, migration of meaning. In the domain of narrative there is no synonymy. In the formation of a chain of *metabolic generators*, displacement is evidently achieved by implicit comparison, and it is, therefore, the metaphorical aspect which triumphs over the metonymical aspect, dominant up until this point. The first kisses which Felicity receives from Theodore, her sweetheart, (very symbolically, the first kiss is never named except by ellipsis: "he kissed her again"; in this narrative all original terms are lacking or vanish), these first kisses find their equivalent in those with which Felicity covers the children of her mistress: "she carried them on her back like a horse and Madame Aubain forbade her to kiss them at every minute, which mortified her" (p. 8). Mortification of pride, mortification of the flesh as well: little by little Felicity will seek out substitutes to express this physical tenderness. She still had Virginia to dress, to care for. After her departure for the boarding school: "she missed no longer having her hair to comb, her boots to lace, missed tucking her into bed" (p. 20). Virginia will only come back to her once she is dead: it is she who lays out the corpse and places it in the bier, taking great care to spread out the hair. "It was fair and of extraordinary length for her age. Felicity cut a large lock of it, of which she slipped half into her bosom, resolved never to relinquish it" (p. 28). From then on, at the same time as a quasi-necrophilia, a sort of fetishism emerges in Felicity. All the objects gathered in her room are fetishes, but more particularly this little plush hat with a long nap, chestnut in color, which belonged to Virginia and is quite eaten away with vermin. The hair was a sort of living matter, the plush is dead, dead but rotted, which is a way of aping the living, the living in a state of decomposition. We do not see Felicity caressing Lulu while the bird is alive (it climbs up her, nibbles her, hangs onto her), but as soon as it is dead and stuffed, and what is more as soon as its condition deteriorates, she comes back for what will be for her a last caress: "although it was not a corpse, the maggots were devouring it; one of its wings was broken, the stuffing was coming out of its stomach. But, now blind, she kissed it on the forehead and held it against her cheek" (p. 44). One sees how Flaubert takes care to record these equivalencies textually, if only by denials ("even though it was not a corpse"). Elsewhere, when Felicity has learned the news of Victor's death, she goes off, broken, but taken over by mechanical force of habit to do her washing in the river: "The meadows were empty, the wind was stirring up the river; at its bottom long grasses were swaying like the tresses of corpses floating in the water" (p. 26). Hair is indeed that by which the dead are still in small part among the living. It is a phase of fixation.

From metonymy to metonymy, Felicity's sexuality regresses, just as her physical life regresses in an equivalent chain. One by one her senses close off from the world. We know nothing about her sense of taste, but we know her voice is rarely heard: she hardly ever speaks. From her first adventure the only direct speech which is attributed to her in amorous dialogue is: "Ah!" Then there are cries of pain, groanings. We know that her voice is shrill, like that of the parrot. Later she will have very brief exchanges with Madame Aubain. Finally, viewed from Chapter I as from all eternity, she is as if dumb: "always silent, her figure upright and her gestures deliberate, (she) seemed a woman of wood, functioning in an automatic fashion" (p. 3). The sense of touch fades at the same time as it fixes on a few objects; she cannot make lace, her fingers break the threads. Then she becomes deaf, except to the voice of the parrot, with which she has "dialogues, it uttering to satiety the three phrases of its repertoire and she responding to it in incoherent words, but words in which her heart poured out" (p. 36). Finally "her vision dimmed. The shutters no longer opened" (p. 43). Cause? Effect? It's always the same manner of writing and describing. She finally goes blind. But what Chapter I does not say, speaking of a woman of wood, is that Felicity, by progressively closing herself off from the world, by withdrawing into herself, by hardening herself, succeeds in isolating and in preserving within herself the only little morsel of being for which the trouble of living will have been worthwhile: at the moment of her death she finds an unexpected flame within herself, a marvelous blossoming, she breathes in the vapor of incense "with a mystical sensuality." She retains the sense of smell. Once again, the last link in the chain is at once the poorest and the richest.

Whether these chains of generators be anaphoric or metabolic, they produce one and the same effect. The reason for the repetition is never indicated, the substitution is never commented upon. It is chance which seems to organize these configurations. Anaphora is one of the figures by which the narrator transforms chance into destiny. It is a reversible figure which must be read by going backward as well as forward in the reading. The final term creates meaning and satisfies in part this need for the "why" dear to classical narrative, when only the "how" is described. But it limits the importance of this "why."

A *Simple Heart* offers finally a curious type of syntax, which reacts to fundamental discontinuity and corrects its effects of dispersal. These effects are for us, as modern readers, both detectable and natural. In a compact form like the novella or the short story, construction is important. One cannot leave the task of replacing what is organized up to what is organic (this is what the construction of *A Sentimental Education* rather tends toward). The novella calls for a conclusion, be it a negative one.[29] It necessitates a compacting of the meaning by a literal bringing together of signs. Nevertheless the problem here, for Flaubert, was in recounting a life, one reduced, moreover, as the synecdoche of the title indicates, to the elements of the simplified, if not a simple-minded affectivity, without forgetting that the word heart signifies courage just as much as it does affectivity. The narrative had to be given at once the density of a novel, the slenderness of a novella, and the exemplary character of the short story. It seems that Flaubert resolved this difficulty by the tightness of the weave and by a *synecdochic organization* that must be examined for a moment. Synecdoche is the figure of the title. It is also that of the work.

There are novelists for whom the division into chapters has scarcely any meaning, if not that of convenience. (This is the case of the chapter divisions in *The Charterhouse of Parma*.) In Flaubert this division is calculated, and more particularly so in the *Three Tales*. We possess a plan prepared by Flaubert for *A Simple Heart*. It is in four parts, not in five. The final agony is included in the fourth part. In writing, Flaubert split off the final agony and made a fifth chapter of it. It seems that there is a reason, which became apparent as the short story was being written. Chapter I, in relation to the rest of the text, constitutes the synecdoche of the whole, Chapter V the synecdoche of the part. As we have said, Chapter I considers the narrative as concluded. Not only is this where the main body of items of information is grouped, but all the essential themes are recorded here; the narrative will only provide the development of these themes: economy, closure, death, religiosity, charity, devotion, stubbornness, silence, devitalization. A single, but capital omission: Felicity is spoken of as if she were dead, but the manner of her death is not told. At the beginning of the text she is, therefore, as if dead even before dying.

A. J. Greimas[30] groups narratives into narratives of a present and *accepted* order, where "the order which exists and which goes beyond man because it is a social or natural order, finds its explanation on a human level," and into narratives of a present and *refused* order. "The plan of the narrative is then projected as an archetype of mediation, as a promise of salvation." The narrative then takes into account "various soterial forms by proposing the solution to every intolerable situation of loss." Chapter I announces a narrative of the type: acceptance into the present order. There is no protest from Felicity: for she is diminished and reduced to silence as often as she endures hardship. With the result that the narrative seems to be topsy-turvy and the last chapter seems to be the ultimate point of concentration and reduction. But by the dialectical design, which is figured by the referral of one type of synecdoche to the other, the last chapter, that of the final agony and the death, figures the part for the whole, and the part is suddenly more than the whole. We have seen how all the chains of generators ended up in the kind of syncretism represented by the confusion of the Holy Ghost and the parrot. It is the only moment of the narrative where metaphor reigns, yet it is the fruit of metonymy. At church Felicity contemplates the Holy Ghost of the stained glass window: a likeness by Epinal completes the confusion. "With its crimson wings and its emerald body it was truly the portrait of Lulu." She hangs the likeness beside the stuffed parrot "so that, at a single glance, she could see them together. They became associated in her thoughts, the parrot finding itself sanctified by this relation with the Holy Ghost, which became more alive in her eyes and more intelligible" (p. 40). If one adds that the Holy Ghost is both a part and the whole of God, synecdoche and metaphor, one sees to what extent the combination of the figures is internally reduplicated. It would be tedious to take up again here all the moments in the final chapter where one element figures all those that have preceded it (blindness, procession, etc.). The figure is clear, deliberate, but also reversible, for Felicity, reduced to a wretched body in its final agony, suddenly seems saved, happy, drowned in bliss. She *seems* saved because Flaubert takes care to write: "she *thought* she saw, in the half open heavens, a gigantic parrot soaring over her head." And by this little word, by this "authorial intrusion," the narrator refers us again to the beginning of the narrative. With the result that our reading, in order to remain faithful, should become circular and recommenced perhaps infinitely, without the meaning ever becoming fixed. We will never know whether we are dealing with a narrative of an accepted or refused order, if we are reading the story of a simple-minded woman or that of a saint, of Felicity or of Charity.

We find ourselves at the threshold of a realistic or symbolic interpretation. Flaubert enjoins us never to cross this threshold. He enjoins us to remain within the illusion. At the conclusion of this analysis the figures are figures of nothing if not of themselves. They refer to one another, they circulate meaning, they do not halt it: what is more they prevent its fixation and help nurture the Flaubertian utopia of a *Book About Nothing*.

Notes

1. Roland Barthes, "Introduction à l'analyse structurale des récits," *Communications*, 8 (1966): 3.

2. In Barthesian terms, one could say that generators have a distributional relationship and that figures are of an integrative nature.

3. Barthes, p. 11.

4. Gustave Flaubert, *Un coeur simple*, in *Trois Contes*, edited by René Dumesnil (Paris: Les Belles Lettres, 1957), p. 4. All quotations refer to this edition.

5. Cf. in particular the articles by Michel Crouzet, "Le style épique dans *Madame Bovary*," pp. 151–71, and Claude Duchet, "Roman et objets," pp. 172–201, in *Europe*, 47, nos. 485–87 (September–November, 1969).

6. This expression, so apt in French, has no direct equivalent in English. We have, however, adopted its counterpart "dénouement," literally, an "unknotting," to describe the climax of a drama. [Translator]

7. Jean-Pierre Richard, "La Création de la forme chez Flaubert," in his *Littérature et Sensation* (Paris: Seuil, 1954), p. 159. Concerning this whole aspect, see pp. 159–62.

8. Pierre Fontanier, *Les Figures du discours* (Paris: Flammarion, 1968).

9. Viktor Chklovski, "La Construction de la nouvelle et du roman," pp. 170–96 in *Théorie de la littérature* (Paris: Seuil, 1965).

10. Chklovski, p. 184.

11. Gustave Flaubert, *Correspondance*, in his *Oeuvres complètes*, 28 vols. (Paris: Conard, 1910–54). Letter to Mme Roger des Genettes, June 19, 1876. VII, 307.

12. *Théorie de la littérature*, p. 268.

13. *Vocabulaire de la psychanalyse* (Paris: Presses Universitaires de France, 1968), pp. 86–87.

14. Pp. 329–36.

15. Don-L. Demorest, *L' Expression figurée et symbolique dans l'oeuvre de Gustave Flaubert* (Paris: Les Presses modernes, 1931), p. 580. Emphasis added.

16. The author is making a pun on the word life, *vie*, and the identical "vi" sound shared by the names of Victor and Virginia [Translator].

17. Svend Johansen, "Écritures d'*Un coeur simple*," *Revue Romane*, 2, ii (1967): 108–20.

18. Flaubert, *Correspondance*. Letter to Louise Colet, January 29–30, 1853. III, 92.

19. Flaubert, *Correspondance*. Letter to Mme Roger des Genettes, first two weeks of October, 1879. VIII, 309.

20. Richard, p. 153.

21. Fontanier, p. 331.

22. Debray-Genette will stress the literal sense of the term *miné*. A more natural translation would be "drained," but this would miss the full impact of the word. Not only has Félicité's resilience been drained, but also her existence has been mined out. [Translator]

23. Terms proposed by Gérard Genette during his seminar on "Le Discours narratif chez Proust" (1969–70): "singulative" means the single narrative of a single event; "iterative" the single narrative of several similar events. Internal focalization ("vision with" in Pouillon's terms) characterizes the narrative commanded by the point of view of the hero. [Genette has since published this seminar in his seminal *Figures III* (Paris: Seuil, 1972) — Editor].

24. This phenomenon is to be compared with the following one: in *L'Éducation sentimentale* in particular, one sees certain objects circulating from one person to another: deprived of their successive possessors, they are also deprived of value in themselves, like the casket which goes from Mme Arnoux to Rosanette, then to Mme Dambreuse. Its meaning comes from the fact that it circulates, not from what it is. It creates a link between three women who ought not to meet. Because of it, the women destroy each other and do away with their happiness.

25. Flaubert, L' Éducation sentimentale (Paris: Les Belles Lettres, 1942), 2 vols., edited by René Dumesnil, I, 27.

26. Forster in fact used the term "story" rather than "narrative." The latter term has been used to be consistent with Debray-Genette's use of the term récit. [Translator]

27. A neologism based on the term décuplement, a tenfold increase; the suffix reinforces the sense of process rather than product. [Translator]

28. Roland Barthes, S / Z (Paris: Seuil, 1970), p. 166.

29. Cf. Chklovski, p. 177.

30. A. J. Greimas, Sémantique structurale (Paris: Larousse, 1966), p. 213.

Psyche into Myth: Humanity and Animality in Flaubert's Saint-Julien
Benjamin F. Bart*

Flaubert's Légende de Saint-Julien l'Hospitalier ("The Legend of Saint Julian the Hospitator," 1877) is a retelling of a medieval legend which was itself a mythic account of a saint's life, recalling those of Oedipus, Saint Christopher, Saint Eustace, and others.[1] Flaubert made numerous additions to his medieval sources: the scenes of Julian's childhood, the story of his wanderings, and in particular the accounts of Julian's two hunts, which prove to be mythic representations of the conflict between humanity and animality. By "myth" or "mythic" I shall mean the projection into story form, or into episode, of fundamental, normally unconscious, aspects of the psyche. Certain scenes in the two hunts have, it seems to me, hidden resonances at the level of myth, to which the reader responds. I shall be dealing with these scenes and also with the ending, which resolves their mythic conflict between humanity and animality; but I shall begin with its origins in Flaubert's unconscious.

For this I shall use one of Flaubert's dreams, which treats of the same problem and gives it a similar mythic form, since in the dream his unconscious is more manifest than it is in the Conte. Thereafter, we shall move back and forth between our conscious understanding of the dream and the mythic elements of the Saint-Julien, particularly in the hunting scenes and the ending, so as to bring to our conscious level their burden of psychic content for Flaubert and — through our common humanity — for us. Finally, I shall make use of works by Flaubert which lie chronologically between the time of the dream and the redaction of the story and which use the same themes to embody in similar myths the same psychic elements.[2]

Flaubert's dream dates from 1845, some thirty years before he wrote

*From Kentucky Romance Quarterly 20 (1973):317–41 (renamed the Romance Quarterly in 1986). Reprinted by permission of the Kentucky Romance Quarterly.

the *Saint-Julien*. I have separated the original running text into successive, numbered sections for ease of reference:

1. Lamalgue [a village] — The poet's house — roses in the garden — the little monkey.

2. I never know whether I'm the one who's looking at the monkey or if the monkey is the one looking at me — monkeys are our ancestors.

3. About three weeks ago I dreamed that I was in a vast forest all full of monkeys. My mother was walking with me. The farther we went, the more they came — there were some laughing and leaping about in the branches.

4. A lot of them came onto our path, and bigger and bigger ones, more and more of them — They were all looking at me — at last I was afraid. They surrounded us in a sort of circle —

5. One of them tried to pat me and took hold of my hand.

6. I shot him in the shoulder and made him bleed. He howled horribly —

7. Then my mother said to me: "Why are you hurting him, your friend, what did he do to you? Don't you see that he loves you? How like you he looks!" And the monkey was looking at me. That rent my soul.

8. and I woke up . . . feeling myself to be of the same nature as the animals and fraternizing with them in a wholly pantheistic and tender communion — .[3]

Flaubert reports that while at the village of Lamalgue (Section 1) he saw a small monkey. This led him to reflections (Section 2) on monkeys in general, which prove to be in part the outcome of a dream he had had some three weeks before. He found that monkeys look at us as much as we at them; in this respect, we and they are equals. Indeed, they are our ancestors.

The dream itself, which he now recounts, deals with monkeys, which were extremely lascivious animals for Flaubert, a view recurring frequently throughout his writings.[4] The sequence opens (Section 3) as Flaubert and his mother walk in a forest. It is full of monkeys, and more keep appearing, but at this stage they are pleasant animals. We may interpret this to mean Flaubert's ego is taking cognizance of the existence — albeit distant — of his animality and particularly his sexuality. In Section 4 the dream becomes threatening: the monkeys grow in number and in size, and crowd in upon Flaubert, who becomes frightened. They then enclose him in a circle.

Ambivalence enters with Section 5: one of the monkeys caresses him and seeks to take his hand. He responds with hostility (Section 6), shooting the creature and making him bleed and howl. At this point his mother intervenes (Section 7) to point to what I shall wish to call the lesson of the dream: the monkey is his friend, who has done nothing to him, who loves him and indeed resembles him. Minimally interpreted, Flaubert's animality, and specifically his sexuality, are part and parcel of himself, although he has tried to deny it.

Next, the monkey looks at him, the second time this has occurred in the dream. Flaubert, wiser now, is broken-hearted. At this painful juncture the dream presumably becomes unbearable, and he wakens (Section 8). The conflict is entirely resolved as he rejoices in a feeling that he is of the same nature as the animals; and he fraternizes with them in a pantheistic and tender communion.[5]

When Flaubert found the animals crowding about him, he reacted fearfully; when they encircled him and touched him, he reacted aggressively, only to learn later from his mother that he should have responded with understanding and communion. His error will be Julian's sin. And the lesson, which Julian, too, will learn, will lead Julian to just such a pantheistic communion and to his salvation.

Animals crowding about one are, then, the essential structure here. Flaubert frequently introduces this situation into his novels. It may lead to one of two diametrically opposed responses, acceptance or repulsion and rejection, the latter occurring particularly when crowding becomes encirclement. Their outcome in our *Légende* will be respectively sin or salvation. Both are here mythic incarnations of reactions to animality.

Several of the changes or additions on the MS page indirectly confirm this interpretation. In Section 5, the important "and took hold of my hand" is an interlinear addition, as more of the dream came back to Flaubert's memory. In section 7, when his mother speaks, it is clear that Flaubert's memories came in jumbled, incomplete fashion. After the first statement, "Why are you hurting him, your friend," Flaubert's next recollection was what actually became the third element, for he began: "don't," no doubt intending to go on with the rest of element three, "don't [you see that he loves you?]." Then he realized that his mother had also included here a reproach. Crossing out "don't," he now included the reproach, which thus constitutes the second element of her statement, "what did he do to you?" He then completed her observation that the monkey loved him. At a later time (but presumably not much later) her final statement, which is the most painful because the most revelatory, did come to the surface of his mind and he added it in the interline: "how like you he looks!"

Lastly, in Section 6 Flaubert wrote first "cried out" (a phrase at least as much human as animal) but crossed it out at once and continued in the line with "howled," a clearly more animal word to report the sound.[6]

The verb *to look at* (*regarder*) and the act of looking play an essential role in the account. At the start, Flaubert looked at the monkey, the monkey at him (Section 2). In the dream, when the monkeys became more numerous and crowded about him, he noted that "they were all looking at me" (Section 4). And after he had wounded the caressing monkey, that monkey, too, "was looking at [him]" (Section 7). Flaubert places more emphasis than most authors on how characters look at one another, but this is not solely in order to display their interrelationships; that is, it is more than merely another aspect of his familiar preference for showing rather than telling. It is also, as the dream may suggest, obsessive with him. For both reasons looking will recur very frequently in this study.[7]

At the end of his dream Flaubert extended his feeling of "fraternizing" to the much more inclusive notion of "a wholly pantheistic and tender communion." This final revelation marks the resurgence of one of Flaubert's most fundamental experiences, his recurrent moments of pantheistic awareness, always accompanied by joy. The first he is known to have recorded took place in Corsica in 1840, some five years before the dream:[8]

> It was then high noon, and we were following the road that goes along the shore to the ancient town of Sagom. The sea was calm; the sun shining on it illumined its azure which appeared even more limpid; all around the rocks which barely projected from the water, its sparkling rays suggested crowns of diamonds; they shone more intense and scintillating than the stars. The sea had a perfume sweeter than roses; we breathed it with delight; we were inhaling into ourselves the sun, the sea breeze, the broad horizon, the scent of the myrtle, *for there are days of happiness when the soul, like the countryside, lies open to the sun* and, likewise, emanates an odor of hidden flowers that supreme beauty brings to blossom there. You saturate yourself with sunbeams, with pure air, with pleasant, ineffable thoughts: *everything in you palpitates with joy and flutters its wings with the elements,* you cling to them, you breathe with them, *the essence of living nature seems to have passed into you in an exquisite marriage,* you smile at the sound of the wind that stirs the crests of the trees, at the murmur of the waves on the strand; you run across the seas with the breeze; something ethereal, vast, *tender* hovers in the very light of the sun and is lost in an immensity as radiant as the roseate mists of dawn which rise toward heaven.[9]

Such experiences recurred over the years.[10]

Pantheism is the resolution the dream provided to the conflict embodied in the dream itself between Flaubert's ego and his instincts, which threatened to overcome his ego, to submerge it, which is to say, to destroy him. These are also the psychic elements which give mythic force to certain passages in the *Saint-Julien.* They come particularly close to the surface in the two hunts as well as in the closing paragraphs of the story. While still a young man, Julian went out on the first hunt, at the end of which the great stag, whom he had mortally wounded, predicted he would kill his parents. At a later time, having fled his home to avoid fulfilling the prediction, he went out on the second hunt, wholly unsuccessful, at the end of which he returned and unwittingly did kill his parents. At the end of the story Julian atones for his crime by taking a loathsome leper into his bed and warming him with his own nude body. His recompense came as the leper, transformed into Christ, rose with him to heaven.

In the first hunt Julian indulges in what Flaubert calls in his notes a "senseless slaughter": he wantonly kills for the pleasure of killing. Animals appear in profusion around him: "an infinite number of animals, more numerous at each step."[11] This is the equivalent of the monkeys, who were also "more and more [numerous]" (Section 4). The passage continues: "They circled around him, trembling, with a look full of gentleness and entreaty." But as Flaubert in the dream, so Julian here: he responds with violence. "But Julian did not tire of killing, by turns drawing his cross-bow, unsheathing his sword, thrusting with his hunting knife. . . ." This, however, is not the end: " — and he thought of nothing, remembered nothing at all. He was hunting in an indeterminate land, for an immeasurable time, by virtue of his own existence alone. . . ." And the passage closes with a pregnant observation: " — everything happening with the effortlessness that you experience *in dreams.*"

Throughout the long sentence psychic content is phrased in mythic form. Two elements are present: the loss of a clear sense of time and space, which is characteristic of dreams, and the direct statement: "with the effortlessness that you experience in dreams." This second element is a recurrent phrase in Flaubert's works: each time, desire is being satisfied (or is about to be so), and each time sexuality is profoundly involved, either overtly or by implication. The various episodes linked by this recurrent phrase serve to elucidate each other.

In the first, and again in the second *Éducation sentimentale*, the notation occurs in episodes where is is no more than a normal, direct characterizing of a state of being. In the first *Éducation* (1843–45), Flaubert noted in a seduction scene: "Slowly — it happened without his thinking about it and *with the supernatural effortlessness that we experience in dreams* — he raised his arm, extended it, and slipped it around her waist" (p. 55). In the second *Éducation* (1869): "Frédéric went from the pub to Arnoux's place, as if he were carried by a warm wind and *with the extraordinary ease that you experience in dreams.*" Approaching the satisfaction of sexual desires may, then, induce this dream-like ease of accomplishment in a Flaubertian hero.

Psychic elements are given more mythic dimensions in the episode in which the phrase recurs in *Salammbô* (1862). Mâtho, having possessed himself of the veil of Tanit, the moon goddess, mounts the stairs of Hamilcar Barca's palace to present the veil to Salammbô. "The sky above his head was afire; the sea filled the horizon; at each step he was surrounded by an even vaster immensity, and he continued to climb the stairs *with the strange effortlessness that you experience in dreams*" (p. 102). More is at issue than the general reader is likely to understand consciously from the phrasing, although Flaubert appears to have hoped that intuition would grasp what only erudition makes manifest.[12] Throughout the book Flaubert expressly links Mâtho to Moloch, the male principle, and Salammbô to Tanit, the female principle. In this episode, when Mâtho-Moloch is going (as he thinks) to take possession of Salammbô-Tanit, the god and the goddess both present themselves to his expanding view, for Moloch is god of fire ("The sky above his head was afire") and Tanit is "the [female] ruler of the seas" ("the sea filled the horizon").[13] At each step that Mâtho took, "he was surrounded by an even vaster immensity," and he apprehended more fully the presence of the god and the goddess. Mythic projection gives body to psychic experience and Mâtho mounts the staircase *with the strange effortlessness that you experience in dreams.*" The recurrent phrase emphasizes the mythic content here, as it will later in the *Saint-Julien*.

The contexts of the examples prior to the *Saint-Julien* state directly the sexuality which was at the base of Flaubert's monkey dream. But the various examples may be used to elucidate and enrich each other. A first clue lies in the phrasing which links them: "the effortlessness that you experience in dreams." In the *Saint-Julien* it links Julian's massacre to the overt sexuality of the other examples and hence to the dream itself, which reinforces the intuition that sexuality is at issue in this scene. Conversely, the overt annihilation in the *Julien* scene reflects back—by the same linguistic parallel—upon the earlier occurrences to suggest that they, too, may be exemplifications of Flaubert's habitual linking of sexuality and annihilation, a suggestion borne out by the later developments of the plots in each case.[14]

In all these examples, the instinctual life is invading consciousness and produces a dream-like state. In addition, in the *Saint-Julien*, the instinctual life is also destroying the conscious perception of time. A further episode here, which occurs well after the first hunt, involves the same fundamental situation. Having fled his parents' castle, Julian abstains from hunting, seeking thereby to avoid increasing his guilt (p. 102). Nonetheless, he is tortured in his dreams by a desire for the chase. In fact Julian dreams Flaubert's own dream, with only indispensable adaptations; but he will imagine himself in ancient biblical settings:

Sometimes, in a dream, he saw himself as our forefather Adam in the middle of Eden, among all the animals. — And by stretching out his arm, he caused them to die. — Or else they filed by in pairs and gradated by height, from the elephants and lions to the ermine and the duck, as on the day when they entered Noah's ark. From the shadows of a cave,

he hurled infallible javelins at them; others came. There was no end to
it — and he awoke *rolling savage eyes* (p. 102).

This is a summation of much from the other episodes. It is a dream; action
is effortless. Animals crowd about; they are more and more numerous.
Murder is endlessly easy; annihilation results. But ferocity and not joy is its
culmination, for Julian's dream cannot come out to the lesson Flaubert
learned from his, since the story at this point requires that Julian shortly go
out on his second hunt, from which he will return to accomplish the
murder of his parents.

   The first hunt was the bloody actualization of Julian's desire to kill.
Flaubert carefully prepares the reader for understanding it. Prior to the
hunt, Julian spends his days and his nights in the company of his pack,
"and he came home in the middle of the night, covered with blood and
dirt, with spines in his hair and smelling like the wild animals. He became
like them" (p. 88). This is to descend to the ferocity of certain kinds of
animals ("the wild animals"), not to integrate animality into the ego.[15]
Contrast Félicité of *Un coeur simple*, one of whose virtues is her "bestial
devotion" to Mme Aubain (p. 42). After a brief paragraph of lesser
examples of Julian's ferocity, he — and the reader — are ready to set out on
the sadistic slaughter of the first hunt.

   When the hunt is over, Julian's response to the prediction of the stag
that he will kill his parents brings the hidden truth perilously close to the
surface again, as he meditates on the curse: "If I wanted to, however . . ."
(p. 94; ellipsis in original). Thus to humanity and its rejection, and
animality and its rejection, are added sadism and parricide, as Julian
becomes a "wild animal."[16]

   The successive versions of the *Tentation de saint Antoine* (particularly
those of 1849 and 1874) also contain the crucial scene of animals crowding
about the protagonist. In the version of 1849, during the Parade of the
Monsters before Anthony, the saint is surrounded by animals; his reactions
are predominantly hostile. In the version of 1874 Flaubert again displays
the Parade to Anthony, but this time Anthony accepts them. In his hunts
Julian will relive Anthony's hostile reactions of the version of 1849 and go
on to his murders. Anthony's reaction of 1874, which echoes the acceptance in the dream, is the lesson which it remains for Julian to learn in the
final pages of the Tale, in order to find his salvation.

   In the version of 1849 at the end of Part II, with the long Part III yet
to go — and this placing is important — Anthony has already seen a number
of monstrous animals (e.g., the Martichoras and the Catoblepas) and is
now about to be inundated by them. The passage is an expansion of the
monkeys crowding about Flaubert in the dream (Section 4). As the
monsters continue to arrive, the mass takes on a strange configuration,
which will recur in the *Julien*: "Heaped up, crowded together, suffocating
under their weight, multiplying as they touched, they clamber over each

other. And that [mass] rises into pyramids *like a mountain*, a great moving heap of diverse bodies, each part of which stirs with an independent motion, and whose complex totality sways with one movement, makes noises and gleams through a heavy atmosphere . . ." (p. 408).

In the *Julien*, this scene recurs during the first hunt. He has come upon a herd of deer trapped within a high-walled valley. As he begins to shoot them down (the "insane slaughter"), "the stags, becoming enraged, fought with each other, reared, climbed onto each other, and their bodies with their tangled antlers formed a broad hillock that shifted and collapsed" (p. 92). Julian again reacts as Flaubert did in the dream: he kills them all. A few moments later, the great stag will utter his dire prediction. In the drafts, the phrasing is totally precise: "Cursed be the murderer of animals, of the innocent. . . ."[17]

In the second hunt (pp. 108–10) Julian finds after repeated failures that "A higher power was taking away his strength." The dream sequence again recurs. Animals crowd about him: a marten, a panther, a serpent, which climbs a tree. "In its foliage there was a *monstrous* jackdaw that *was looking at* Julian," a parallel to the monkeys who become larger and larger in the dream and who then stared at Flaubert (Section 4). The two themes continue intertwined. "And here and there a quantity of large sparks appeared among the branches, as if the firmament had made all its stars rain down *into the forest*. They were *animals' eyes*, of wildcats, squirrels, owls, parrots, *monkeys*." Julian's weapons are useless (in contrast to the first hunt and to Flaubert's gun in the dream) and he reacts with unbridled rage as instinct again overwhelms ego: "He cursed himself, would have liked to strike himself, screamed invective, suffocated with rage."

The next paragraph is particularly probant, for it is related to a scene from the *Tentation* which occurs in different forms in the two different versions. First the *Julien* passage, in which the continuation of the dream is apparent: "And all the animals he had been pursuing presented themselves, forming *a tight circle* around him . . . He remained in the middle, *frozen with terror*, unable to make the slightest movement. With a supreme effort of will, he took a step. Those who were roosting in the trees opened their wings, those who were treading the earth moved their limbs; and they all accompanied him." Each, by his specific form of movement, is emphasizing his specific form of animality, as were the monkeys who leaped about the branches in the dream (Section 3).

This invading, particularized animality takes on a nightmare quality: "The hyenas walked in front of him, the wolf and the wild boar behind. To his right, the bull was swaying his head, and the snake at his left was undulating through the grass, while the panther, arching his back, advanced with velvet footsteps, and with great strides. He [Julian] went as slowly as possible so as not to annoy them; and from the depths of the thickets he saw emerging: porcupines, foxes, vipers, jackals, and bears."

Terror now intervenes; animality becomes even more oppressive. "Julian started to run; they ran. The snake was hissing, the smaller predators ["bêtes puantes"][18] were drooling." As Julian experiences it, faithful to Flaubert's dream, the animals now become menacing: "The boar rubbed his ankles with his tusks, the wolf his palms with the hairs on his muzzle. The *monkeys* pinched him, grimacing. . . ." And then the threatening beasts begin to blur the distinction between animality and humanity, for they take on a human character: "irony showed through their crafty manner. While *observing him out of the corner of their eyes*, they seemed to be ruminating on a plan of revenge." Julian is overcome: " — And dazed by the buzzing of the insects, struck by birds' tails, stifled by the animals' breath, he walked with outstretched arms and closed eyes like a blind man, without even having the strength to call out for mercy."

By placing the future saint thus in a state such that he cannot even appeal to God for grace, Flaubert invokes the larger context of the sin Julian is about to commit. It is the ironic parallel to his state in his earlier killings, when his actions had "the effortlessness that you experience in dreams." The reference to the dream experience was an enlargement of context to suggest that the killings are the living out of fantasy, the rejection of the bond with animality and the concomitant desire for parricide, which will shortly rise to consciousness after it is verbalized by the stag. In the second hunt, when Julian can no longer appeal for grace, he will return home, exasperated beyond endurance, actually to commit his desired crime: "since animals were unavailable, he would have wanted to massacre men" (p. 110).

In the 1849 version of the *Tentation* Anthony had felt a terror similar to Julian's on being surrounded by the hostile animals. Anthony's experience can illuminate the mythic resonances of Julian's. As the monsters first begin to appear before Anthony, the theme and much of the vocabulary display the parallel at once: "The Chimera *barks*, the Sphinx *growls*, enormous butterflies start to *buzz* in the air, lizards come forward, bats *flutter in circles* with their young, toads *hop* and *roll their huge eyes* . . . vipers *hiss* . . . giant spiders walk" (p. 397).

Anthony is "horrified" just as Julian was. Anthony's experience is enormously physical, a repulsion of the flesh before this animality: "A horrible terror is invading me. Oh! I'm cold! My skin is trembling on my body! . . . how many of them there are! It's like a rain oozing in large drops; on the ground there are sticky tracks with gleaming slime." But it is the *Pig* [Anthony's pet in the earlier versions] who is charged with making explicit the fear of death: "Mercy! those horrid animals are going to swallow me raw!" (p. 398). And then Anthony gives a fuller account of his fear of this invading animality: "They are increasing, on my head, at my sides, everywhere, just everywhere; I don't dare to walk, for I would roll over on those dragging bodies, and as I fell I would crush those soft palpitating things beneath my hands; and I don't dare to breathe, for *I would swallow* all those vibrating, pointed wings; they are ringing in my ears." This is to make explicit what was implicit in Julian's repulsion. Anthony continues: "I'm choking, I can't see any more, I can't hear any more . . . So who is exhaling those breaths, stinking like a winter fog? What scraping sounds! What sighs! I see *huge eyes* revolving, limbs twisting, breasts leaping like waves, and insubstantial men more transparent than bubbles of air."

The next notation is, as it were, a stage direction, in which the dream sequence is reaffirmed: "Indeed, shapes of all kinds appear, some seeming to split off from inside the others; as they multiply, they become progressively more distinct." The sexual character, noted in Anthony's speech, is here more explicit. It will grow in importance. But already what will underlie the *Julien* passage, the rejection of oneness with all of animality, is apparent. And the *Tentation* has also phrased directly the fear of the loss of self, the fear of death, which animality involves.

As in Flaubert's dream, the animals now crowd in upon Anthony; who watches them, this time "stupefied": "What an abundance! What variety! What shapes! . . . they arrive, they whirl, they heap up . . ." (p. 407). Looking is central here, too: "their *gaze* has depths where my soul whirls, you'd say they were souls." This is akin to Flaubert's observation on seeing the monkey at Lamalgue (Section 2). As the vision continues, the dream sequence (Section 4) still provides the pattern for the mythic projection:

> While Anthony *looks at the animals*, they *swell*, *grow*, *enlarge*, and there come yet *more formidable* and *more monstrous* ones . . . (p. 407)

> And others, in confusion, pell-mell, sliding by like a lightning flash, carried off like dry leaves; howling squalls of them come, full of marvellous anatomies . . . [19]

> And those that have gone by return, those that have not yet come arrive, they fall from the sky, spring from the earth, climb down from the rocks (p. 408).

As at the start of the Parade, each now displays and emphasizes his own peculiar form of animality, of monstrosity (I abridge greatly): "The Cynocephalids start to bark . . . the Martichoras roars . . . the Basilisk hisses . . . the beasts of the sea start wiggling their fins, the reptiles exhaling their venom, the toads leaping . . . teeth grind, wings vibrate, chests fill, claws extend, flesh slaps against flesh. . . ." And now their sexuality, which was absent from the hunting passage but which so marks the ending of the *Julien*: "some give birth, others copulate, or devour each other in a single gulp" (p. 408). Here the relationship between sexuality and eating, taking into the body, is explicit: and as before, there is the concomitant of all animality, death.[20]

Anthony, who had earlier been "horrified," then "stupefied," now bursts forth: "The blood in my veins is beating so hard [sic] that it's going to break them, my head is bursting in pieces, my soul is overflowing above me. I would like to depart, go away, flee!" (p. 409). But already in 1849 something of the lesson of the dream lingered, for instead of actually fleeing, he exclaims: "I too am an animal, life is teeming in my belly, and I feel internal roilings such as there are in rivers." This is Flaubert's earlier "feeling myself to be of the same nature as the animals" and, indeed, the pantheistic communion of the moment of awakening from the dream (Section 8). Anthony's ecstasy grows: "I need to bark, to bellow, to howl . . . [I would like] to twist my body and divide myself everywhere, to be in everything, to emanate myself with odors, to unfold like plants, to vibrate like sound, to shine like the day, to model myself in all shapes, to enter each atom, to circulate in matter, to be matter myself to know what it thinks."

At first sight this appears to be the full wisdom of the dream lesson, the integration of ego and instinct, the acceptance, by the spirit, of animality, including sexuality and even monstrosity.[21] But this would be to read into the passage more than is fully there. Dream and fiction have indeed been very close, and the endings are similar; but they are not identical. Two reservations must be made. First, Anthony does wish to be matter, but only in order to know "what it thinks." His goal is not being as an end in itself: it partakes more of the nature of an intellectual curiosity . . . which the Devil at once undertakes to satisfy. Second, and more critical, this is only part way through the *Tentation* of 1849, only one of almost innumerable temptations, and the vision is brushed away as rapidly as it came.

Not so in 1874! The scene will be altered in its tone in the new version, will partake of joy at the end and not of terror, and its lesson, obscured and set aside in 1849, will become the final version in 1874, as it will be the lesson of the ending of the *Julien*. As before, Anthony sees much the same monsters performing much the same gyrations, emphasizing in much the same way their animality and their rampant sexuality. The introductory elements are similar to the earlier version: "And all kinds of fearsome beasts rise up . . ." (p. 197) and there follows much the same list, albeit condensed. Then, as before, "They arrive in squalls, full of marvelous anatomies": we appear to be following an identical experience, even to the animals climbing upon one another, copulating, devouring one another. Indeed, the final statement brings out yet more forcefully and with greater condensation the horror of their clammy touch in a foretaste of Julian's embrace of the leper: "He feels the slime of slugs on his calves, the coldness of vipers on his hands; and spiders spinning their webs enclose him in their net" (p. 198). The slugs had appeared at the start of the Parade in 1849; the others, appearing at the end (as here), had been merely: "the vipers hiss . . . giant spiders walk" (p. 397). Now even the spiders enclose Anthony in their web!

The encirclement has taken place, the sequence of the dream seems about to be repeated, when suddenly it is broken: "But the circle of monsters opens, the sky suddenly becomes blue . . ." (p. 198). The frightening entrapment is reversed, peace replaces fear, and the sky becomes blue overhead. More and more animals appear. But then the hallucination changes form: "The plants are no longer distinguishable from the animals" (p. 200). The next move is inexorable: "the plants blend with the stones." As all of nature fuses into one, to make his meaning explicit Flaubert comments of Anthony: "And he is no longer afraid!" Lying flat upon the ground, the saint observes nature closely and perceives the vibration of the molecules.[22]

Anthony becomes "delirious" and exclaims "O happiness! happiness! I've seen life being born. . . ." Now as his veins again threaten to burst and as, again, he longs to fly, swim, bark, bellow, the vision rises to ever greater power, and his final line in the book is "[I would like] to be matter!" Its position makes it the ultimate lesson of the long night of visions as it had been earlier for the dream. Being matter, being at one with all of nature, at one with all of himself, is goal enough, the final end in itself. The dawn rises, the clouds part; and in the heavens "right in the center, and in the very disc of the sun, shines the countenance of Jesus Christ" (p. 201).

What Anthony in 1849 did not fully possess and what he did learn fully in 1874 is precisely what Julian still lacked at the time of the second hunt: an understanding of how religion, specifically how a pantheistic intuition, may infuse such an experience of animality to relieve the revulsion and thus make possible that tender communion Flaubert felt on awakening from his dream.

Midway in time between the *Tentation* of 1849 and of 1874, *Salammbô* (1862) had contained a further exemplification of animality crowding about the hero, Mâtho. As *Salammbô* is intended to display the full splendor of love, its description of encroaching animality need show no revulsion, no drawing back.[23] It occurs in a passage immediately preceding Mâtho's mounting the staircase to Salammbô's room. Mâtho, incarnation (as we have seen) of the male principle and of Moloch, has entered the temple of the moon goddess, Tanit, to steal the sacred veil to give to Salammbô, incarnation of the female principle and of Tanit. The familiar themes recur, but now the emphasis on sexuality is overt as Mâtho, accompanied by Spendius, observes the paintings covering the walls of the temple chamber:

> A blinding light made them lower their eyes. Then they perceived all around them an infinity of beasts, gaunt, *panting*, bristling with claws, and *confusingly overlapping* in a mysterious disorder that *was frightening*. Snakes had feet, bulls had wings, fish with human heads were devouring fruit, flowers bloomed in crocodiles' maws, and elephants with their trunks raised passed by in the middle of the sky, haughty as

eagles. A fearsome effort swelled their incomplete or multiple limbs. They seemed, sticking out their tongues, to be *trying to make their souls come out of their bodies*; and every possible shape was seen there, as if the container holding all germination, splitting open in a sudden hatching, had emptied itself onto the walls of the room (pp. 97–98).

The beasts "confusingly overlapping" recall Anthony's vision in 1849. The monstrous amalgams of animals had already also appeared there, derived from Breughel, e.g., "alligator heads supported by ducks' feet . . . winged bellies flitting about . . . women's bodies having a full-blown lotus blossom instead of a face" (p. 408). Breughel's concept of monstrosity in his painting of the *Tentation* pushes the horror to new heights. Flaubert had not yet seen the painting at the time of his dream: the critical experience came one month later to add its formulations to Flaubert's psychic and hence mythic structures.

Monstrous though the amalgams of animals in *Salammbô* may be for the reader, they do not so affect Mâtho. The explanation lies in Flaubert's concept of love as a total physical experience and a total spiritual and religious experience as well, each aspect fusing with the other and completing it.[24] Over and over Flaubert makes this point; it is integral to Mâtho's successful experience in the temple of Tanit, for though the monsters do display "a mysterious disorder that was frightening," Mâtho is not repulsed by either the monstrosity of these animals or their sexuality. Instead, he pushes ahead in his search for the veil, symbol of Tanit and of Salammbô. It all hangs together: after having possessed himself of the veil, he made his way to Salammbô's palace and mounted the stairs "with the effortlessness you experience in dreams."

Julian, at the time of the second hunt, knew even less of all this than did the Anthony of 1849. After murdering his parents, Julian must learn, through his penance, what the Anthony of 1874 knew, to which will be added, even more overtly, the sexual component present in *Salammbô*. He must integrate his body and his soul and accept his own place in a nature no longer conceived as inanimate, but rather understood pantheistically as one and all animate.

The problem may be phrased as Julian's relationship to nature, which he finds profoundly hostile, for it bodies forth his own animality. He is echoing his creator, for Flaubert had often known revulsion at nature quite as much as "a wholly pantheistic and tender communion." In 1840 he wrote: "There are days when I am overcome with *tenderness* upon seeing animals." At about the time of his dream (1845): "Sometimes I look at animals and even trees with a *tenderness* that goes as far as sympathy. . . ."[25]

Thereafter, however, there are few favorable comments on nature. Though these pantheistic moments were immensely powerful and filled with peace and joy, they were moments only, and as the years passed they became—or so it would appear—less and less frequent. Far more often,

Flaubert, much like Baudelaire, found nature unacceptable, and far inferior to the artificial: "I am not a man of Nature; 'her marvels' move me less than those of Art." Sometimes Flaubert is clearly embarrassed over having a warmer feeling: "Would you believe that I miss the country and that I feel like seeing greenery and flowers? It makes me blush for shame. That's the first time in my life that this shopkeeper's sentiment has surged from my soul." It was far more typical for him to note: "I who *hate nature.* . . ." A longer observation is perceptive: "I'll start by declaring that the beauties of Nature thoroughly bug me . . . Nature bores me to tears or rather crushes me." Elsewhere he analyzes this fear in terms which become transparent when linked to the dream. Invasive nature, animality threatening to overcome the ego, spells imminent death: "When I lie down on the grass, it seems to me that *I'm already beneath the ground* and that heads of lettuce are beginning to sprout from my stomach. Your troubadour [Flaubert's phrase for himself in these letters to George Sand] is a man *unwholesome* by nature. I like the country only when I'm traveling, because then the independent state of my person allows me to pass over *the awareness of my nothingness.*"[26]

Only in the 1870's do other attitudes begin to reassert themselves. The experiences and actions Flaubert reports appear hyperbolic, but they are no more than a return to older feelings: the frequency of their occurrence is warrant of their validity. One year before beginning the *Julien* he wrote of an experience in a Swiss hotel: "And then my companions . . . those foreign gentlemen who live in the hotel! All German or English, armed with walking sticks and opera glasses. Yesterday, I was tempted to kiss three calves I met in a pasture, out of a sense of humanity and a need for expansiveness."[27] The phrase "out of a sense of humanity" marks the critical change. Embracing the calves leaps back thirty years to the *tenderness* he expressed in the early 1840's for "animals and even trees." Humanity having disgusted him in the form of his fellow guests at the hotel, he had felt "a need for expansiveness" toward calves. The psychological structure of the event he transferred one year later, intact, to Julian.

Flaubert did not always hold to his renewed acceptance of nature during the 1870's. Even while in Brittany working on the *Julien* and frequently rejoicing in his natural surroundings,[28] he also felt the old fears, which he lent to Julian: "Under other circumstances, this landscape would have enchanted me, but nature is not always good to contemplate. She reimmerses us *in the feeling of our nothingness and of our powerlessness.*" During these years he was sometimes puzzled when he discovered within himself an openness to nature: "this makes three times that I've come back from Rouen [to his home in Croisset] on foot, along the river, admiring Nature! This year [1876] the autumn delights me! Why?" On another occasion the analysis is more profound and the phrasing more explicitly sexual, surprised though Flaubert obviously was at when he had written: "I feel a sensual pleasure (the term is not too strong) when I admire the sun striking the river, I listen to the cackling of hens with beatitude, and I breathe in the good smell of the garden."[29] Two further letters from this decade return to his feeling of closeness to animals: "You can't imagine how I'm becoming 'a lover of nature.' I look at the sky, the trees, and the greenery with a pleasure I've never had! I'd like to be a cow in order to eat grass."[30] And, "The weather was splendid! — I stayed fixed in contemplation before nature — and I was seized with such tenderness for the little calf lying next to its mother . . . that I kissed it on the forehead, the aforesaid calf!"[31]

Against this background the resonances of the final pages of the *Julien* become clearer. The dream (Section 8) and the parallel sequence of responses during Flaubert's Swiss visit underlie a first movement. Julian, fleeing after his murder, is repulsed by all. However, "the need to mingle with the life of others made him go down into the town. But the bestial air of the faces . . . the indifference of the conversations chilled his heart . . . and he went back toward the country" (p. 116). Now, with the end only a few pages off, Julian must quickly learn the lesson which Flaubert had known intermittently ever since the dream: "*With transports of love* he contemplated the colts in the pastures, the birds in their nests, the insects on the flowers." He is learning to integrate his full being, but his sin still requires penance. Hence the next sentence reads, as it must: "All, at his approach, ran off, hid in fear, flew off quickly." And not only must there be a penance adequate to Julian's sin; the further issue of sexuality must be more fully integrated than it was in the phrase "with transports of love."

The hideous leper has come to Julian's cabin, has even demanded to be put into Julian's bed. Now he requires Julian to lie down nude on top of him to warm him: "Julian stretched out completely on top, mouth to mouth, chest to chest" (p. 124). The position is sexual; Julian's acceptance is now as full as was his earlier rejection.

The transcendent final paragraph completes the integration and thus brings the Tale to its necessary conclusion:

> Then the Leper embraced him; and suddenly his eyes became bright as stars; his hair lengthened like rays of the sun; the breath from his nostrils had the fragrance of roses; a cloud of incense rose from the hearth, the waves were singing. During this an abundance of delight, a superhuman joy came down like a flood into the swooning soul of Julian; and he whose arms were still holding him tight, grew larger, larger, touching the opposite walls of the cabin with his head and his feet. The roof flew off, the firmament unfolded. — And Julian rose toward the blue expanses, face to face with Our Lord Jesus who was carrying him off into heaven (pp. 124–25).

Much in the passage is by now familiar: the importance of eyes, the increasing size, the radiance of the ending of the *Tentation* of 1874, and the *blue expanses*. The remainder of the language is consonant with these, the resonances clear always in the reader's unconscious but now more manifest. As the waves sing in exultation, the psalms come to mind; but pantheism is also being affirmed. The clarity of the stars (*stella maris*), the scent of roses, the overwhelming perfumes of the Song of Solomon all remind the reader of the ancient phrasings of the mystics translating their love for Mary. But before being phrasings of mystic love of God, these were phrasings of human love for humans.

In addition, these phrases had long been the clichés through which Flaubert phrased his characters' efforts to speak of their love for their mistresses. Two texts go back to Flaubert's first *Éducation sentimentale* of 1843–45, that is, to about the time of the dream. Jules speaks of his mistress: "she's the one with whom one should feel oneself *ascend toward the stars*, toward the light, *toward eternal extasy* . . . and, blending into her soul, to disseminate oneself like the *incense* that goes away, that goes away slowly, forever, *ascending in order to die in a pure and limitless expanse*."[32] Anthony too, it may be recalled, had said, "I would like . . . to emanate myself with odors," a desire whose occurrences in the *Tentation* and here cast light upon each other. In this first *Éducation* Henri, too, had spoken of his mistress: "suddenly we found ourselves close to each other, and in effect I sensed that *her mouth had the scent of roses. A luminous fluid flowed from her eyes*. . . ." And later, "*Her eyes shone like torches* . . . we took delight . . . in that inexhaustible happiness."[33]

This coupling in the *Éducation* of religion, sexuality, and spiritual love was consciously available to Flaubert then. It found further formulation in the dream. Shortly thereafter, during a trip through Brittany in 1847, he had been moved by the profound love for the Virgin which he found there. In it, too, he could find a substratum of sexuality: "Religion entails nearly carnal sensations; prayer has its forms of debauchery . . . and the men who come to kneel before that clothed statue in the evenings also experience poundings of the heart and vague intoxications there. . . ." Anthony would know all this in the version of 1849. Similarly in Brittany Flaubert had seen a statue of an ancient fertility goddess and was moved to write of "that eternal religion of the human entrails . . . [it] cannot die, for this enduring dream . . . is the cult of one's being; the worship of Life through the principle that gives it."[34] It is this permanent, underlying current of the religious instinct allied to sexuality and, through pantheism, to the totality of creation, which had been the basis of Flaubert's dream, which had won peace for Anthony in 1874, and which now marked God's acceptance of Julian's penance in the final vision of the Tale.

For the central fact of this final paragraph is pantheism, the "wholly pantheistic and tender communion" to which Flaubert had wakened at the close of his dream. The concepts and indeed the very words he used to transcribe his pantheistic experiences are the true base from which this paragraph is drawn, far more than from the Song of Solomon or the phrasing of the mystics or the images Flaubert put in the mouths of his lovers.[35] It is enough to repeat here the central expressions from the pantheistic experience of 1840, which we considered earlier, for this to be manifest: "more scintillating than the stars . . . a perfume sweeter than roses . . . the soul . . . emanates an odor of hidden flowers . . . pleasant, ineffable thoughts . . . joy . . . the murmur of the waves . . . roseate mists of dawn which rise toward heaven."[36]

Flaubert was wont to read the ending of the *Julien* in so thunderous a voice that the ceiling shook. Zola recalled that he completed it "with a veritable thunderclap."[37] Perhaps this is something of what he meant when he said that art consoled one for life. His life was hideous; he said so.[38] And moments were rare of awakening from the profound teachings of the dream life into a tender, fraternal, pantheistic communion with creation. But in his art he could know — to the exclusion of all else — the pantheistic exultation of Julian's ascent to heaven in the arms of his Savior.

Notes

1. I should acknowledge from the outset of this paper the very great assistance I have received from Cynthia S. Bart. Her training in humanistic psychology at Duquesne University she constantly placed at my disposal: many of the suggestions I here offer are as much hers as mine.

2. The present article derives from a paper prepared for the Kentucky Foreign Language Conference in April, 1972. I have treated aspects of the mechanics by which the mythic materials are made more readily acceptable in "Space, Time, and Reality in Flaubert's *Saint-Julien*," *Romanic Review*, 59 (1968):30–39.

3. Unless otherwise specified, all references to Flaubert's works will be to the Conard edition, 28 vols. (Paris, 1910–54). The account of the dream is published in *Notes de voyages*, I, 15. I have emended that text to conform, except for minor corrections in spelling and punctuation, to the original manuscript at the Bibliothèque historique de la Ville de Paris, Carnets de Voyage de Gustave Flaubert, no. 1, "Voyage en Italie, mai 1845," folio 13 recto and verso.

4. E.g., *Oeuvres de jeunesse*, I, "Quidquid volueris," especially pp. 220–23, 232–33, 235–39; 252, 513. *Tentation de saint Antoine*, pp. 30, 37, 387, 392, 583, 587. *Trois Contes*, p. 13. *Bouvard et Pécuchet*, p. 583. *Correspondance*, VIII, 97.

5. It is entirely possible, perhaps even probable, that Flaubert's recollection of the dream is fragmentary. Even so, it has a number of meanings on a number of levels. For a discussion of the background of the dream, see Benjamin F. Bart, *Flaubert* (Syracuse, N.Y.: Syracuse University Press, 1967), Chapter 6; certain aspects of the dream and its meanings are considered on pp. 670–75. In the present study, I shall be discussing only those aspects directly related to animality, its acceptance and rejection. Thus, specifically, I shall not treat here the crucial role of Flaubert's mother.

6. To complete the account of the MS, in Section 2, Flaubert originally wrote; "I don't know," but crossed out "don't" and strengthened his statement to "never." In Section 4, to emphasize "bigger and bigger ones," he added an interlinear "and." Lastly, in Section 3, the precise indication, "About three weeks ago," is an interlinear addition.

7. The prominence of eyes and of looking in the *Saint-Julien* is particularly suggestive in Flaubert, who sought always to avoid repetitions. In addition to four examples I shall examine in the present study, there are nine others, which it is instructive to study side by side. The gypsy who predicts Julian's future has "flaming pupils." The mastiffs show their ferocity by "rolling their pupils." Like the gypsy, the great stag, too, has "flaming eyes." To display an

opposite temperament, the very brief description of Julian's wife opens: "Her great black eyes shone like two gentle lamps." As Julian approaches his father whom he has just murdered, "[he] saw between his half-open lids a lustreless pupil, that burned him like fire." Continuing the images of fire and burning, the leper has "two eyes redder than glowing coals." While crossing the river in the storm, "[Julian] always perceived the leper's pupils." And similarly, as the leper neared death, "his eyes no longer shone." Lastly, in opposite vein, when the leper is transformed into Christ: "his eyes suddenly became as bright as stars."

8. See Jean Bruneau, *Les Débuts littéraires de Gustave Flaubert, 1831–1845* (Paris: Colin, 1962), pp. 301–02.

9. *Par les champs et par les grèves*, pp. 424–25. The italics, not present in the original, draw attention to elements common to this description and to the aura at the end of the dream experience. Throughout this study I shall so use italics. There are none in any of the original texts, with two exceptions which are noted.

10. It is possible that Flaubert was reporting a similar pantheistic moment, though the terms are not entirely clear, in a letter he wrote to his niece Caroline while he was in Brittany in 1875 and in fact drafting the opening pages of the *Saint-Julien*. He was in great spiritual anguish over their common financial catastrophe:

> Yesterday, I took a boatride, charming. The sea was like a lake, the temperature warm and the sun splendid. During two whole hours, *I forgot myself, thank God!* I spent a lot of time, lying flat on my stomach on the grass of an islet, looking at the waves rebounding from the rocks, and the gulls flying in the sky. The roadstead was covered with little boats returning from fishing for sardines and the crescent moon appeared, illuminating an entire side of the horizon. *How much good that would do you . . . to come spend a few days here!* (*Correspondance*, VII, 270–71. October 7, 1875).

11. Page 91. In all quotations from the *Saint-Julien* I shall give the paging of the Conard edition, as for the other works of Flaubert. For the text, however, I shall use the corrected readings which I shall present in my edition of the *Conte*, currently in preparation. The differences are in general minor in the passages cited; hence the Conard may be consulted without difficulties. Flaubert's manuscripts relating to the *Trois Contes* are for the most part in the Bibliothèque Nationale, Paris, "Nouvelles Acquisitions Françaises," 23663 (Henceforth abbreviated NAF). The present citation is from folio 492 recto.

12. Gaston Bachelard's studies would support Flaubert here.

13. Similarly, when Salammbô gives herself to Mâtho, Moloch is present in the thunder and Tanit in the moon. Salammbô will exclaim to Mâtho as he possesses her: "Moloch, you're burning me!" (p. 265). In his review of *Salammbô*, Sainte-Beuve objected to the thunder in this passage. Flaubert's reply shows that — as I have suggested — he counted on his reader either to know that Moloch is the god of thunder or to intuit his presence from the thunder: "Note, moreover, that Moloch is the soul of this story, Fire, Thunder. Here the God himself, in one of his forms, is acting: he tames Salammbô. So the thunder was where it should have been" (*Correspondance*, V, 64. December 23–24, 1862.) Flaubert no doubt felt a similar justification for "the sky . . . was enveloped with fire."

14. Flaubert's constant linking of sexuality with annihilation is fully discussed and exemplified in Victor Brombert, *The Novels of Flaubert, A Study of Themes and Techniques* (Princeton, N.J.: Princeton University Press, 1966), passim.

15. The drafts, here as so often, show Flaubert starting with clear and direct statements of precisely what he means (an analysis) but then moving from this limited account to far broader, more generalized statements (mythic projections). The reader, though perhaps less sharply stimulated by them, responds more freely, is set more readily to "dreaming" as Flaubert said he wished him to be (*Correspondance*, IV, 314–15). Letter to Mlle Leroyer de Chantepie, February 18, 1859). Thus Flaubert's initial note for this

development is a direct, analytic statement: "becomes like a savage. His puberty shows itself in that way" (NAF, 23663, folio 429 recto). Next (and typically) he seeks a means of showing it to the reader: "barks like his dogs and hurls himself upon the animals emerging from their dens" (folio 418 recto). Only after this, and gradually, does the more generalized final text emerge. Less violent, to be sure, it is thereby more broadly suggestive and, as such, more fully mythic.

16. In the interests of simplicity, I shall not treat here the issues of sadism and parricide, reserving them for another study.

17. NAF, 23663, folio 429 recto.

18. The reader who is not familiar with French hunting terms may easily misunderstand the precise connotation of "bêtes puantes" (small predators; literally, "stinking beasts"). Joseph La Vallée, one of Flaubert's principal sources for this passage, explains it: "one designates with the name of 'false beasts' the fox, the badger, the otter, the marten, the polecat, the stone-marten, even to the mere weasel, to all that breed full of trickery and cunning, the terror of our chicken coops and our fishponds, to that entire brood, that huntsmen call in an even more informal way bêtes puantes" (La Chasse à courre, 2nd edition [Paris: Hachette, 1859], p. 134).

19. These monsters, inspired from Breughel, I shall consider below.

20. There now follows the passage describing the monsters climbing upon one another to form a living, moving mountain, which served to clarify the earlier passage from the first hunt in the Saint-Julien. [The Martichoras is a gigantic red lion with a human face and three rows of teeth; the Cynocephalids are African baboons whose elongated muzzles suggest a dog's head — Editor.]

21. As with the issues of sadism and parricide earlier, so here in the interest of simplification I prefer to postpone to a later study Flaubert's fascination with monsters in relation to this matter.

22. This passage from the Tentation lends further force to my pantheistic interpretation of the episode cited in note 10.

23. The descriptions of the leprous Hannon [a Carthaginian leader — Editor] serve quite another purpose, of course.

24. The concept is most clearly expressed in Une Nuit de Don Juan, published in Oeuvres de jeunesse, III, especially pp. 324–25. It dates from 1850–51.

25. Souvenirs, notes et pensées intimes (Paris: Buchet, Chastel, 1965), p. 95; Correspondance, I, 177–78 (Letter to Alfred Le Poittevin, May 26, 1845).

26. In order, the quotations come from: Correspondance, VII, 158 (Letter to Turgeniev, July 2, 1874); V, 18 (Letter to his niece Caroline, May 1862; italics in original); V, 136 (Letter to Caroline, April 18, 1864); Supplément à la Correspondance, III, 132 (Letter to Caroline, July 1, 1874); Correspondance, VI, 33 (Letter to George Sand, June–July 1869).

27. Correspondance, VII, 159 (Letter to Turgeniev, July 2, 1874).

28. See above, note 10.

29. In order, the quotations come from: Correspondance, VII, 268 (Letter to Mme Roger des Genettes, October 3, 1875); Supplément à la Correspondance, III, 291 (Letter to Mme Brainne, October 17, 1876); Correspondance, IV, 187, [this last reference appears to be a misprint; I have not been able to locate the passage in question — Editor.]

30. Correspondance, VII, 383–84 (Letter to Caroline, December 31, 1876). The reader will recall that Saint Anthony expressed similar desires.

31. Correspondance, VI, 300 (Letter to Caroline, October 26, 1871), with minor corrections from the autograph letter.

32. Oeuvres de jeunesse, III, 69.

33. Oeuvres de jeunesse, III, 113–14. Henri was soon to discover how ephemeral this

"happiness" was in fact. At this moment, however, he knew little of the lesson the dream would teach to Flaubert a year or two later.

34. *Par les champs et par les grèves*, pp. 153 and 197; *Tentation*, pp. 208ff.

35. The question of medieval or nineteenth-century works which might be "sources" for this passage has been much debated. The issues are too complex to treat here [see Benjamin F. Bart and Robert Francis Cook, *The Legendary Sources of Flaubert's "Saint Julien"* (Toronto: The University of Toronto Press, 1977) — Editor]. Suffice it for the moment that, if certain texts did affect Flaubert and linger in his memory, then they did so because their phrasings matched his own long-established concepts and phrasings, as I am seeking to show here. It is precisely these phrasings which are involved in this question of "sources." For a perceptive investigation of further aspects of this matter, see Sergio Cigada, "L'Episodio del lebbroso in 'Saint Julien L'Hospitalier' di Flaubert," *Aevum*, 31 (1957):465–91.

36. There are many later pantheistic passages in Flaubert, too numerous to be adduced here; I shall return to the subject elsewhere. One brief passage from *Novembre* will suggest their relevance: "I would have liked to become absorbed by the light of the sun and to lose myself in that azure immensity, with the odors rising from the surface of the waves; and at that moment I was gripped by an insane joy . . . as if all the happiness of the heavens had entered my soul" (*Oeuvres de jeunesse*, II, 190).

37. Emile Zola, *Les Romanciers naturalistes* (Paris: Bernouard, 1927), p. 177.

38. Specifically in *Correspondance*, IV, 182 (Letter to Mlle Leroyer de Chantepie, May 18, 1857). For numerous variations on this theme, see Charles Carlut, *La Correspondance de Flaubert. Étude et répertoire critique* (Columbus, Ohio: Ohio State University Press, 1968), pp. 194–97.

Bouvard et Pécuchet

The Museum's Furnace: Notes toward a Contextual Reading of *Bouvard and Pécuchet*

Eugenio Donato*

THE LIBRARY

Flaubert's *Bouvard and Pécuchet* describes the systematic pursuit by two office clerks of a number of activities — agriculture, arboriculture, garden architecture, chemistry, anatomy, physiology, geology, archeology, and others — which span the totality of human knowledge by systematically exhausting its various domains. Yet neither the well-meant, systematic enterprises of the two clerks nor their immense resiliency in the face of failure allows them ever to gain mastery over any of the regions of the encyclopedia. The encyclopedia, assumed to be the ultimate principle of reality, turns out to be a constantly elusive mirage. The odyssey of the two asexual bachelors stages the concept of an encyclopedic knowledge both as that which preexists and determines the various activities in which the two clerks engage and also as the teleological end point which they indefatigably attempt to attain, without its ever being at any time present to them.

The office clerks systematically fail in each and every one of their endeavors; each field of knowledge reveals itself to be contradictory, unsystematic, or simply unable to give an adequate representation of the objects it is supposed to describe. A bookish knowledge of agriculture in no way permits them to grow crops, archeology is full of contradictions, the writing of history impossible. Having finally recognized the failure of their enterprise, they return to their original activity of copying; however, this time they simply copy anything and everything that comes to hand. Having begun with the dream and hope of a total, finite, rational domain of knowledge, they come to realize that not only is knowledge as a given totality unavailable but that also any act of totalization is by definition incomplete, infinite, and everywhere marked by accident, chance, and randomness:

*From *Textual Strategies*, edited by Josué Harari (Ithaca: Cornell University Press, 1979), 213–38 abridged. Reprinted by permission of Cornell University Press.

They copy papers haphazardly, everything they find, tobacco pouches, old newspapers, posters, torn books, etc. (real items and their imitations. Typical of each category).

Then, they feel the need for a taxonomy. They make tables, antithetical oppositions such as "crimes of the kings and crimes of the people"—blessings of religion, crimes of religion. Beauties of history, etc.; sometimes, however, they have real problems putting each thing in its proper place and suffer great anxieties about it.

—Onward! Enough speculation! Keep on copying! The page must be filled. Everything is equal, the good and the evil. The farcical and the sublime—the beautiful and the ugly—the insignificant and the typical, they all become an exaltation of the statistical. There are nothing but facts—and phenomena.

Final bliss.[1]

Most readings of *Bouvard and Pécuchet* take their point of departure from Flaubert's remarks about the composition and significance of the work. The result of the author's meanderings through the library: "I'm aghast at what I have to do for *Bouvard and Pécuchet*. I read catalogues of books that I annotate". "I am, sir, *inside a labyrinth*!" "I have gotten indigestion from books. I burp in-folio"; "Reading is an abyss; one never gets out of it. I am becoming as dumb as a pot." The novel is to portray "the story of these two men who copy a kind of farcical version of a critical encyclopedia."[2]

. . . .

THE MUSEUM

The reading of *Bouvard and Pécuchet* in terms of the metaphor of the *Encyclopedia-Library*, despite its relating the novel to a crucial textual problematic and allowing for the reading of certain passages in terms of primarily linguistic or representational considerations, falls short, however, of being completely satisfactory. The reason for this is twofold. On the one hand, the *Encyclopedia-Library* is never thematized as a master-term that explicitly controls the deployment of the various regions of knowledge; on the contrary Flaubert systematically stages the *Encyclopedia-Library* as one nonprivileged term in an indifferent series. On the other hand, a good number of the failures of Bouvard and Pécuchet cannot be attributed to the incapacity of linguistic or symbolic representation to account for reality. For example, when wind and rain destroy their fruit crops, or when a storm destroys their wheat crop, there is no way of accounting for the storm within any representational system. The forces at play within nature are absolutely other than those at work in the deconstruction of taxonomies, rhetoric, and semiology.

The clerks' original dream of a pastoral existence excludes the activity of writing, that is to say, of the most complex and resistant of language's representational forms: "Waking with the lark, they would follow the plough, go out with a basket to gather apples, watch the butter being made, the corn threshed, the sheep sheared, the beehives tended, and they would revel in the mooing of cows and the scent of fresh-mown hay. No more copying!" (*BP*, 30).[3] Carried away by their illusion, they also reject from the start any need for books. Flaubert in the *Dictionnaire des idées reçues* writes: "Library — always have one in one's home, especially when living in the country." Bouvard, on the contrary, on the verge of his new rural life decides that "we'll have no library." In their pastoral dream, Bouvard and Pécuchet dismiss the mediation of books and aspire instead to the mastery of a science which acts directly on nature. Significantly, they start their adventures equipped with an odd assortment of scientific instruments: "They purchased gardening implements and a mass of things 'which might come in useful,' such as a tool-box (every house should have one), followed by a pair of scales, a land-chain, a bath-tub in case of illness, a thermometer, and even a barometer, 'on the Gay-Lussac system,' for meteorological experiments, should the fancy take them" (*BP*, 30–31).

The odd assortment of books that belonged to Pécuchet before he undertook his rural adventure hardly amounts to a library. The books, in fact, are part of a group of heterogeneous objects that anticipate the "*bric-a-brac* shops" they will later visit: "and in the corners were scattered a number of volumes of the Roret Encyclopaedia, the Mesmerist's Handbook, a Fenelon, and other old tomes, as well as a pile of papers, two coconuts, various medallions, a Turkish fez, and shells brought from Le Havre by Dumouchel" (*BP*, 21). It can be argued, of course, that Bouvard and Pécuchet are defeated by the very thing whose importance they fail to account for in the first place. As I suggested earlier, there is no doubt that such a remark is regionally correct and that the efforts of the two clerks are sometimes undone by an unstable representational or symbolical system that they fail fully to understand or to recognize. Nevertheless, when the theme of the *Encyclopedia-Library* appears in the novel, it is thematized in such a way as to require a separate set of remarks. To return to the passage quoted above, the clerks' library — if one can call it that — is on the one hand contrasted with their scientific instruments, that is, with an otherness which is not obviously inscribed in the texture of representation; but more important, it appears in a series of heterogeneous elements. The difficulty resides, precisely, in reading a series of heterogeneous elements, since through their heterogeneity they offer what is absolutely other to the homogeneous representational space of the *Encyclopedia-Library*.

Later in the novel, when Flaubert describes the various buildings and public collections that Bouvard and Pécuchet visit, the library is again placed in a heterogeneous series:

> They sauntered past the old *bric-a-brac* shops. They visited the Conservatoire des Arts et Métiers, Saint-Denis, the Gobelins, the Invalides and all the public collections.

In the galleries of the Museum they viewed the stuffed quadrupeds with astonishment, the butterflies with pleasure, the metals with indifference; fossils fired their imagination, conchology bored them. They peered into hot-houses, and shuddered at the thought of so many foliages distilling poison. What struck them most about the cedar was that it had been brought over in a hat.

They worked up an enthusiasm at the Louvre for Raphael. At the Central Library they would have liked to know the exact number of volumes. [BP, 25–26]

The bric-a-brac is emblematic of the whole series. Again, it is not the bric-a-brac which is in the library; it is the latter that belongs to a series which can be characterized as bric-a-brac. Interestingly, however, the series contains one term that itself contains a heterogeneous series, namely the *Museum* (the Museum of Natural History). The term which is then representationally privileged, which allegorizes the series, is the museum and not the library, since the former contains a series of which the latter is only a term. It is then perhaps in the concept of the *Museum* that we must search for an encyclopedic totality.

If Bouvard and Pécuchet never assemble what can amount to a library, they nevertheless manage to constitute for themselves a private museum. The museum, in fact, occupies a central position in the novel; it is connected to the characters' interest in archeology, geology, and history and it is thus through the *Museum* that questions of origin, causality, representation, and symbolization are most clearly stated. The *Museum*, as well as the questions it tries to answer, depends upon an archeological epistemology. Its representational and historical pretensions are based upon a number of metaphysical assumptions about origins — archeology intends, after all, to be a science of the *archēs*. Archeological origins are important in two ways: each archeological artifact has to be an original artifact, and these original artifacts must in turn explain the "meaning" of a subsequent larger history. Thus, in Flaubert's caricatural example, the baptismal font that Bouvard and Pécuchet discover has to be a Celtic sacrificial stone, and Celtic culture has in turn to act as an original master pattern for cultural history:

. . . whence it must be concluded that the religion of the Gauls had the same principles as that of the Jews.

Their society was very well organized. . . . Some uttered prophesies, others chanted, others taught botany, medicine, history and literature: in short, "all the arts of their epoch." Pythagoras and Plato were their pupils. They instructed the Greeks in metaphysics, the Persians in sorcery, the Etruscans in augury, and the Romans in plating copper and trading in ham.

But of this people which dominated the ancient world, there remain only a few stones. [BP, 127–128]

These stones will become the archival material displayed in the museums which are the outward manifestation of an implicit archeological knowledge or essence.

The outstanding characteristic of the Flaubertian *Museum* is its irreducible heterogeneity. This heterogeneity becomes, in fact, caricatural in Flaubert's early scenarios for the novel. To quote from one of them:

> Six months later the house looked entirely different. They possessed a collection. *Museum*.
>
> Old junk, pottery of all sorts, shaving cups, butter plates, earthenware lamps, wardrobes, a halberd, one of a kind! Bludgeons, panoplies of primitive origins. Works of spun glass. Chest of drawers and Chippendale trunks, prison hampers. Saint-Allyre's petrified objects: a cat with a mouse in its jaws, stuffed birds. Various curios: chauffeur's cap, a madman's shoe. Objects drawn from rivers and people, etc.[4]

I have quoted this early draft because of its brevity; the lengthy description of the Museum of Bouvard and Pécuchet contains as heterogeneous a collection of objects as that of the draft, and interestingly enough contains also a library as one of the objects of the Museum.

. . . .

The set of objects of the Museum displays is sustained only by the fiction that they somehow constitute a coherent representational universe. The fiction is that a repeated metonymic displacement of fragment for totality, object to label, series of objects to series of labels, can still produce a representation which is somehow adequate to a nonlinguistic universe. Such a fiction is the result of an uncritical belief in the notion that ordering and classifying, that is to say, the spatial juxtaposition of fragments, can produce a representational understanding of the world. Should the fiction disappear, there is nothing left of the *Museum* but "bric-a-brac," a heap of meaningless and valueless fragments of objects which are incapable of substituting themselves either metonymically for the original objects or metaphorically for their representations.

Flaubert's critique seems radical enough to question, by means of the *Museum*, the possibility of reaching any truth, essence, or origin through a representational mode. If the *Museum* as concept has at its origin the same metaphysical ambition that the *Library* has in other contexts, namely, to give an adequate ordered rational representation of reality, nevertheless its project is doomed from the start because representation within the concept of the museum is intrinsically impossible. The museum can only display objects metonymically at least twice removed from that which they are originally supposed to represent or signify. The objects displayed as a series are of necessity only part of the totality to which they originally belonged. Spatially and temporally detached from their origin and function, they signify only by arbitrary and derived associations. The series in which the individual pieces and fragments are displayed is also arbitrary and incapable of investing the particular object with anything but irrelevant fabulations.[5] Again, the critique implied here goes beyond a critique which would limit itself to linguistic representation, even though it includes it. Linguistic representation carries within itself, in the *Library*, its own memory, its own origin, its own *archē*—displaced or hidden as it may be. The *Museum*, on the other hand, testifies to an archeological memory that cannot be recovered except through fabulation. The chapter on Bouvard and Pécuchet's museum, in fact, repeats other statements by Flaubert to the same effect. For example, in a chapter in *Par les champs et par les grèves*, he described the ruins of Carnac, ironizing all attempts to understand them:

> Thus we find this famous field of Carnac that has occasioned the writing of more stupidities than it contains rocks, and one certainly does not come across such rocky paths every day. But, in spite of our natural penchant for admiring everything, we saw in it only a hardy joke, left there by an unknown age to excite the spirit of antiquarians and stupefy travelers. In front of it one opens naive eyes and, all the while finding it quite uncommon, must admit at the same time that it is not very pretty. We understood then the irony of these granite boulders that, since the age of the Druids, have laughed in their green lichen beards at seeing all the imbeciles that came to stare at them. Scholars' lives have been spent in an attempt to determine their past usages; don't you admire this eternal preoccupation of the unfeathered biped with finding some sort of usefulness for everything? Not content with distilling the ocean to salt his stew, and assassinating elephants to make knife-handles out of them, his egotism is again provoked when he is faced with some debris or other whose utility he can't figure out.[6]

It should be obvious from such a passage that the cornerstone of Flaubert's critique is in a way remarkably similar to Nietzsche's critique of representation — namely, the anthropocentrism of meaning. If the *Museum* fails at reaching the nature and essence of the objects it displays, it is because it tries to understand them in relation to the spectator rather than in relation to the objects themselves. "Meaning," the result of metonymic or metaphoric displacements, is anthropomorphic and anthropocentric, and it is because of its anthropocentrism that it is necessarily doomed to failure. Archeology, ultimately, is not an objective science but a fantasy of the perceiving subject.[7]

. . . .

In *Bouvard and Pécuchet*, and in the nineteenth century generally, the archeological metaphor is closely linked with geology and its specific epistemology. It is, in fact, the scientific nature of geology which guarantees the displacement of its metaphors toward archeology. The central name in geology is that of Cuvier, whom the two clerks, of course, had read: "Cuvier . . . had appeared to them in the brilliance of an aureole, on the peak of a science beyond dispute" (*BP*, 108). This is not surprising, since Cuvier's *Discours sur les révolutions de la surface du globe* was a very widely read text whose influence in the earlier part of the century was comparable to that of Claude Bernard's *Introduction à la médecine expérimentale* in the latter part. Cuvier described his enterprise as that of an archeological antiquarian:

> Antiquarian of a new type, I found it necessary to learn at the same time to restore these monuments of past revolutions and to decode their sense; it was my task to collect and to put together in their original order the fragments which composed them, to reconstruct the antique creatures to which these fragments belonged; to reproduce them conserving their proportions and their characteristics; to compare them finally to those which live today at the earth's surface. . . . I was sustained, in this double work by the fact that it promised to be of equal import both to the general science of anatomy, the essential basis of all those sciences which deal with organized bodies, and to the physical history of the earth, the foundation of mineralogy, of geography, and even, one could say, of the history of men, and of everything that it is most important for them to know concerning themselves.
>
>   If it is of interest to us to track down in the childhood of our species the nearly eradicated traces of so many extinct nations, would it not be of greater interest to search in the darkness of the childhood of the earth for the traces of revolutions that took place prior to the existence of all nations? . . . Would there not be some glory for man in knowing how to overstep the limits of time, and in rediscovering, by means of a few observations, the history of this world and a series of events which preceded the birth of the human race?[8]

Cuvier's text is exemplary; for him, geology is a form of archeology. The function of the geologist is to reconstruct a continuous temporal history out of the fragments handed down to him. His task, like that of the archeologist, is twofold: to reconstruct the entities to which the fragments belonged and then to arrange those same entities in a series so as to discover the history of the globe—a history which, incidentally, is of necessity as anthropocentric as that proposed by archeology: "All of these ages have been separated from each other by cataclysms, of which our deluge was the last. It was like a fairy-tale in several acts, having man for the finale" (*BP*, 98). To the geologist, the earth in its entirety is a museum.

When Bouvard and Pécuchet, their fancy having been caught by geology, attempt such a reconstruction in imitation of Cuvier, they fail, but their failure is the failure of the epistemology of the *Museum* to offer an adequate continuous representation between Words and Things. That is to say, attempting to understand the history of the globe through geological fragments is as futile as trying to understand human history through archeology. Disordered fragments lead only to a multitude of contradictory fabulations, something that even the two clerks seem to understand, since to Bouvard's "Geology is too restricted!" Pécuchet replies, "Creation takes place in an up-and-down and haphazard manner. We should do better to start on something else" (*BP*, 112). Their only blindness is in not seeing that what they will pursue next through archeology is the same thing they attempted to find in geology, namely, a continual temporal order where there are actually only disconnected fragments.

The figure of the *Museum* is so pervasive that Bouvard and Pécuchet's failure at the various branches of agriculture can also be read as a failure of the *Museum*, or, more exactly, their failure at agriculture should signal to the reader from the start the failure of the *Museum*. Mouchard had already put forth the argument that the two clerks' concern with agriculture, being aesthetic, deals primarily with the question of selecting and ordering, that is to say with precisely the activities upon which the *Museum* is based.[9] I believe the argument can be generalized, and that perhaps the fact is that we still have a theological nostalgia for the *Museum* that has in part prevented us from seeing the obvious. If the Museum of Natural History is singled out, it is because, as I stated earlier, the ideology of the *Museum* was first applied to Nature. The Museum of Natural History was, strictly speaking, the first French museum.[10] Its function was to give an ordered representation, a spectacle of Nature. By displaying plants, metonymically selected and metonymically ordered, it meant to produce a *tableau* of Nature. The botanical failure of Bouvard and Pécuchet points directly to the failure of understanding Nature. In spite of our hopes and wishes, Nature will always escape any attempt on our part to comprehend it through the representation we give of it to ourselves, in our cultured, cultivated, tame fields and gardens.

Soon after their failure in the various branches of botany, Bouvard and Pécuchet undertake a study of anatomy. The order of succession seems random only if one does not take the *Museum* into account. Edward Said has already perceptively pointed out how anatomy in the eighteenth century epistemologically belongs to the realm of the laboratory and the museum: "Both linguists and anatomists purport to be speaking about matters not directly obtainable or observable in nature. . . . The text of a linguistic or an anatomical work bears the same general relation to nature (or actuality) that a museum case exhibiting a specimen mammal or organ does. What is given on the page and in the museum case is a truncated exaggeration . . . whose purpose is to exhibit a relationship between the science (or scientists) and the object, not one between the object and nature."[11] This is also true, in a caricatural way, of the anatomical episode in *Bouvard and Pécuchet*. In the first place, the two clerks do not study the anatomy of a "natural specimen" but of a mannequin, that is to say, a representation: "It was brick-coloured, hairless, skinless, striped with numerous blue, red and white filaments. This was not so much a corpse as a kind of toy, horrible-looking, very spick-and-span, and smelling of varnish" (*BP*, 76–77). The function of each part of the mannequin, instead of having any relation to a presumed nature, is the cause of imaginary fabulations; for example, "the brain inspired them with philosophical reflections" (*BP*, 78). More important, however, throughout the eighteenth and beginning of the nineteenth centuries anatomy was, along with botany, very much a part of the *Museum*. Anatomy stands in the same relation to animals and humans that botany does to plants. Significantly, the Museum of Natural History had from its very beginnings a chair of anatomy attached to it."[12] By taking up anatomy after the various branches of botany, Bouvard and Pécuchet in fact exhaust what were the domains of knowledge associated with the Museum of Natural History and its major epistemological ideology from approximately the time of Buffon to that of Cuvier.

In summary, then, *Bouvard and Pécuchet* retraces the changes, the evolution, the archeological metaphor on which the *Museum* is based. Representation of Nature, representation of the globe, representation of history, the *Museum* believed it possible to make visible the implicit order of Nature and of History. It failed. It failed not only at its pretense of displaying the order of Nature and History, but in comprehending them as well. Behind our gardens and our fields hides a Nature to which we cannot have access. As for the past of our globe or of human societies, it is given to us only in the form of senseless fragments without a memory, and any attempt of ours to reconstruct a history is nothing but vain fabulation. We are irrevocably cut off spatially from Nature and temporally from our past. There is no continuity between Nature and us, any more than between our past and us. And in this sense, beyond language, Flaubert is an epistemological nihilist.

THE FURNACE

Bouvard and Pécuchet fail systematically: they fail in their dealings with Nature, with the world, with society, and, up to a point, in their private lives. Some of the failures seem to be intrinsic to their pursuits; if they fail at history, geology, or archeology it is because these enterprises are epistemologically doomed from the start. Their botanical failures seem to be of a different kind. If our cultured nature has no epistemological privilege, it nevertheless need not fail as long as our concerns, like those of the count of Faverges or of the peasants who surround Bouvard and Pécuchet, are pragmatic rather than theoretical. However, as we mentioned earlier, their botanical enterprises fail in part because of storms, wind, and rain. Storms, wind, and rain belong to Nature proper, and not to the spectacle of Nature that the cultured botanical museum and garden offer. Storms, in fact, are there to remind us that the two are discontinuous. Once, when Flaubert's own garden at Croisset was badly damaged by a storm, he wrote in a letter to Louise Colet:

> Not without some pleasure, I beheld my destroyed espalier trees, all my flowers cut to pieces, and the vegetable garden in total disarray. In beholding all these little artificial arrangements created by man which five minutes of Nature sufficed to overturn, I admired true order reestablishing itself within false order. These things tormented by us — sculptured trees, flowers growing where they have no desire to, vegetables from other lands, got a type of revenge in this atmospheric rebuff. All this has a *farcical side* to it which overcomes us. Is there anything more ridiculous than bell-glass covers for melons? So, these poor bell-glass covers have had quite a time of it! Ah! Ah! To what fantasies of little useful purpose this Nature whom we exploit pitilessly, whom we make ugly with so much impudence, whom we disdain with such fine speeches, abandons herself when the temptation seizes her! This is right. It is widely believed that the sun has no other useful purpose on earth except to make cabbages grow. [13]

An essential form of our contact with Nature is through the forces it brings into play which cannot be understood as such, but which wreak havoc with our ordinary representations of Nature.

If we were to search for other instances of the unaccountable manifestations of such a force in the novel, we should easily find them in the way the two clerks encounter, time and again, fire and heat and all of their literary and historical metaphors without ever realizing exactly what it is they face, nor ever knowing how to come to terms with it.

Their first encounter with fire occurs when the hay spontaneously ignites. As in the case of the storm, they no more have a way of understanding this event's origin than of coping with its results. Their second encounter, this time in the form of an explosion, is far more significant. During their experiment at distillation, the container explodes:

> Suddenly, with the detonation of a shell, the still burst into a score of pieces which leapt to the ceiling, cracking the pots, knocking over the ladles, shivering the glasses; the coals were scattered, the stove demolished. . . .
>
> The pressure of the steam had broken the apparatus — naturally so, as the cucurbit turned out to be blocked at the mouth. . . .
>
> When they recovered their speech, they asked themselves what could be the cause of so much ill-luck, especially the last? And they could make nothing of it, except that they had escaped death. Finally, Pécuchet said: "Perhaps it is because we never studied chemistry!" [*BP*, 72–73]

What is particularly relevant, of course, is Pécuchet's inability to determine the cause of the explosion. Steam is a concern not of chemistry but of thermodynamics. Thermodynamics, on the other hand, is the one science they are not capable of recognizing, because it constitutes the new science which will sweep away the old Newtonian physics as well as all the epistemologies based upon the temporality it predicates. The tools that Bouvard and Pécuchet take with them to the country are in themselves significant. They are tools that belong to the old physics of mechanical devices and not to the new physics of heat and fire.

The point, of course, is not to make Flaubert the proponent of one system as opposed to the other. The case for Flaubert's knowledge of the new physics and what it entailed could easily be stated and is rather uninteresting — the hasty extrapolation of the second law of thermodynamics, according to which the solar system will cool down and our universe will die a frozen death, an idea that the nineteenth-century imagination found striking, is even mentioned in *Bouvard and Pécuchet*. What is at stake is something different. The new physics brought with it a new concept of time and history, differing from and subverting the one postulated by archeology and the *Museum*. What is significant is the fact that Flaubert subscribes to a view of history which assumes a temporality similar to that predicated by the new physics.

Before we turn to that subject, however, a remark is in order. Heat, as the object of thermodynamics, possesses in the literary imagination of the nineteenth century a number of metaphorical equivalents, in particular, revolutions, gold, and sexuality. It is interesting to note that Bouvard and Pécuchet encounter all three of these metaphors without understanding them. They live through the revolution of 1848 without realizing its historical implications. They disperse, through their financial failures, a fortune in gold without realizing it. Finally, their attempts at integrating sexuality into their lives are resounding failures.

Let us return to the problem of history. The Newtonian model of time displays its object as forever identical to itself, based upon an eternal, circular, and recurring movement. Time, the clock as an emblem, moves from point to point, each point considered identical to the others. In this sense, the Newtonian model moves from point of presence to point of presence and does not have, intrinsically, a temporality that describes systems as changing. As Laplace would have it, given Newtonian mechanics: "An intelligence that, at a given instant was acquainted with all the forces by which Nature is animated and with the state of the bodies of which it is composed would — if it were vast enough to submit these data to analysis — embrace in the same formula the movements of the largest bodies in the Universe and those of the lightest atoms: nothing would be uncertain for such an intelligence, and the future like the past would be present to its eyes."[14] It is easy to see how the model of Newtonian physics and the *Museum* depend epistemologically on the same temporal scheme, for the *Museum* also makes of time a spatial continuum in which each point is equivalent to each other point.

The revolution introduced by thermodynamics is a revolution at the very heart of history. The second principle, so striking to the romantic imagination, states that energy goes from a differentiated to an undifferentiated state. The consequences are enormous; henceforth, systems will move inexorably in a given direction. The process of a history patterned after the new science will be an abolition of differences. Finally, the system has no memory. From the state of the system at a given moment, it is impossible to deduce what conditions were at its origin. In Michel Serres's characterization:

> The final equilibrium à la Fourier or Boltzmann implies an ignorance of initial conditions and of duration. Whatever the origin of history may be, its end is unequivocal, determined, everywhere identical and necessary, no matter what the length of the process is. Universal equilibrium, monotonous distribution, maximum entropy . . . Inevitable, the boltzmanian world is without individualizing memory, it wipes out progressively both memory banks and differences. It has its discrete events, without causal preconditions; it is subject to this single linear law which gives a distribution over an orderless space as the end-point of history. And no matter how long the time necessary, one only need wait; and whatever one may do. . . .[15]

What thermodynamics makes impossible is a history conceived as archeology. In the long run, the metaphors of thermodynamics will rob Cuvier's geology, as well as the museums of natural or human artifacts, of any epistemological privilege, reducing them to the status of a bric-a-brac collection of disparate objects, which they always were and had remained for the author of *Bouvard and Pécuchet*, despite the illusions of an archeological history.

In contrast to Newtonian history, based upon points of presence, thermodynamics will substitute a notion of history based upon the metaphors of decay, decadence, corruption; in a word, a notion of history based upon any metaphor that can be read as abolishing differences.

Bouvard at one point is overtaken by a "frenzy for manure," and furiously begins to produce fertilizer out of manure, excrement, and anything else he can find that is in an advanced state of decomposition: "In the compost-trench were flung together boughs, blood, entrails, feathers — everything that could be found. He employed Belgian dressing, Swiss fertilizer, lye, pickled herrings, seaweed, rags; he sent for guano, and tried to manufacture it; then, pushing his tenets to the extreme, would not let any urine be wasted. He suppressed the privies. Dead animals were brought into the yard with which he treated the soil. Their carcases were scattered over the country in fragments. Bouvard smiled in the midst of the stench" [*BP*, 50].

Bouvard, who was unable to recognize the forces which ushered in the new science, is unable to recognize his emblematic fabrication of the metaphor of the very history in which he is caught and which determines his failures. What escapes the characters does not escape the author, who recognizes in the products of Bouvard the very metaphors of the history in which his work is inscribed: "We are not dancing on a volcano, but on the floorboard of a latrine that seems to me quite rotten. Pretty soon society will go drown itself in nineteen centuries of excrement and they'll scream themselves hoarse."[16] It is then precisely at the level of the metaphors of decomposition that we must localize the lucid irony that constitutes the distance between the characters and the author, who can but write from where he stands and compose with what history has handed down to him.

> But finally is it not necessary to recognize all the rooms of the heart and the social body, from the cellar to the attic, not even leaving out the latrines; above all not forgetting the latrines! In them are worked out a magical chemistry, fertilizing decompositions are made in them. Who knows to what excremental ooze we owe the perfume of roses and the taste of melons? Has anyone ever counted how many contemptible actions must be contemplated to build the greatness of a soul? How much nauseating pollution one must have swallowed, how much chagrin one must have felt, how many tortures one must have endured, to write one good page? [446]

It is with the rotting by-products of history that one grows tasty melons, not with the botanical taxonomies cherished by Bouvard who "had grown different species next to one another, the sweet variety got mixed with the bitter, the big Portuguese with the great Mongolian, and the presence of tomatoes completing the anarchy, there resulted abominable hybrids of a pumpkin flavour" (*BP*, 48).[17] In the same way that it takes excrement to grow proper melons, it takes the rotting by-products of history and the ruins of the Museum to construct a book such as *Bouvard and Pécuchet*.

In conclusion, then, *Bouvard and Pécuchet* stages within itself the conflict of two epistemologies, one characterized by the *Museum*, the other by a *Force* that escapes the domain of representation, and the undoing of one by the other.

Bouvard and Pécuchet does not so much argue for one system as opposed to the other; rather it denounces the optimism of the first system in the name of the implicit nihilism of the latter. In part an epistemological nihilism that denounces the possibility of ever attaining an essential knowledge of the world, it manifests itself more explicitly as a historical nihilism. The *Museum* displayed history as an eternally present spectacle with transparent origins and anthropocentric ends. The history ushered in by thermodynamics is a different one. Origins are forever erased, differences disappear, and the end foreseen is an indifferent universe governed by the laws of chance and statistics. More important, in this perspective, nihilism becomes an event at the end of time, and as such, *Bouvard and Pécuchet* is a book at the end of time about the end of time.

This permits us, perhaps, to read the ending of the novel, from whence we began, as the final state of indifferent events governed purely by chance: "Everything is equal . . . exaltation of the statistical. There are nothing but facts — and phenomena." In this sense the ending of *Bouvard and Pécuchet* and the creation of *The Copy*,[18] "the orderless space" of the text, rather than being emblematic of a literature yet to come, intends, instead, to be damningly prophetic.

Notes

1. *Oeuvres complètes de Gustave Flaubert*, 16 vols. (Paris: Club de l'Honnête Homme, 1971–76), VI, 607. Flaubert died before finishing *Bouvard et Pécuchet* but left a number of scenarios for the ending of the novel [of which this is one — Editor]. I have slightly modified the text and have not taken into account words or expressions erased by Flaubert nor reproduced the diacritical marks the editors have used to indicate words and expressions added by Flaubert at a later date. Translations are mine.

2. The quotations in this paragraph come from the nine-volume edition of Flaubert's *Correspondance* in the *Oeuvres complètes de Gustave Flaubert* (Paris: Conard, 1910–54), 28 vols., henceforth referred to by Roman numeral for the volume, and Arabic for the page. In order, they are: VI, 412. Letter to Flaubert's niece Caroline, September 8, 1872; IV, 214. Letter to Jules Duplan, August 5, 1857; IV, 189. Letter to Jules Duplan, May 1857; III, 228. Letter to Louise Colet, June 6–7, 1853; VI, 402. Letter to Mme Roger des Genettes, August 18, 1872.

3. All quotations from [the completed text of] *Bouvard et Pécuchet* come from the translation ("Bouvard and Pécuchet") of T. W. Earp and G. W. Stoner (New York: New Directions, 1954), indicated by "*BP*" and the page number in parentheses, as here: *BP*, 30.

4. Flaubert, *Oeuvres complètes* (1971–76): VI, 662.

5. To the best of my knowledge, the first to underscore the epistemological importance of archeology and museums is Raymond Schwab in *La Renaissance orientale* (Paris: Payot, 1950). In particular, he writes:

> The scriptural document . . . ceases to have sole and absolute reign. The advent of the archeological method forcefully heightens the authority and efficiency of history . . . The museum is no longer so much a conservatory of models as a storehouse of information; the masterpiece, formerly a source only of pleasure and a standard of taste, now must share the same room with household artifacts: it is placed side by side with the commercial object on an exhibit table; it is removed from the class of aeroliths in order to become a number in these series . . . The object is contrasted to the text, the inscription to the chronical [sic], the statue or the vase to the narrative, the king's deeds to his legend (p. 410).

6. Flaubert, *Oeuvres complètes* (1971–76), X, 99.

7. The metonymic displacement of the archeological objects of the museum which makes them unsuitable for an objective science makes them, on the contrary, very suggestive to the literary imagination. The archeologist's loss is the novelist's gain: witness *Salammbô*.

In 1851, Flaubert went to England with his mother to visit the "Great Exhibition of the Works of Industry of All Nations." There is no particular rationale to the objects that caught Flaubert's fancy. Seznec notes, for example, that in the Indian section Flaubert "pauses for a long time in front of a harnessed elephant; then examines a chariot, then instruments of music, a canon [sic] on a camel's saddle, a coat of mail, a divan, a vest, some fans, three Indian dancing girl dresses, and some turbans." Even taking into account the "unusual nature of the Exposition," the question remains as to why Flaubert chose to describe one object rather than another. I believe Seznec's answer to be very convincing. The function of the objects chosen by the novelist is to permit him to reconstruct a *fictional image* of a particular culture: "I am inclined to believe that an object is chosen on account of its special power of evocation. This knick-knack, that accessory, is the fragment of a civilization which, by itself, it is capable of suggesting. 'Is not *all of China* contained in a Chinese woman's slipper decorated with damask roses and having embroidered cats on its vamp' (III, 325. Letter to Louise Colet, August 26, 1853). In basing itself on objects, the imagination reconstructs that universe whose quintessence they express" (Jean Seznec, *Flaubert à l'exposition de 1851* [Oxford: Clarendon Press, 1951], pp. 16–17).

8. Georges Cuvier, *Recherches sur les ossemens fossiles* . . . , 5 vols. (Paris: E. d'Ocagne, 1834–36), I, 93–95.

9. Claude Mouchard, "Terre, technologie, roman: A propos du deuxième chapitre de *Bouvard et Pécuchet," Littérature,* 15 (1974): 68. " 'Pécuchet spent . . . delightful hours there unpodding the seeds, writing tickets, arranging his little pots. He used to rest on a box at the door and meditate improvements' [*BP*, 46]. From Rousseau to Goethe or Jünger, we note the contemplative meticulousness of botany and the charms of manipulating the plant kingdom. The concerns of classifying and conserving plants are very close, in the nineteenth century, to those which regard the library. In this way, these few lines enter into a game of mirrors with many other passages of *Bouvard et Pécuchet,* and even with the entire book in its ever-present tendency to classify."

10. For a history of the Museum of Natural History, see Joseph Philippe François Deleuze, *Histoire et description du Muséum royal d'histoire naturelle* (Paris: A. Royer, 1823). Michelet in a curious passage gives a good illustration of how for his generation the first museum with a pedagogical function that comes to mind is the Museum of Natural History: "The young people from the provinces, who arrived trembling with excitement, found the immense creation of the museums and of the libraries ready to welcome them . . . These museums, these gardens, were our education for us, the children of Paris. When from dreary neighborhoods, from dark streets, we went there to dream before so many beautiful enigmas, what things did we not feel instinctively, from our hearts! Did we understand? Not everything . . . It was there and nowhere else that history first made a deep impression on me" (quoted by Schwab, pp. 412–13).

11. *Orientalism* (New York: Pantheon, 1978), p. 142.

12. A nineteenth-century description of the gallery of anatomy attached to the Museum of Natural History gives a clear illustration of its similarity to collections of bric-a-brac: "the gallery of comparative anatomy, established by Cuvier . . . is made up of several rooms; the first of them presents bones and skeletons of gigantic fossils, skeletons of cetaceans and of whales; then come skeletons of all the human races, of heads of birds, of reptiles, of fish, of mammals, etc, etc. Other rooms are devoted to ovology, to phrenology, to teratology. The anatomy gallery contains approximately twenty-five thousand specimens, six thousand of which are stuffed, five thousand in alcohol, the rest in wax or in plaster" (Pierre Larousse, "Jardin des plantes de Paris," in his *Grand Dictionnaire universel du XIXe siècle,* 17 vols. [Paris: Administration du Grand Dictionnaire universel, 1866–90], IX, 906–07).

13. III, 275–76. Letter to Louise Colet, July 12, 1853.

14. Quoted in David Layzer, "The Arrow of Time," in *Scientific American,* December, 1975, p. 69. The opposition between a geological history and a thermodynamic history runs throughout the nineteenth century. The opposition is made even more evident by curious attempts, such as Renan's, at synthesizing the two. For Renan there are three histories: the history of the universe before the creation of the earth (Laplace's history), the history of the world before the advent of man (geological history—the history of Cuvier), and finally the history of man (the history of the sun—thermodynamic history): "The history of our planet before the advent of man and of life is in some respects beyond our reach for it hinges on a less delicate order of things. It is the geologist who, in this context, becomes a historian. With the help of general physics, he narrates the transformations that the earth has undergone since the first day it existed as an independent globe . . . One can truthfully say that the geologist holds the secrets of history. . . .

The *System of the World* of Laplace is the history of a preterrestrial era, the history of the world before the formation of the planet Earth, or if one prefers, of the Earth in its unity with the Sun. In fact, we have reached a point in our reasoning where the history of the world is the history of the sun" (Letter to Marcellin Berthelot in Ernest Renan, *Oeuvres complètes*, edited by Henriette Psichari, 10 vols. [Paris: Calmann-Lévy, 1947–61], I, 638–39).

15. *Hermes III: La Traduction* (Paris: Minuit, 1974), p. 62. Serres had most convincingly argued for the importance of understanding thermodynamics in order to understand the nineteenth century. My argument is derived entirely from his analysis. On this same subject, see also his *Jouvences sur Jules Verne* (Paris: Minuit, 1974). For a less analytic but more descriptive treatment of the influence of thermodynamics on the romantic imagination, see S. Brush, "Thermodynamics and History," in *The Graduate Journal*, 7, (1967): 477–566.

16. Flaubert, *Correspondance*. edited by Jean Bruneau (Paris: Gallimard, 1973–   ), I, 708. Letter to Louis Bouilhet, November 14, 1850.

17. For a reading of this passage in terms of linguistic taxonomies, see Eugenio Donato, " 'A Mere Labyrinth of Letters': Flaubert and the Quest for Fiction / A Montage," *MLN*, 89 (1974): 892.

18. Flaubert had projected a second volume for *Bouvard et Pécuchet* which was to be made up of a collage of quotations and was to continue the "Book" composed by Bouvard and Pécuchet.

SELECTED
BIBLIOGRAPHY

This listing extends through 1984. To update it, readers should consult (1) Otto Klapp, *Bibliographie der französischen Literaturwissenschaft*, 1956– , annual, usable by those who know no German, the most complete and prompt compilation (appears in October following the year covered), including book reviews; supplement with (2) The Modern Language Association of America, *Bibliography*, vol. 2, annual, currently running two years late, includes dissertations and has recently inaugurated an exhaustive index to subjects and approaches in a separate volume; and (3) The Modern Humanities Research Association (of England), *The Year's Work in Modern Language Studies*, running two and a half years late, includes comments and descriptions, although it is incomplete and quirky.

PRIMARY SOURCES

Translations

Additional translations can readily be found in *Books in Print* and *Paperback Books in Print*.

Dictionary of Accepted Ideas. Translated by Jacques Barzun. New York: New Directions, 1968. A penetrating introduction and masterful renderings of clichés.

The Letters of Gustave Flaubert, 1830–1857. Edited and translated by Francis Steegmuller. Cambridge, Mass.: Harvard University Press, 1980.

Madame Bovary. Background and Sources. Essays in Criticism. Translated by Eleanor Marx Aveling. Revised and edited by Paul de Man. New York: W. W. Norton, 1965. Authoritative. Excellent collection of secondary sources. Highly recommended.

The Temptation of Saint Anthony. Translated and with an introduction by Kitty Mrosovsky. London: Secker and Warburg, 1980. A good, wide-ranging introduction presents backgrounds and surveys the major criticism well.

Works in French

Flaubert's works are available from the Paris publishers Garnier (in the economy editions of the Collection Folio and in the regular Classiques Garnier series) and Gallimard (in the expensive Pléiade leatherbound edition in two volumes). Both the Pléiade and the Garnier are acceptable for scholarly work.

They do not include the Correspondence, however, and are not cited as often as the following (complete works listed first):

Oeuvres complètes de Gustave Flaubert. 16 vols. Paris: Club de l'Honnête homme, 1971–76. Includes valuable documentation and contemporary critical reactions. Unfortunately, the texts are unreliable.

Oeuvres complètes. 2 vols. Paris: Seuil, 1964. Edited by Bernard Masson.

Oeuvres complètes. 28 vols. Paris: Conard, 1910–54. This invaluable edition, cited by most of the critics in the present anthology, is now being superseded by those listed above. Since there are at least four different printings, with varying numbers of volumes and starting dates, and since libraries often combine volumes from different sets in their holdings, the volume number given for a particular work may not correspond to the volume number of that work in your library.

Bouvard et Pécuchet. Edited by Claudine Gothot-Mersch. Paris: Gallimard, 1979. Authoritative. Includes "Dictionnaire des Idées reçues." Renews discussion of genesis.

Correspondance. Edited by Jean Bruneau. Paris: Gallimard, 1973– . Two volumes (1973 and 1980) have appeared thus far, extending through 1858. Definitive. Valuable selections from letters *to* Flaubert.

L' Éducation sentimentale. Edited by A. W. Raitt. Paris: Imprimerie Nationale, 1979. 2 vols. A valuable introduction, notes, and overview of critical discussions.

Madame Bovary — Nouvelle Version. Edited by Jean Pommier and Gabrielle Leleu. Paris: Corti, 1949. Interweaves unpublished scenes and passages with the final text to create a vastly expanded version of the novel.

SECONDARY SOURCES

General Studies

Bart, Benjamin F. *Flaubert*. Syracuse, N.Y.: Syracuse University Press, 1967. The definitive biography. Extensive use of unpublished manuscript materials. Psycho-sexual approach. Helpful comments on all the literary works except *Madame Bovary*.

— — —. "Flaubert's Concept of the Novel." *PMLA* 80, no. 1 (March 1965):84–89. Lucid. Emphasizes Platonist idealism. Style generates plot and the type generates the individual character.

Barthes, Roland. *Le Degré zéro de l'écriture*. Paris: Seuil, 1953. "L'Artisanat du style," 89–94. Translated as *Writing Degree Zero* by Annette Lavers and Colin Smith (London: Jonathan Cape, 1967), 68–72. Flaubert exemplifies the crisis of literature around 1850 ("What is it good for?"), attempting to justify the enterprise of writing by the work it has cost. Craftsmanship supersedes genius as an ideal.

Becker, George Joseph, ed. *Documents of Modern Literary Realism*. Princeton, N.J.: Princeton University Press, 1963. "Modern Realism as a Literary Movement" (3–38) provides a valuable overview.

Bernheimer, Charles. *Flaubert and Kafka: Studies in Psycho-poetic Structure*.

New Haven, Conn.: Yale University Press, 1982. An important statement using the psychology of object relations ("object" meaning "significant others") to go beyond the defensive strategies of deconstructionism, which seeks godlike invulnerability by assimilating itself to Thanatos. Of general interest to critics.

Bourget, Paul. "Gustave Flaubert." In *Essais de psychologie contemporaine*, 97–147. Paris: Plon, 1899 (1884). See pp. 111–20 on Flaubert's nihilism, a notion later borrowed by Barthes and Sartre.

Brunot, Ferdinand. *Histoire de la langue française des origines à nos jours*. 13 vols. Paris: Armand Colin, 1972. Vol. 13, part 2, pp. 7–46 provide a valuable enumerative overview of hundreds of Flaubert's stylistic features.

Butor, Michel. *Improvisations sur Flaubert*. Paris: Éditions de la Différence, 1984. A lucidly-written mosaic of brilliant, fragmentary observations, in lapidary style, interlarded with long quotations and banalities. Best on the travel journals, *L' Éducation sentimentale*, and the *Trois Contes*.

Culler, Jonathan. *Flaubert: The Uses of Uncertainty*. London: Elek, 1974. An influential, pioneering, deconstructionist study demonstrating how Flaubert's realistic fiction thwarts interpretation. Rich in ideas. Weak on the fantasy literature.

Demorest, Don-Louis. *L' Expression figurée et symbolique dans l'oeuvre de Gustave Flaubert*. Paris: Conard, 1931. Reprint. Geneva: Slatkine Reprints, 1967. A monumental study of Flaubert's metaphors.

Derrida, Jacques. "An Idea of Flaubert's 'Plato's Letter.'" *MLN* 99, no. 4 (September 1984):748–68. Deconstructs the notion of Flaubert's idealism.

Du Bos, Charles. "Sur le milieu intérieur dans Flaubert." In *Approximations*, 1:165–82. Paris: Plon, 1922. Reprint. Paris: Fayard, 1965. Translated in the Norton Critical Edition of *Madame Bovary* [see above], pp. 360–71. A pioneering phenomenological study.

Du Camp, Maxime. *Souvenirs littéraires*, 2 vols. Paris: Hachette, 1906 (1882–83). See vol. 1, chaps. 7, 9–14; vol. 2, chaps. 21, 25, 28–30. Du Camp has been much maligned for being jealous, insidious, and opportunistic, but his memoirs provide a mine of information on Flaubert, quite readable and often borrowed without acknowledgment by later critics.

Durry, Marie-Jeanne. *Flaubert et ses projets inédits*. Paris: Nizet, 1950. Valuable. Reproduces notebooks and adds commentary. Covers 1862–74.

Genette, Gérard. "Le Travail de Flaubert." *Tel Quel* 14 (1963):51–57. A capable essay on his style, by a leading French Structuralist critic.

Gothot-Mersch, Claudine. "Aspects de la temporalité dans les romans de Flaubert." In *Flaubert: la dimension du texte*, ed. P. M. Wetherill, 6–55. Manchester University Press, 1982. Substantial. Flaubert respects neither chronology nor dates but seeks instead symbolically appropriate seasons for events.

— — —. "Sur le narrateur chez Flaubert." *Nineteenth-Century French Studies* 12, no. 3 (Spring 1984):344–65. An important overview.

Houston, John Porter. "Flaubert." In *The Traditions of French Prose Style*, 204–31. Baton Rouge, La.: The Louisiana State University Press, 1981. Clear, interesting. Situates his style in literary history.

James, Henry. "The Minor French Novelists." *Galaxy* 21 (1876):224–29. Finds Flaubert boring and disgusting.

Lemaître, Jules. "Gustave Flaubert." In *Les Contemporains: Études et portraits littéraires. Huitième série*, 59–120. Paris: Boivin, 1914 (1879). Treats his three major novels perceptively and defends his realism, pp. 91–93.

Murphy, S. "L' Éducation de la femme et les sentiments de l' homme." *Dalhousie French Studies* 5 (1983):12–37. Forceful feminist view of how Flaubert condemns his society.

Prendergast, Christopher. "Flaubert: Quotation, Stupidity and the Cretan Liar Paradox." *French Studies* 35 (1981):261–77. Takes issue with Barthes and Derrida, claiming Flaubert creates paradoxical indeterminacy rather than deconstructive irony.

Proust, Marcel. "A propos du style de Flaubert." In *Chroniques*, 193–206. Paris: Gallimard, 1928. (First published in the *Nouvelle Revue Française*, January 1920.) Rich in perceptive insights.

Richard, Jean-Pierre. "La Création de la forme chez Flaubert." in his *Littérature et sensation*. Paris: Seuil, 1954. A classic phenomenological study, widely cited.

Saintsbury, George. "Gustave Flaubert." In *Essays on French Novelists*. London: Percival, 1891. (First published in *Fortnightly Review* 29 [1878]:575–95.) Keenly sensitive.

Sartre, Jean-Paul. *L' Idiot de la famille; Gustave Flaubert de 1821 à 1857*. 3 vols. Paris: Gallimard, 1971–72. Monumental psychoanalytical (vols. 1–2) and sociological (vol. 3) approach. Sees in Flaubert an hysterical neurotic; the nihilism of his *Madame Bovary* reflects the bankrupt ideology of the bourgeoisie. The University of Chicago Press is producing a flawed translation; a better approach for the reader who has no French is Hazel E. Barnes's admirable *Sartre & Flaubert* (Chicago: University of Chicago Press, 1981), a critical summary.

Schor, Naomi, and Henry F. Majewski, editors. *Flaubert and Postmodernism*. Lincoln: University of Nebraska Press, 1984. An outstanding collection of twelve essays, of which four are listed here as they were published separately. Covers nearly all works of Flaubert.

Seznec, Jean. "Flaubert and the Graphic Arts." *Journal of the Warburg and Courtauld Institute* 8 (1945):175–90. Magisterial, wide-ranging, and lavishly illustrated.

Sherrington, R. J. *Three Novels by Flaubert. A Study of Techniques*. London: Oxford University Press, 1970. Best on *Madame Bovary*. Outstanding study of point of view and the evolution of Flaubert's treatment of it.

Thibaudet, Albert. *Gustave Flaubert (1821–80): Vie, oeuvres, style*. Paris: Plon, 1935 (substantially revised from the 1914 and 1922 editions). The best sections are on *Madame Bovary* and on style (the latter added in 1935). A landmark work, now dated.

Warning, Rainer. "Irony and the 'Order of Discourse' in Flaubert." *New Literary History* 13, no. 2 (Winter 1982):253–86. Discusses the irony of irony: in a humdrum context, Emma Bovary's delusions and her readings revalorize her.

White, Hayden. "The Problem of Style in Realistic Representation: Marx and Flaubert." In Berel Lang, ed., *The Concept of Style*, 213–29. Philadelphia: The University of Pennsylvania Press, 1979. Claims that both men's discourses attempt to correlate events with (1) their mythic archetypes, and (2) types of cognition, despite words' ever-changing relationships with the things they are supposed to signify.

Williams, D. A. "Flaubert—'le premier des non-figuratifs du roman moderne?' " *Orbis litterarum* 34, no. 1 (1979):66–86. Attacks the myth of Flaubert's modernity, making a cogent distinction between the French New Novel and the nineteenth-century novel.

Zola, Emile. *Les Romanciers Naturalistes*, 125–30. Paris: Fasquelle, 1881. (First published in *Le Messager de l' Europe*, November 1875.) Admiring and specific homage from the leader of the French Naturalist School.

Critical Reception

Debray-Genette, Raymonde, comp. *Flaubert*. Paris: Firmin Didot & Didier, 1970 ("Miroir de la Critique"). Good introduction; critical bibliography; anthology of extracts of major critics from George Sand to Foucault.

Gervais, David. *Flaubert and Henry James: A Study in Contrasts*, 1–88, 119–46, 198–223. London: Macmillan, 1978. An effective defense against James's five attacks; characterizes Flaubert's sense of the tragic.

Raitt, A. W. "État présent des études sur Flaubert." *L' Information Littéraire* 34, no. 4 (1982):198–206; 35, no. 1 (1983):18–24. A major review article. Includes several neglected German works.

Weinberg, Bernard. *French Realism: The Critical Reaction, 1830–1870*. London, New York: Oxford University Press; Modern Language Association of America, 1937. Pages 140–41, 159–76 are valuable.

Early Works

Brombert, Victor. "Usure et rupture chez Flaubert: l' exemple de *Novembre*." In *Essais sur Flaubert* . . . , ed. Charles Carlut, 145–54. Paris: Nizet, 1979. The purity and profanation of language. A good study.

Bruneau, Jean. *Les Débuts littéraires de Gustave Flaubert: 1831–1845*. Paris: Colin, 1962. Includes a substantial study of the first *Éducation sentimentale* (1845). A fine conclusion traces Flaubert's artistic development from youth to maturity.

Diamond, Marie J. *Flaubert: The Problem of Aesthetic Discontinuity*. Port Washington, N.Y.: Kennikat Press, 1975. Studies the conflict between Flaubert's lyrical and comic literary selves. Valuable updating of Bruneau. Coverage up to 1849.

Perrone-Moisés, L. "L' autre Flaubert. *Quidquid volueris*: l'éducation scripturale." *Poétique* 53 (1983):109–22. A Lacanian reading. Condemns ethnocentrism. The ape is the anti-bourgeois par excellence. Like Lautréamont, the early Flaubert exemplifies the death of romanticism, which remains in a mummified form in his work.

Bouvard et Pécuchet.

Gothot-Mersch, Claudine. "Bouvard et Pécuchet: sur la genèse des personnages." In *Flaubert à l' oeuvre*, 135–67. Paris: Flammarion, 1980. Exemplary genetic criticism.

Correspondance

Carlut, Charles. *La Correspondance de Flaubert. Étude et répertoire critique.* Columbus: Ohio State University Press, 1968. Valuable index of topics, names, and motifs, with commentary.

Deutelbaum, Wendy. "Desolation and Consolation: The Correspondence of Gustave Flaubert and George Sand." *Genre* 15, no. 3 (Fall 1982):281–302. Enlightening comments on Flaubert's androgyny and his relationship to it.

L' Éducation sentimentale

Bem, Jeanne. "Flaubert et les signes." In *Clefs pour "L' Éducation sentimentale,"* 76–92. Paris; Tübingen: Place; Gunter Narr Verlag, 1981. In a novel of circulation and prostitution, interchangeable signs reflect the triumph of capitalism. Good bibliography.

Brooks, Peter. "Retrospective Lust, or Flaubert's Perversities." In *Reading for the Plot: Design and Intention in Narrative*, 171–215. New York: Alfred A. Knopf, 1984; Random House, 1985. Through his systematic perversion of plot, Flaubert marks a turning-point in the history of the novel. In *L' Éducation sentimentale* the will of the characters (unlike Balzac's) does not move the plot. Only the act of narration itself keeps the narrative going. Inspired by Culler. Rich in ideas.

Bruneau, Jean. "La Présence de Flaubert dans *L' Éducation sentimentale.*" In *Langages de Flaubert*, ed. Michael Issacharoff, 33–42. Paris: Lettres Modernes; Minard, 1976. Excellent study of autobiographical elements.

Cento, Alberto. *Il Realismo documentario nell' "Éducation sentimentale."* Naples: Liguori, 1967. Important study of sources; fine introduction.

Crouzet, Michel. "*L' Éducation sentimentale* et le 'genre historique.' " In *Histoire et langage dans "L' Éducation sentimentale,"* 77–110. Paris: SEDES, 1981. Densely argued treatment of the historical novel.

Goodman, Paul. *The Structure of Literature*, 127–62. Chicago, Ill.: Chicago University Press, 1954. A classic Chicago School (Neo-Aristotelian) analysis in which categorizations are an end in themselves, but which offers many interesting remarks on plot and character.

Torgovnick, Marianna. *Closure in the Novel.* Princeton, N.J.: Princeton University Press, 1981. See chapter 5, pp. 101–2, 108–20. A good analysis of how Flaubert "throws the book at the reader" and refuses to depict conventional happiness. Compared with Thackerey's *Vanity Fair.*

Vial, André. "Flaubert, émule et disciple émancipé de Balzac: *L' Éducation sentimentale.*" *Revue d' histoire littéraire de la France* 48 (July–September 1948):233–63. A masterful study of Flaubert's mingled admiration and rivalry. Balzac's *Le Lys dans la vallée* and *Illusions perdues* inspire *L' Éducation sentimentale*, in which Balzacian clichés of will and fatality are ridiculed.

Madame Bovary

Auerbach, Eric. "*Madame Bovary*." In *Mimesis*, 482–91. Princeton, N.J.: Princeton University Press, 1953 (1946). Reprinted in *Flaubert: A Collection of Critical Essays*, ed. Raymond Giraud, 132–40. Twentieth Century Views. Englewood Cliffs, N.J.: Prentice-Hall, 1964. (Better than the Norton selection.) A famous characterization of Flaubert's particular brand of realism, based on a close reading of one scene.

Bal, Mieke. "Descriptions: Pour une théorie de la description narrative; à propos de *Madame Bovary* de Flaubert." In *Narratologie*, 87–112. Paris: Klincksieck, 1977. Fine essay, revealing how the narrative voice functions even in descriptions seemingly focused by the observing character; and how description, like *mise en abyme* (internal reduplication), can signify the entire work in which it occurs.

Baudelaire, Charles. "*Madame Bovary*, par Gustave Flaubert." *L' Artiste*, 18 October 1857. Translated and reprinted in the Norton Critical Edition of *Madame Bovary* (see above), 336–43. A classic essay on the masculine qualities of the heroine, and on the difficulties of affirming the ideal of Art for Art's Sake in a materialistic era.

Béguin, Albert. "On Rereading *Madame Bovary*." In the Norton Critical Edition of *Madame Bovary*, 292–97. Reprinted from *La Table Ronde*, 27 March 1950, 160–64. A beautiful lament for Flaubert's self-mutilating sacrifices of his rich psychological insights, producing a great poem of *ennui*.

Duchet, Claude. "Roman et Objets: l'exemple de *Madame Bovary*." *Europe* 47, nos. 485–87 (September–November 1969): 172–201. Excellent. Rich in detail. Sound, clear statement of method.

Falconer, Graham. "Flaubert assassin de Charles." In *Langages de Flaubert*, ed. Michael Issacharoff, 114–36. Paris: Lettres modernes, Minard, 1976. How Flaubert sacrificed an originally more sensitive, articulate Charles Bovary (traces of whom appear in the last pages) so as to bring out the psychological portrait of Emma.

Gothot-Mersch, Claudine. *La Genèse de "Madame Bovary."* Paris: Corti, 1966. An indispensable examination of the stages of composition of the novel, dispelling many common misconceptions.

Peterson, Carla L. "The Heroine as Reader in the Nineteenth Century Novel: Emma Bovary and Maggie Tulliver." *Comparative Literature Studies* 17 (1980):168–83. A good, clear feminist reading. Novel-reading is a natural outlet for intelligent women denied autonomy and a serious education; Emma's suicide is an act of self-assertion which the men around her can't prevent.

Poulet, Georges. "The Circle and the Center: Reality and Madame Bovary." *Western Review* 19 (Summer 1955):245–60. Reprinted in his *Metamorphoses of the Circle*. Baltimore, Md.: Johns Hopkins University Press, 1966. The classic phenomenological essay. Reprinted in the Norton Critical Edition, pp. 392–407. Takes issue with Auerbach. "Flaubert is the first who builds his novels around a series of centers encompassed by their environments," which contract and expand in the consciousness of the author and of his heroine.

Ricardou, Jean. "Le Texte en conflit." In *Nouveaux problèmes du roman*, 24–88.

Paris: Seuil, 1978. Important theoretical statement supported by detailed textual analysis: paradoxically, description in the novel tends to destroy the realistic illusion it purports to create. But description and narration are inseparable.

Schor, Naomi. "For a Restricted Thematics: Writing, Speech, and Difference in *Madame Bovary*." In *The Future of Difference*, ed. Hester Eisenstein, 167–92. Boston: G.K. Hall, 1980. (First printed in French, 1976.) A playful feminist-Lacanian reading contrasts Emma Bovary ("f-emme" deprived of the "f" or phallus) and Homais ("homme" plus "ais," the added phallus); and her inefficacious writing (letters to Léon) with Homais's effective writing (with it he achieves his goals).

Steegmuller, Francis. *Flaubert and Madame Bovary: A Double Portrait*. New York: Farrar, Straus and Giroux, 1968. Very readable and entertaining. For undergraduates.

Tanner, Tony. "Flaubert's *Madame Bovary*." In *Adultery in the Novel. Contract and Transgression*, 233–367. Baltimore, Md.: Johns Hopkins University Press, 1979. Stimulating, uneven. Best on "fetishism," pp. 284–96.

Williams, D.A. *Psychological Determinism in "Madame Bovary."* Hull, England: Hull University Press, 1973. Clear, well argued. See especially pp. 51–57.

— — —. "The Role of Binet in *Madame Bovary*." *Romanic Review* 71, no. 2 (March 1980):149–66. A rich discussion of this minor figure, a parody of artistic self-consciousness.

Salammbô

Bart, B.F. "Male Hysteria in *Salammbô*." *Nineteenth-Century French Studies* 12, no. 3 (Spring 1984):313–21. Underlines the frustration and helplessness that shape the conduct of the apparently virile barbarian leader.

Holdheim, William Wolfgang. "Description and Cliché." In *The Hermeneutic Mode: Essays on Time in Literature and Literary Theory*, 132–47. Ithaca, N.Y.: Cornell University Press, 1984. Flaubert's "aggressive reification of the human" and predominant use of cliché in descriptions in *Salammbô* sketch the "pseudo-cognitive act" of signifiers aspiring to autoreferentiality. On the genre of the historical novel, see also his *Die Suche nach dem Epos: Der Geschichtsroman bei Hugo, Tolstoi und Flaubert* (Heidelberg: C. Winter, 1978).

Lukács, György. "Salammbô." In *The Historical Novel*, 184–95. London: Merlin Press, 1962. Reprinted in *Flaubert*, ed. Raymond Giraud, 141–53. Twentieth Century Views. Englewood Cliffs, N.J.: Prentice-Hall, 1964. To Lukács, the work illustrates the decadence of romantic realism. Flaubert lacks a sense of history; sadism gives events a "pseudo-monumentality."

Neefs, Jacques. "Le Parcours du Zaïmph." In *La Production du sens chez Flaubert*, 227–52. Paris: Collection 10 / 18 (Colloque de Cérisy), 1975. First-rate, Studies the goddess's veil as an embodiment of power and desire that centers the work.

Rousset, Jean. "Positions, distances, perspectives dans *Salammbô*." *Poétique* 6 (1971):145–54. The significance of space in the novel. One of the best studies of it.

Sainte-Beuve, Charles Augustin. "*Salammbô.*" In *Nouveaux Lundis*, 4:31–95. Paris: Levy, 1864–84. (First published 8, 15, and 22 December 1862.) See pp. 31–34, 79–95 — the rest is plot summary. Accuses Flaubert of plagiarism, coldness, artifice, and gratuitous cruelty. Flaubert's answer, in a letter dated 23–24 December, 1862, is indispensable for understanding his view of the novel.

Schor, Naomi. "Salammbô enchaînée; ou, Femme et ville dans *Salammbô.*" In *Flaubert: La Femme, la ville*, ed. Marie-Claire Bancquart, 89–104. Paris: Presses Universitaires de France, 1983. A lucid feminist psychoanalytic reading in a broad context of nineteenth-century fiction.

Strong, Isabelle. "Flaubert's Controversy with [the archeologist] Froehner: The Manuscript Tradition." *Romance Notes* 16, no. 2 (Winter 1975):283–99. Solid documentation for Flaubert's sources in his replies to his adversary.

La Tentation de saint Antoine

Bem, Jeanne. *Désir et savoir dans l'oeuvre de Flaubert. Étude de "La Tentation de saint Antoine.*" Neuchâtel: La Baconnière, 1979. An enormously rich, wide-ranging, suggestive psychoanalytic study based on the theories of Freud and his French revisionists.

Chastel, Andre. "L' Épisode de la Reine de Saba dans *La Tentation de saint Antoine* de Flaubert." *Romanic Review* 40 (December 1949):261–67. Excellent discussion.

Danger, Pierre. "Sainteté et castration dans *La Tentation de saint Antoine.*" In *Essais sur Flaubert en l'honneur du professeur Don Demorest*, 185–202. Paris: Nizet, 1979. A lively, provocative Freudian study.

Dumesnil, René, and Don-L. Demorest. "Bibliographie de Gustave Flaubert." *Bulletin du bibliophile et du bibliothécaire*, 1937–38. See particularly 1938, pp. 25–32, 75–82, 134–42, 168–75, 311–17, and 404–14, for an excellent study of the multiple manuscripts of the work.

Flaubert, Gustave. *Oeuvres complètes.* 28 vols. Paris: Conard, 1910–54. Vol. 17, pp. 655–65 presents an excellent discussion of the historical accuracy of the *Tentation.* See also accounts of the Saint's life in the *Catholic Encyclopedia* and in Hastings's *Encyclopaedia of Religion and Ethics.*

Foucault, Michel. "Un 'Fantastique' de bibliothèque." *Cahiers Renaud-Barrault* 59 (March 1967):2–33. Pp. 16–26 lucidly discuss the nesting layers of the *Tentation*, although Foucault exaggerates their complexity and also the bookishness of Flaubert.

Jung, Carl Gustav. *Psychological Types or the Psychology of Individuation*, 18–33, 70–75. London: Kegan Paul, 1946. An overview of the Gnostic heresies which dominated the Alexandrian Period when Anthony lived; and a discussion of how the hermit's battles against tempting demons exemplify psychic repression.

Merivale, Patricia. "Learning the Hard Way: Gothic Pedagogy in the Modern Romantic Quest." *Comparative Literature* 36, no. 2 (Spring 1984):146–61. Traces the tradition of "teaching through fear" by allegorical pageants, rituals, and visions, from Mozart's *The Magic Flute* and Goethe's *Faust* to Hesse's *Steppenwolf* and John Fowles's *The Magus.* Illuminating.

Porter, Laurence M. "The Devil as Double in Nineteenth-Century Literature: Goethe, Dostoevsky, and Flaubert." *Comparative Literature Studies* 15 (Fall 1978):316–35. How the Devil-figure steadily becomes less real until the religious revivals of the twentieth century. Situates him in the history of ideas.

— — — . "A Fourth Version of Flaubert's *Tentation de saint Antoine.*" *Nineteenth-Century French Studies* 4, nos. 1–2 (Fall 1975–Winter 1976; Festschrift for Jean Seznec):53–66. Describes the previously unrecognized 1869 version and how it illuminates Flaubert's creative process.

Seznec, Jean. *Nouvelles Études sur "La Tentation de saint Antoine."* London: The Warburg Institute, 1949. Essential study of Flaubert's sources.

— — — . *Les Sources de l' Épisode des Dieux dans "La Tentation de saint Antoine."* Paris: Vrin, 1940. Definitive.

Trois Contes

Bart, Benjamin F. and R. F. Cook. *The Legendary Sources of Flaubert's "Saint Julien."* Toronto: Toronto University Press, 1977. Definitive. Discusses the artistic elaboration of legends, and shows that Flaubert's essential sources were nineteenth-century rather than medieval.

Berg, William J., Michel Grimaud, and George Moskos. *Saint / Oedipus: Psychocritical Approaches to Flaubert's Art.* Ithaca, N.Y.: Cornell University Press, 1982. Offers a Sartrean, Jungian, Freudian, and Post-Freudian reading of the *Saint Julien.* Best are Berg's Freudian reading, Grimaud's discussion of the problems of translation, and his bibliography of psychoanalytic approaches in French studies.

Chambers, Ross. "Simplicité de coeur et duplicité textuelle. Étude d'*Un coeur simple.*" *MLN* 96, no. 4 (May 1981): 771–91. Ingenious and elegant.

Issacharoff, Michael. *L' Espace et la nouvelle.* Paris: Corti, 1976. Contains: (1) "*Hérodias* et la symbolique combinatoire des *Trois Contes* de Flaubert," pp. 21–38. *Hérodias* is the key to the other stories, which echo its central opposition of imprisonment and spatial liberation. (2) "*Trois Contes,* et le problème de la non-linéarité," pp. 39–60. Sees the stories as a deliberate triptych despite their apparent unrelatedness.

Peterson, Carla L. "The Trinity in Flaubert's *Trois Contes*: Deconstructing History." *French Forum* 8, no. 3 (September 1983):243–58. Original. Compares the three tales to Joachim de Flora's tripartite history (ancient period — God the Father; medieval period — Christ; modern period — the Holy Ghost) [which also influenced Alfred de Vigny]. Flaubert transformed a progressive schema to a cyclical one, pessimistic regarding history but optimistic regarding art.

Forthcoming Studies to Watch For

Bruneau, Jean, editor. *Correspondance,* vol. 3. Paris: Gallimard. Every volume is a major event in Flaubert criticism.

Conroy, Mark. *Modernism and Authority: Strategies of Legitimation in Flaubert and Conrad.* Baltimore, Md.: The Johns Hopkins University Press.

Donato, Eugenio. A posthumous volume of his collected essays, forthcoming, should be the best Flaubert book in years.

Furst, Lilian R. *Fictions of Romantic Irony*. Cambridge, Mass.: Harvard University Press.

Ginsburg, Michal Peled. *Strategies of Representation: A Study of Flaubert's Works*. Stanford, Calif.: Stanford University Press.

Wing, Nathaniel. Chapter on *Madame Bovary* in his forthcoming book from Cambridge University Press. A lucid post-structuralist reading.

INDEX